COMMON SENSE, RIGHTS OF MAN, AND OTHER ESSENTIAL WRITINGS OF THOMAS PAINE

With an Introduction by Sidney Hook and a New Foreword by Jack Fruchtman Jr.

SIGNET CLASSICS

SIGNET CLASSICS
Published by New American Library, a division of
Penguin Group (USA) Inc., 375 Hudson Street,
New York, New York 10014, USA
Penguin Group (Canada), 90 Eglinton Avenue East, Suite 700, Toronto,
Ontario M4P 2Y3, Canada (a division of Pearson Penguin Canada Inc.)
Penguin Books Ltd., 80 Strand, London WC2R 0RL, England
Penguin Ireland, 25 St. Stephen's Green, Dublin 2,
Ireland (a division of Penguin Books Ltd.)
Penguin Group (Australia), 250 Camberwell Road, Camberwell, Victoria 3124,
Australia (a division of Pearson Australia Group Pty. Ltd.)
Penguin Books India Pvt. Ltd., 11 Community Centre, Panchsheel Park,
New Delhi - 110 017, India
Penguin Group (NZ), 67 Apollo Drive, Rosedale, North Shore 0632,
New Zealand (a division of Pearson New Zealand Ltd.)
Penguin Books (South Africa) (Pty.) Ltd., 24 Sturdee Avenue,
Rosebank, Johannesburg 2196, South Africa

Penguin Books Ltd., Registered Offices:
80 Strand, London WC2R 0RL, England

Published by Signet Classics, an imprint of New American Library,
a division of Penguin Group (USA) Inc.

First Signet Classics Printing, July 2003
20   19   18   17

Introduction copyright © New American Library, a division of Penguin Group
(USA) Inc., 1969
Foreword copyright © Jack Fruchtman Jr., 2003
All rights reserved

 REGISTERED TRADEMARK—MARCA REGISTRADA

Printed in the United States of America

CONTENTS

FOREWORD

With his wide-ranging interests in politics, society, and religion as well as science and technology, Thomas Paine was the most colorful and successful pamphleteer in the age of the American and French Revolutions. Arguably America's first "bestseller," *Common Sense* sold as many as 150,000 copies and the *Rights of Man* well into the hundreds of thousands, but Paine never earned a penny from their extraordinary sales. Often reprinted in England, they were also translated into French, Dutch, Russian, and many other European languages. His writing was as fiery as it was earthy. A master wordsmith, Paine wrote directly to plain people, not to monarchs, aristocrats, or the wealthy. He wanted to persuade his readers of their human rights and democratic equality, and he wanted them to abandon the discredited ideas of hereditary rule, rank, and privilege.

Yet this bestselling author had no formal training as a writer. Nor did he have sufficient schooling to be a philosopher. We remember him today as a crusading journalist who gave birth to several familiar slogans that we associate with his turbulent era: "we have it in our power to begin the world over again," "the birthday of a new world is at hand," and "these are the times that try men's souls." Most vividly, he gave life to the phrase that we typically associate with the eighteenth-century Enlightenment: "the Age of Reason." Even in our own time, American politicians (including presidents of the United States), journalists, and teachers use Paine's words to amplify and give authority to their own ideas.

Friends and Enemies

Paine had many friends and many enemies. He was a lightning rod who attracted either grand praise or shocked anger. When he was with those he liked and respected, even if he was gruff and unpolished, he could be polite and courteous. He loved to spend time in taverns, where he told stories, usually about men in politics, and sang songs. More important, he debated current issues with his friends while eating a plate of oysters and drinking his fair share of Madeira or beer.

Born in Thetford, England, in 1737, Paine spent his first thirty-seven years as a man in quest of a mission. Wandering from his hometown to London and throughout the English Midlands, he searched for a profession that would be both lucrative and satisfying. He first tried and failed to follow his father's trade of making stays for women's corsets. He also tried to teach in a grammar school, but gave it up after a few months. His two marriages both ended in failure: his first wife died in childbirth, and he and his second wife separated shortly after the dry goods store her father owned went bankrupt under Paine's management. He served on two occasions as an excise tax collector, but he was dismissed both times: once for allowing goods to pass through without collecting the tax and once for leaving his post to advocate before Parliament an increase in the wages of his fellow tax collectors. This plea to Parliament, though filled with facts about the rough and dangerous life that the tax-men faced, was ignored. While it became his first major piece of writing, it was not printed until 1793, twenty-one years after he wrote it.

These experiences throughout the English countryside shaped his thinking about life, politics, and society. He lived for a while in Lewes, where he was elected to the town council, whose meetings were held in the White Hart Inn, where decisions were made, drinks and food passed around, and debate ongoing.

It was on one of his trips to London, when he met Benjamin Franklin, the American colonial agent for Pennsylvania, that his life dramatically changed. Despite his modest birth and common-man pleasures, Paine traveled from then on in the highest intellectual and social circles in America, England, and France. Soon Franklin, his closest friend and greatest mentor, was taking him to his favorite inn, where his Club of Honest Whigs met to wine and dine and discuss the great political, social, and scientific issues of the day. There, Paine met several political radicals such as Richard Price and Joseph Priestley, who demanded the total reform of the English government.

When Paine finally immigrated to America in the fall of 1774, he carried with him a letter of introduction from Franklin, who himself returned to Philadelphia the following year.

As a writer and editor for the monthly *Pennsylvania Magazine*, Paine was soon recognized as the man who could best express the reasons for America's separation from Britain. In drafting *Common Sense*, he was assisted not only by Franklin but also by the renowned physician and republican writer Dr. Benjamin Rush; David Rittenhouse, the astronomer, who noted the transit of Venus; and the Boston firebrand Samuel Adams. Though published anonymously (most people thought that Franklin or John Adams had written it), the pamphlet was soon identified with the newly arrived Thomas Paine. George Washington, Thomas Jefferson, and many others praised it.

But not everyone agreed. *Common Sense* argued for American independence, just as Rush, Franklin, and Sam Adams desired. But it did so in such charged language that some American leaders thought it went too far. John Adams wrote a blistering response in his *Thoughts on Government*. In a letter to James Warren, Adams wrote that " 'Common Sense' . . . will do more Mischief. . . . He is a keen Writer but very ignorant of the Science of Government." Franklin's Tory son, William, then serving as the royal governor of New Jersey, was appalled by "the inflammatory Pamphlet in which the horrid Measure [of independence] is strongly and artfully recommended." Another writer, James Chalmers, despised Paine because he had disputed the English Constitution, "the pride and envy of all mankind."

Still, when regarded from a more modern perspective, *Common Sense* was the January heat of 1776 that balanced the July light of Thomas Jefferson's Declaration of Independence. It might even be said that while Jefferson's abstract diction justified rebellion, Paine's explosive words got rebel men and muskets into the field.

So when Paine finally sailed from America in 1787, he left behind a new country, a trail of friends, and a host of enemies. His reason for leaving his "adopted country," as he called it, was to promote his design of an iron bridge without piers to replace wooden bridges that broke apart during the winter months when their piers stood in icy waters. Although his design was heartily approved by both the Royal Society of London and the Royal Academy of Sciences in Paris, the bridge was never built. In the meantime, Paine became deeply involved in European politics two years later with the outbreak of the French Revolution. The first part of his *Rights of Man* (1791) responded directly to Edmund Burke's great work condemning the French Revolution.

Paine and Burke had become close friends just after Paine's return to England. Paine had long admired the member of Parliament from Bristol for his strong defense of the Americans during the revolutionary crisis in the 1770s. Burke thought the Americans had a right to independence if they wanted it, especially because separation would bring no changes to the historic structure of the British government. The two men had even traveled together throughout England, inspecting various ironworks for Paine's bridge project. But after 1790 these friends became implacable enemies and never spoke to each other again.

Paine's *Rights of Man* was a sharp refutation of Burke's *Reflections on the Revolution in France*: as Burke defended tradition, church, and aristocracy, Paine attacked them with the weapons of innovation, free thought, and democracy.

Meantime, Paine's English radical friends in the London Corresponding Society, who demanded political reform of the English government, and his French revolutionary colleagues in the Jacobin Club all extolled his ideas. Richard Brinsley Sheridan, a famous playwright and member of Parliament, defended them. The leader of the ill-fated 1798 Irish Rebellion, Edward Lord Fitzgerald, was so profoundly moved that he traveled to Paris to meet the great man.

While living in Paris, Paine was watched by English spies, who reported back to the British ministry. By the end of 1792, the English government, tired of Paine's unyielding attacks, tried and convicted him in absentia for treason. It dared him to return to England. If captured, he faced imprisonment or, worse, the gallows. But his troubles were not solely with the English.

At the time of his trial, the French Revolution fell into the Reign of Terror. Its leaders, Robespierre and Saint-Just, saw enemies and traitors all around them. France was at war against all of Europe, including

England, after the execution of King Louis XVI in January 1793. Meanwhile, uprisings against the revolutionary regime opened a new front, a civil war within France itself. Soon thousands were arrested, some accused of nothing more than refusing to wear the *bonnet rouge*, the revolutionary red cap. Hundreds faced the guillotine.

In December, Paine himself was arrested for simply being English, although he considered himself an American. Confined to the Luxembourg Prison (a former palace and today the home of the French senate), he languished in fear for his life for more than a year. He wrote the American ambassador, Gouverneur Morris, the only foreign diplomat to remain in France during the Terror, begging for help. But Morris, who hated Paine as much as Adams did for his extreme, fiery language, caustically wrote that he hoped that Paine "may see [his own dim future] in the fate" of those already executed.

Finally released from prison after the fall of the Jacobins and the end of the Terror, Paine wrote an open letter to President George Washington, still the most famous, most popular man in America, criticizing him for failing to help him. He claimed that he had done as much as any man to further the goals of the Americans in combating the British during the Revolutionary War and had deserved the president's assistance. After the letter appeared in print in America, most newspaper editorials supported the president and condemned Paine. A friend to America, Paine now had a continent full of new American enemies.

At last, Paine's longtime friend Thomas Jefferson, whom he had known from the early days of the American Revolution, was elected president in 1800. Two years later, he sent a ship to France to pick up his old comrade. Paine returned to America and lived the rest of his life railing against enemies like John Adams and Gouverneur Morris. He died in New York City in 1809.

Politics and Society

Thomas Paine's political agenda was as controversial as his personality. Some scholars have correctly seen him as the great advocate of American independence and human rights. But most overlook the most important part of his message. While separation from England was certainly a key to understanding *Common Sense*, and the title of his work *Rights of Man* clearly tells us that he despised any attempt to limit our rights and liberties, Paine went further. He was so sickened by the misery, poverty, and degradation caused by hereditary rank and privilege that he championed revolution not only in America, but worldwide.

We can see this as early as *Common Sense* (1776) just by his language. While he certainly condemns the English government's mistreatment of the American colonies and even refers to King George III as "the Brute of Britain," "Savage," and "Pharaoh," he has bigger game in his sights. The world was ruled by monarchies, and monarchies had to be destroyed. Aristocracies deserved the same fate because, like monarchies, they were based on heredity. Not only the English king, but all kings everywhere were useless. "In England a king hath little more to do than to make war and give away places; which in plain terms is to impoverish a nation and set it together by the ears. A pretty business indeed for a man to be allowed eight hundred thousand sterling for a year, and worshiped into the bargain" (p. 21). Surely a fine condem-

nation of George III, but he does not stop there.
Immediately, he launches into a universal assault that
goes beyond England: "Of more worth is one honest
man to society and in the sight of God, than *all the
crowned ruffians that ever lived*" [emphasis added]
(p. 21).

We have seen how his critic James Chalmers attacked Paine for denouncing the English Constitution.
Paine was mild in his *Common Sense* attack compared
to what he would say in the *Rights of Man*. In *Common Sense*, he had argued that the division of power
among King, Lords, and Commons was hardly defensible: the King and Lords were two ancient tyrannies
that dominated the Commons. In answering Burke, he
argued that while the British might talk about their
great and "happy" constitution that divided power between an executive and two legislative branches,
"[the] continual use of the word *Constitution* in the
English Parliament shews there is none; and that the
whole is merely a form of Government without a Constitution, and constituting itself with what powers it
pleases. As long as England had no *written* document,
no one can rightly argue that England ever had a constitution" (pp. 239–40).

Paine's philosophical objective was a government
that truly respects and protects human rights. One
practical way to achieve it, he thought, was by institut-
ing a freely elected single-house legislature. Like his
mentor, Franklin, who had argued for a unicameral
Pennsylvania assembly, Paine believed that such a national legislature would more easily avoid divisiveness
and be more answerable to the people, the true source
of government.

For Paine, ridding the world of kings and aristocrats
was the only way to advance the cause of human
rights. Edmund Burke attacked the French Revolution
because it was based solely on abstract rights. He believed that reform came as a long, slow historical evo-

lution of political and social institutions. To uproot
them in the name of human rights undermined hundreds of years of custom and history. Institutions
lasted because they worked.

Paine's counterargument to Burke was the most famous of some forty-five published responses: "It requires but a very small glance of thought to perceive
that altho' laws made in one generation often continue
in force through succeeding generations, yet that they
continue to derive their force from the consent of the
living" (p. 141). This was Paine's famous reiteration
of Jefferson's principle that the earth belonged to the
living. Any attempt by one generation to bind the
next—to rule from the grave—was the moral and political equivalent of despotism. Kings and members of
Parliament had no authority to bind anyone except
themselves. "I smile to myself when I contemplate the
ridiculous insignificance into which literature and all
the sciences would sink, were they made hereditary,"
he mused, "and I carry the same idea into Governments" (p. 284).

Rights and liberties were the essence of a person's
humanity. Every person is born with them because
they came into being "under the auspices of [their]
Creator." They were the "illuminating and divine
principle of the equal rights of man" (p. 167) and they
were the same for all human beings regardless of their
social or economic status. Once a government becomes so tyrannical that these rights no longer exist,
"a Nation has at all times an inherent, indefeasible
right to abolish" (p. 252) that government and set up
a new one.

At the same time, to help those citizens caught in
the wellspring of poverty, he proposed in the second
part of the *Rights of Man* (1792) a series of social
welfare programs, such as monetary assistance for the
poor, young married couples, children, and the elderly.
He even suggested that public money should be set

aside to pay for the funerals of those who could not afford them. In his last great work, *Agrarian Justice* (1797), he went even further to argue that the government should create a special fund from high inheritance taxes to pay for public assistance.

Paine ended his *Rights of Man* by extolling the two major revolutions of his time. He expected that all the other European nations would soon follow: "To use a trite expression, the iron is hot all over Europe. The insulted German and the enslaved Spaniard, the Russ and the Pole, are beginning to think. The present age will hereafter merit to be called the Age of Reason, and the present generation will appear to the future as the Adam of a new world" (p. 344). Soon, even South America would create independent republics. No less than world revolution would reform the entire world in this new and advanced era.

Religion

If revolution was the main part of Thomas Paine's agenda, what are we to make of his reference to the Creator in the origins of human rights or to the criticism he faced when he returned to America as being anti-Christian? Enemies like John Adams and Gouverneur Morris and even his old friend Sam Adams condemned him for being a "nonbeliever." Morris declined to help Paine while he was imprisoned in the Luxembourg because he thought that Paine "amuses himself with publishing a pamphlet against Jesus Christ."

In fact, this pamphlet was another two-volume work, *The Age of Reason* (1794–95), in which Paine explained in some detail and with great bravado and irreverence his hatred of organized religion. He was careful to attack only churches, not God, but even so, John Adams characterized him as "profligate and impious." Although baptized in the Church of England, Paine followed his father's religion and became a Quaker (a member of the Society of Friends), though on his own terms. He was attracted by the inner-light spirituality of the Friends and their belief that every person possessed a divine spark that impelled him to do good for all people, but he firmly rejected their pacifism, especially when he chose to support American efforts to fight the British.

As a Quaker, Paine announced his belief in God and an afterlife in the opening lines of *The Age of Reason*. Even more important, he was certain that God chose some men in particular to perform good works. In the *Rights of Man*, for example, he revealed that he thought he was such a man: "For my own part," he wrote in this work,

> I am fully satisfied that what I am now doing, with an endeavour to conciliate mankind, to render their condition happy, to unite Nations that have hitherto been enemies, and to extirpate the horrid practice of war, and break the chains of slavery and oppression, is acceptable in his [God's] sight; and being the best service I can perform I act it cheerfully. (p. 348)

Soon after the publication of the second part of the *Rights of Man*, a major shift in his religious beliefs occurred that took him from the Quakerism of his father to the Deism of Franklin, Jefferson, Voltaire, and many of the other great names of the century. When this transition occurred is impossible to trace because he never said. He may not even have noticed it himself. Perhaps he became a Deist when he first wrote about religion in the first part of *The Age of Reason*. (He had told John Adams in 1776 that someday he would do so, but "it will be best to postpone it to the latter part of life.")

As a Deist and a republican writer and activist, Paine believed that religious beliefs had to be reasonable and that God had given human beings control over their lives to perform good deeds. Paine believed that a truly religious man need not belong to a church or even attend religious services. He now gave up as absurd his belief that he had been God's chosen instrument to lead the world to revolution. A man was his own instrument. A man must devote his life, as he had, to performing good works and leave the world a better place than he found it. His writings display his dedication to the principle that people everywhere would see that rights and liberty form the very foundation of human life and that no person should ever willingly relinquish them without a fierce struggle. By his rational analysis of God, government, and society, Thomas Paine personified the Age of Reason.

—Jack Fruchtman Jr.

INTRODUCTION

I

Thomas Paine lived in a blaze of political glory and died in relative obscurity. His philosophy inspired two of the greatest revolutions in human history—the American Revolution and the French Revolution. In gratitude both the United States and France bestowed great honor as well as citizenship upon him. Yet his memory has been dimmed in the first nation, and all but forgotten in the second. If any man is entitled to be called the Father of American Independence, it is Thomas Paine, whose *Common Sense* stated the case for freedom from England's rule with a logic and a passion that roused the public opinion of the Colonies to a white heat. Just as essential in preserving the cause of independence was the series of pamphlets, *The American Crisis,* published to sustain the morale of Washington's army and the patriotic cause in the darkest days of the conflict. The first of them, written on a drumhead by the flickering light of a campfire during Washington's retreat before greatly superior forces, with its ringing opening sentence: "These are the times that try men's souls," galvanized the soldiers before whom it was read, at Washington's orders, into spirited and successful resistance and counterattack.

Paine's pamphlet *Rights of Man* brought him international fame—but in England, where his earlier works had been forgiven after the recognition of American sovereignty, only infamy. Written as a reply to *Reflections on the Revolution in France,* by Edmund Burke—whom Paine had regarded as "a friend of mankind" because of his defense of the American cause—it presented the severest indictment of hereditary monarchy and privilege that had ever been penned until that time. In consequence he was elected a deputy to the French National Convention. He was the chief, if not the sole author—Condorcet was a collaborator—of the *Declaration of the Rights of Man and of the Citizen,* which Burke vehemently attacked.

In virtue of his devotion to the provisions of that declaration, Paine opposed the incipient terrorist practices of the French revolutionists and courageously pleaded against the proposed execution of Louis XVI and Marie Antoinette. On Robespierre's orders he was arrested and jailed. Although some of his American friends intervened on his behalf, the French authorities refused to recognize his American citizenship or to release him. By a lucky chance he escaped the guillotine—his cell had been improperly marked. After Robespierre's downfall he was released and restored to his post in the Convention, but by this time he had become disillusioned by the fanaticism and extremism that had betrayed the rights of man he had so zealously defended against Burke's animadversions.

It was during the days immediately preceding his arrest, when Paine was convinced that he would be sacrificed on the bloody altars of the Jacobins, that he composed the first part of *The Age of Reason.* The action and its significance can be compared to Condorcet's composition of his great work on *The Outlines of the Progress of the Human Spirit** as he lay hiding

*Esquisse d'un tableau historique des progrès de l'esprit humain.

from those who had come to execute him in the name of human progress. In a letter to Samuel Adams in 1803 Paine relates the dramatic circumstances under which he wrote the first part of *The Age of Reason:*

> My friends were falling as fast as the guillotine could cut their heads off, and I every day expected the same fate . . . I appeared to myself to be on the death-bed, for death was on every side of me, and I had no time to lose.

By one of the greatest ironies in intellectual history, this work—which Paine in a dedicatory epistle put under the protection of "My Fellow Citizens of the United States of America" as he slipped the manuscript to a friend under the eyes of his captors and which he wrote to combat the atheism and infidelity of the French revolutionists—became the cause of his unpopularity in the only country he adopted as his own. Never was there so gross and inexcusable an act of historical ingratitude as that suffered by Thomas Paine at the hands of his former comrades-in-arms on the occasion of his second visit to America.

The irony was all the greater because Thomas Paine's *Age of Reason* expressed the religious faith of the great architects of the American Revolution—of philosopher-statesmen like Thomas Jefferson, Benjamin Franklin, John Adams, and others. It was an impassioned plea for Deism and the religion of reason, and a criticism of the literal reading of the Old and the New Testament, a criticism which grounded orthodoxy in primitive superstition and sublimated violence and lust. Paine was a man of naive but moving natural piety. He had already proclaimed in *Rights of Man,* while contending that religion was a private matter, that *"every religion is good that teaches man to be good,"* but in his *Age of Reason* he made quite explicit his fervent belief in the existence of God and the immortality of the soul. Paine had underestimated the hold that institutional religion had on the belief and behavior of the American people even though religion was not a part of the legal establishment as it was in England. His experience in America was to teach him that religious intolerance does not disappear merely because religion is disestablished. Although he loved America, he did not understand her very well and overlooked the fact that for most of his countrymen religious tolerance at that time did not flow from conviction—as was the case for Jefferson and his circle—but from the plurality of religious sects, no one of which was strong enough to crush the others.

At any rate when Theodore Roosevelt, to his lasting discredit, referred to Thomas Paine, without having read him, as "a filthy little atheist," he was slandering someone whose belief in the traditional doctrines of the existence of a Supreme Power and the immortality of the Soul was much more unqualified than the belief of two thinkers who have been characterized as the leading Protestant theologians of the twentieth century—Paul Tillich and Reinhold Niebuhr.

II

Thomas Paine was a typical figure of the Enlightenment. He was not a profound thinker but a remarkable popularizer whose gift for bold and graphic expression made him a natural pamphleteer. It was the cause of American independence that drew him into politics and his pen onto paper. Although he firmly believed that the American colonists had right on their side, it was not merely as an American or in behalf of narrow American interests that he threw himself so completely into the struggle, but as a free man, a cosmopolitan citizen of the world, who was convinced that when he struck a blow for freedom in America he was doing so for England and France or wherever arbitrary authority ruled. "My principle is universal. My attachment is to all the world, and not to any particular part, and if what I advance is right— no matter where or who it comes from."

What was the source of his principle? Theoretically, it stemmed from his ambiguous doctrine of natural rights. Psychologically, it was rooted in the man himself—proud and sensitive, simple yet dignified—who turned aside a fortune by refusing to profit a penny from any of the pamphlets that he wrote. The excesses of his style flowed from a hatred "of cruel men and cruel measures." He was a compassionate and modest person, prepared to risk his life in action, who sought no compensation or rewards except the goodwill and good judgment of his fellowmen.

Of all his writings only his *Rights of Man* remains topical, and relevant to contemporary concerns. It is not a profound work. Paine answers Burke brilliantly and effectively but does not do justice to the subtleties of Burke's position. And although he properly defines human rights, he offers little by way of justification for them.

Insofar as Burke attacked the French Revolution on the grounds that it opposed the principle of hereditary succession, undermined the authority of the past, discarded hereditary rights, and scorned hereditary wisdom, Paine is on solid ground in revealing the insufficiency and arbitrariness of Burke's position. He emphasizes that every people has a right to govern itself and that it can set up any regime, republican or monarchical, to which it delegates power. Actually Burke admits that this is a right which the people of England and of other countries once had. But—and with this we reach the nub of the difference between

Burke and Paine—for Burke, once this choice was made—as the English Parliament had made it in 1688—any further right to change was forsworn: "The English *nation* did, at the time of the Revolution, most solemnly renounce and abdicate it, for themselves, and for *all their posterity, forever.*" Burke has no difficulty in citing the official documents of the past in which Parliament claims "to bind" the nation and its posterity to perpetual fealty.

Paine has no difficulty in showing that Burke confuses right by delegation with the right by assumption, "that of binding and controlling posterity to the end of time." He is most eloquent in repudiating the claim of authority based on anything but consent. This was the principle already expressed in the Declaration of Independence:

> Every age and generation must be as free to act for itself, *in all* cases, as the ages and generation which preceded it. The vanity and presumption of governing beyond the grave, is the most ridiculous and insolent of all tyrannies.

Both in his defense of government by consent and in his repudiation of the tyranny of the past, Paine invokes the rights of man. It is his discussion of the rights of man that gives Paine's work its perennial importance, for the implicit or explicit appeal to human rights underlies every large movement of human protest in history, and we can be confident that it will continue to be so in the future.

Paine's analysis of human rights was not undertaken as a theoretical exercise but delivered in the course of the polemical defense of a revolution in which he had great hope and whose excesses he was prepared to condemn as vigorously as most of its critics. We must therefore not look for precision in his language but sympathetically enter into the intent of his thought.

His discussion may most fruitfully be considered under three heads: (1) What are human rights or natural rights? (2) What is their origin? (3) What is their objective justification?

Paine is at his best in identifying and defining human or natural rights. They are "those which appertain to man in right of his existence. Of this kind are all the intellectual rights, or rights of the mind, and also all those rights of acting as an individual for his own comfort and happiness, which are not injurious to the natural rights of others." This is obviously circular. What Paine clearly means is that a natural right is a moral claim to the exercise of certain human powers and to the enjoyment of certain goods. It is a claim against all men and governments. Civil rights are natural rights that appertain to man in virtue of his being a member of society. They are moral claims individuals recognize as necessary to safeguard and to implement more effectively their natural rights. "The rights of men in society are neither divisible nor transferable, nor annihilable, but are discardible only." Human beings can forgo asserting their rights. They may, in extreme cases, even voluntarily enslave themselves to others. But if they do, they do not extinguish their rights, which they or others may subsequently reclaim for them, and above all, they do not extinguish the natural rights of their posterity. "If the present generation, or any other, are disposed to be slaves, it does not lessen the right of the succeeding generation to be free: wrongs cannot have a legal descent."

From whence come these rights? Strictly speaking this is an illegitimate question which Paine should not have asked. For if rights are natural, coeval with the existence of man as such, they have no origin. Paine asks the question because he is following Burke, for whom rights are always special or partial, historical, and limited. Paine has no difficulty in exposing the arbitrariness and invalidity of the view that any human being or beings, whether a tyrant or a tyrannical corporation, has the authority to endow human beings with rights. Trace human rights back as far as you wish and you will discover that human beings already had them, or, if they were denied by a king or bishop, that they should have had them. No one can grant human rights to human beings, who already possess them once we classify them as men. History is irrelevant. If we undertake historical excursions, then we must go beyond antiquity to the beginning of man, "when man came from the hand of his Maker."

The natural rights of man according to Paine derive from the *equality* and *unity of man,* by which he means:

> . . . that men are all of *one degree,* and consequently that all men are born equal, and with equal natural rights, in the same manner as if posterity had been continued by *creation* instead of *generation;* and consequently every child born into the world must be considered as deriving its existence from God. The world is as new to him as it was to the first man that existed, and his natural right in it is of the same kind.

Two things must be said about Paine's attempt to justify the rights of man. On the basis of his own theory, a religious justification is superfluous. God may have created man in his own image, but the rights of man do not depend on that creation. If the rights of man are also possessed by God, they would be divine and man would not possess them. If men as such have them in virtue of their being men, this would be unaffected by the existence or nonexistence of God.

Nor are the rights of man logically justified because all men are equal in the sight of the Lord. Men could all be recognized as equal in the sight of the Lord but not before the Law. The inference from one to the other is not logical. The strength of Burke's position appears in his repudiation of any religious, logical, or metaphysical justification of human rights. For Burke "government is a contrivance of human wisdom," and the "rights of man" are the reasonable claims that men make when they choose between goods and between evils, when they make decisions concerning the better when goods conflict, or decisions concerning the lesser evil when choice is limited to alternatives *both* of which are evil. To Paine this is tantamount to saying that government is ruled by no principle and that it is the expression of arbitrary power.

Paine is unjust to Burke's position on this point, for even if one holds that the natural rights of man are absolute, the conflict of rights is an inescapable fact of moral and political experience. In the end our wisdom must decide which rights are to be given priority and emphasis. Where Burke erred—and here Paine's criticism is completely warranted—is in ascribing a kind of hereditary wisdom to hereditary political and social rights. But, as Paine caustically argues, ". . . it is impossible to make wisdom hereditary . . . that cannot be a wise contrivance, which in its operation may commit the government of a nation to the wisdom of an idiot."

Once the question is posed not as, What is natural to man? but as, What is reasonable for man? questions of origin become largely irrelevant. What man *is now* and what he is likely *to become,* and not what he originally was, are pertinent in considering what he *should do* and how he should live now. Contemporary human needs and wants, not hereditary forms, are focal for Paine. Society is described as the set of institutions that enables men to gratify their needs and wants. Like Jefferson, whom he strongly influenced, Paine felt that government, whose scope should be restricted merely to state power, was an intrusion into society, unfortunately made necessary by violations of the moral duties men owed to each other. Both Paine and Jefferson underestimated the role of government in strengthening the social institutions required to gratify contemporary human needs and wants. The state of England was such, however, that Paine at the close of his *Rights of Man* proposes that the government undertake measures for the amelioration of distress—which entitles him to be considered almost despite himself a forerunner of the Welfare State. In his views on land rent and agrarian justice, shortly afterward, he strikingly anticipates the doctrines of Henry George.

This inconsistency in Paine is a tribute to his sense of compassion for human suffering, but it reveals a political naiveté, probably strengthened by his reading of Rousseau, that blinded him to the realities not only of American life but of life in modern society. For him it is not the absence of government which is anomalous and must be explained, but its presence. "The instant formal government is abolished," he writes, "society begins to act." In the absence of formal government, Paine relies upon the diversity of human needs and the necessity of reciprocal help to gratify them to provide the bonds that hold society together. He assumes that these bonds must be harmonious and ignores the possibility that the social bonds themselves may reflect not only dependence of some upon others but exploitation and enslavement. The unconscious assumption is that until government interferes with its operations, society can be considered as one great happy family capable of resolving its disputes without establishing governments and states. "The more perfect civilization is, the less occasion has it for government, because the more does it regulate its own affairs, and govern itself." The tumults and riots that afflict society, in Paine's view, are the consequence not of absence of government but of its presence. How is this possible if, as Paine admits, poverty and unhappiness are the ultimate source of social disorder? "Whatever the apparent cause of any riots may be, the real one is always want of happiness." His reply is that even here government is at fault because poverty is caused by excessive and inequitable taxation. Presumably, under an equitable tax-system there would be no poverty or social distress. Aside from the dubious economics involved, this overlooks the obvious fact that a tax system cannot be enforced without the existence of a government. Paine cites the instance of America as a community which suffered from excessive government under the British, yet carried on without difficulty when the authority of government was destroyed during the War of Independence. It is quite clear, however, that the subsequent development of the United States could never have taken place under the aegis of a *laissez-faire* regime such as Paine favored.

III

It may be instructive to examine Thomas Paine's position on some special questions of topical importance such as the right to revolution, civil disobedience, and the limits of dissent. Since the legitimacy of government rests upon the freely given consent of the governed, any government that is imposed upon the people by conquest or fraud or usurpation, no matter how benevolent its intention or beneficial its rule, is *morally* illegitimate. The people have a moral right—"the simple voice of nature and reason"—to overthrow it and to act on that right whenever their discretion and judgment deem it wise to do so. For basically—in a logical if not a historical sense—all men are legislators.

"In this first parliament every man by natural right has a seat."

The actual making and enforcing of laws cannot be done by society at large. For that we need government. But what kind of government men should have, what kind of constitution should be adopted, modified, or amended, is a subject always before a country *as a matter of right*. This leaves men free to discuss and advocate any system of government they please, provided its establishment rests upon the free consent of their fellows and is not imposed upon them by dictators or would-be saviors. Paine rather optimistically believed that if monarchy and aristocracy were to be judged by their fruits in experience mankind would reject them in favor of republican regimes. Meanwhile, men must be free to say, to read, and to print what they think about existing governments and to make any proposals to change or modify them without let or hindrance by civil authority. Such rights "cannot without invading the general rights of the country, be made subjects for prosecution."

Paine grounds the ultimate authority of government in "a convention of the whole nation fairly elected." But why trust the decision to such a convention, why risk the danger that prejudice and passion will triumph and the convention of the whole nation degenerate into a mob? Paine's answer is the answer of an optimistic democrat to the pessimistic Plato, who is convinced that the generality of mankind is too unintelligent and/or too vicious to be entrusted with the power of self-government. Paine believes that prejudice is the result of moral ignorance. "No man is prejudiced in favor of a thing, knowing it to be wrong." Once prejudices are compelled to face the test and challenge of reason, they will give way. This faith in the power of reason to affect prejudice reflects the assumptions of the Enlightenment. It is oversimple in that it does not understand the springs of action—

which, often concealed and obscure, flow from vested personal and social interest, vanity, ambition, and sheer love of power. Less weak is Paine's retort to those who hold that a people is unfit for freedom because men are afflicted with some natural depravity. Even if this were so, it would be better to trust the many than the few, who are also infected with the plague of self-interest and selfishness. Although Paine's arguments can be developed to a point where they possess considerable validity, he really begs the question in his defense of the natural virtue of man, uncorrupted by customary prejudices.

Once we start from the premise that the only right or justified government is one based on consent, all is smooth sailing. Revolutions then are justified because they restore to men the power of choice. But once the mechanisms by which popular sovereignty expresses itself have been established, then—within the provision that men's natural rights—the rights to speech, press, and assembly—be scrupulously preserved—there is no longer a right to forcible revolution. That is why Paine opposed not only the royalist conspiracies to overthrow the French Republic but the conspiracy of Babeuf. He agreed with Babeuf that it was a serious flaw to limit suffrage in any way, but he denounced him because instead of "seeking a remedy by legitimate and constitutional means" he sought to establish "a directorship usurped by violence." This crucial point is overlooked by those who assume that the Boston Tea Party is a precedent for similar action when one encounters a bad or iniquitous law. For Paine, the Boston Tea Party and the resort to revolution was justified only because there were no means by which grievances could peacefully be redressed. The crimes of tyranny are a standing justification for resistance. But where tyranny has been replaced by government based on consent, then although such government may enact measures that are unjust, so long as criticism and the right to dissent are not abridged, so long as means exist to repeal or amend them, they should be obeyed. For if one's private judgment becomes the sole arbiter of what should be obeyed or not obeyed, good laws as well as bad laws will be undermined.

> I have always held it an opinion (making it also my practice) that it is better to obey a bad law, making use at the same time of every argument to show its errors and procure its repeal, than forcibly to violate it; because the precedent of breaking a bad law might weaken the force, and lead to a discretionary violation of those which are good.

In this connection, it is interesting to note that Paine, whose own antecedents were Quakers, speaks very harshly of the Quakers in and around Philadelphia. The Quakers were not required by the newly independent State, in its struggle for survival against England, to engage in any action contrary to the spirit of their religion. Paine severely castigates them for advising their members to resist the American authorities in carrying out their tasks of defense against British aggression, and for actions which made them in his eyes "three-quarter Tories." In terms of our own times, Paine was zealous in defending civil disobedience if it meant refusal to do what strained a man's religious conscience. But he condemned actions that, under the plea of conscience, interfered with the prosecution of the war for freedom and independence. The Quakers could refuse on grounds of conscience to bear arms in any war under any circumstances, but to the extent that they prevented others from bearing arms, according to Paine, they were insofar forth guilty of treason.

IV

Thomas Paine has not yet received his due measure of homage from the peoples and nations of the world whose aspirations he expressed with such force and clarity. His passion for human freedom shines through everything he wrote. An autodidact, he acquired sufficient knowledge of literature and science to make him one of the company of the immortals of the Enlightenment. Like Franklin and Jefferson he was an inventor, the first one to create a working model of an iron bridge. He was a true cosmopolitan who felt that he was personally engaged wherever injustice was committed or freedom denied. He was the great phrasemaker of his age, and his complete sincerity and dedication to the cause of human dignity and freedom were evident in the details of his daily life.

To most Americans Paine has been seen through a mist thrown up around him by the confluence of different streams of thought. It is safe to predict, however, that if he is read, these mists will vanish, and the man and his thought emerge in clearer and sharper focus as one of the great figures in American political thought.

—Sidney Hook

COMMON SENSE

1776

INTRODUCTION

Perhaps the sentiments contained in the following pages, are not *yet* sufficiently fashionable to procure them general favor; a long habit of not thinking a thing *wrong,* gives it a superficial appearance of being *right,* and raises at first a formidable outcry in defence of custom. But the tumult soon subsides. Time makes more converts than reason.

As a long and violent abuse of power, is generally the Means of calling the right of it in question (and in Matters too which might never have been thought of, had not the Sufferers been aggravated into the inquiry) and as the King of England hath undertaken in his *own Right,* to support the Parliament in what he calls *Theirs,* and as the good people of this country are grievously oppressed by the combination, they have an undoubted privilege to inquire into the pretensions of both, and equally to reject the usurpation of either.

In the following sheets, the author hath studiously avoided every thing which is personal among ourselves. Compliments as well as censure to individuals make no part thereof. The wise, and the worthy, need not the triumph of a pamphlet; and those whose sentiments are injudicious, or unfriendly, will cease of themselves unless too much pains are bestowed upon their conversion.

The cause of America is in a great measure the

cause of all mankind. Many circumstances hath, and will arise, which are not local, but universal, and through which the principles of all Lovers of Mankind are affected, and in the Event of which, their Affections are interested. The laying a Country desolate with Fire and Sword, declaring War against the natural rights of all Mankind, and extirpating the Defenders thereof from the Face of the Earth, is the Concern of every Man to whom Nature hath given the Power of feeling; of which Class, regardless of Party Censure, is the

AUTHOR.

P. S. The Publication of this new Edition hath been delayed, with a View of taking notice (had it been necessary) of any Attempt to refute the Doctrine of Independance: As no Answer hath yet appeared, it is now presumed that none will, the Time needful for getting such a Performance ready for the Public being considerably past.

Who the Author of this Production is, is wholly unnecessary to the Public, as the Object for Attention is the *Doctrine itself,* not the *Man.* Yet it may not be unnecessary to say, That he is unconnected with any Party, and under no sort of Influence public or private, but the influence of reason and principle.

Philadelphia, February 14, 1776

Of the origin and design of government in general. With concise remarks on the English constitution

Some writers have so confounded society with government, as to leave little or no distinction between them; whereas they are not only different, but have different origins. Society is produced by our wants, and government by our wickedness; the former promotes our happiness *positively* by uniting our affections, the latter *negatively* by restraining our vices. The one encourages intercourse, the other creates distinctions. The first is a patron, the last a punisher.

Society in every state is a blessing, but government even in its best state is but a necessary evil; in its worst state an intolerable one; for when we suffer, or are exposed to the same miseries *by a government,* which we might expect in a country *without government,* our calamity is heightened by reflecting that we furnish the means by which we suffer. Government, like dress, is the badge of lost innocence; the palaces of kings are built on the ruins of the bowers of paradise. For were the impulses of conscience clear, uniform, and irresistibly obeyed, man would need no other lawgiver; but that not being the case, he finds it necessary to surrender up a part of his property to furnish means for the protection of the rest; and this he is induced to do by the same prudence which in every other case advises him out of two evils to choose the least. *Wherefore,* security being the true design and end of government, it unanswerably follows, that whatever *form* thereof appears most likely to ensure it to us, with the least expence and greatest benefit, is preferable to all others.

In order to gain a clear and just idea of the design and end of government, let us suppose a small number of persons settled in some sequestered part of the earth, unconnected with the rest, they will then represent the first peopling of any country, or of the world. In this state of natural liberty, society will be their first thought. A thousand motives will excite them thereto, the strength of one man is so unequal to his wants, and his mind so unfitted for perpetual solitude, that he is soon obliged to seek assistance and relief of another, who in his turn requires the same. Four or five united would be able to raise a tolerable dwelling in the midst of a wilderness, but *one* man might labour out the common period of life without accomplishing any thing; when he had felled his timber he could not remove it, nor erect it after it was removed; hunger in the mean time would urge him from his work, and every different want call him a different way. Disease, nay even misfortune would be death, for though neither might be mortal, yet either would disable him from living, and reduce him to a state in which he might rather be said to perish than to die.

Thus necessity, like a gravitating power, would soon form our newly arrived emigrants into society, the reciprocal blessings of which, would supersede, and render the obligations of law and government unnecessary while they remained perfectly just to each other; but as nothing but heaven is impregnable to vice, it will unavoidably happen, that in proportion as they surmount the first difficulties of emigration, which bound them together in a common cause, they will begin to relax in their duty and attachment to each other; and this remissness will point out the necessity of establishing some form of government to supply the defect of moral virtue.

Some convenient tree will afford them a State-House, under the branches of which, the whole colony may assemble to deliberate on public matters. It is more than probable that their first laws will have the title only of REGULATIONS, and be enforced by no other penalty than public disesteem. In this first parliament every man, by natural right, will have a seat.

But as the colony increases, the public concerns will increase likewise, and the distance at which the members may be separated, will render it too inconvenient for all of them to meet on every occasion as at first, when their number was small, their habitations near, and the public concerns few and trifling. This will point out the convenience of their consenting to leave the legislative part to be managed by a select number chosen from the whole body, who are supposed to have the same concerns at stake which those have who appointed them, and who will act in the same manner as the whole body would act, were they present. If the colony continue increasing, it will become necessary to augment the number of the representatives, and that the interest of every part of the colony may be attended to, it will be found best to divide the whole into convenient parts, each part sending its proper number; and that the *elected* might never form to themselves an interest separate from the *electors,* prudence will point out the propriety of having elections often; because as the *elected* might by that means return and mix again with the general body of the *electors* in a few months, their fidelity to the public will be secured by the prudent reflexion of not making a rod for themselves. And as this frequent interchange will establish a common interest with every part of the community, they will mutually and naturally support each other, and on this (not on the unmeaning name of king) depends the *strength of government, and the happiness of the governed.*

Here then is the origin and rise of government; namely, a mode rendered necessary by the inability of moral virtue to govern the world; here too is the design and end of government, viz. freedom and security. And however our eyes may be dazzled with show, or our ears deceived by sound; however prejudice may warp our wills, or interest darken our understanding, the simple voice of nature and of reason will say, it is right.

I draw my idea of the form of government from a principle in nature, which no art can overturn, viz. that the more simple any thing is, the less liable it is to be disordered, and the easier repaired when disordered; and with this maxim in view, I offer a few remarks on the so much boasted constitution of England. That it was noble for the dark and slavish times in which it was erected, is granted. When the world was overrun with tyranny the least remove therefrom was a glorious rescue. But that it is imperfect, subject to convulsions, and incapable of producing what it seems to promise, is easily demonstrated.

Absolute governments (tho' the disgrace of human nature) have this advantage with them, that they are simple; if the people suffer, they know the head from which their suffering springs, know likewise the remedy, and are not bewildered by a variety of causes and cures. But the constitution of England is so exceedingly complex, that the nation may suffer for years together without being able to discover in which part the fault lies; some will say in one and some in another, and every political physician will advise a different medicine.

I know it is difficult to get over local or long standing prejudices, yet if we will suffer ourselves to examine the component parts of the English constitution, we shall find them to be the base remains of two ancient tyrannies, compounded with some new republican materials.

First.—The remains of monarchical tyranny in the person of the king.

Secondly.—The remains of aristocratical tyranny in the persons of the peers.

Thirdly.—The new republican materials in the persons of the commons, on whose virtue depends the freedom of England.

The two first, by being hereditary, are independent of the people; wherefore in a *constitutional sense* they contribute nothing towards the freedom of the state.

To say that the constitution of England is a *union* of three powers reciprocally *checking* each other, is farcical, either the words have no meaning, or they are flat contradictions.

To say that the commons is a check upon the king, presupposes two things:

First.—That the king is not to be trusted without

being looked after, or in other words, that a thirst for absolute power is the natural disease of monarchy.

Secondly.—That the commons, by being appointed for that purpose, are either wiser or more worthy of confidence than the crown.

But as the same constitution which gives the commons a power to check the king by withholding the supplies, gives afterwards the king a power to check the commons, by empowering him to reject their other bills; it again supposes that the king is wiser than those whom it has already supposed to be wiser than him. A mere absurdity!

There is something exceedingly ridiculous in the composition of monarchy; it first excludes a man from the means of information, yet empowers him to act in cases where the highest judgment is required. The state of a king shuts him from the world, yet the business of a king requires him to know it thoroughly; wherefore the different parts, by unnaturally opposing and destroying each other, prove the whole character to be absurd and useless.

Some writers have explained the English constitution thus: The king, say they, is one, the people another; the peers are an house in behalf of the king, the commons in behalf of the people; but this hath all the distinctions of an house divided against itself; and though the expressions be pleasantly arranged, yet when examined, they appear idle and ambiguous; and it will always happen, that the nicest construction that words are capable of, when applied to the description of some thing which either cannot exist, or is too incomprehensible to be within the compass of description, will be words of sound only, and though they may amuse the ear, they cannot inform the mind, for this explanation includes a previous question, viz. *How came the king by a power which the people are afraid to trust, and always obliged to check?* Such a power could not be the gift of a wise people, neither can any power, *which needs checking,* be from God; yet the provision, which the constitution makes, supposes such a power to exist.

But the provision is unequal to the task; the means either cannot or will not accomplish the end, and the whole affair is a felo de se; for as the greater weight will always carry up the less, and as all the wheels of a machine are put in motion by one, it only remains to know which power in the constitution has the most weight, for that will govern; and though the others, or a part of them, may clog, or, as the phrase is, check the rapidity of its motion, yet so long as they cannot stop it, their endeavours will be ineffectual; the first moving power will at last have its way, and what it wants in speed, is supplied by time.

That the crown is this overbearing part in the English constitution, needs not be mentioned, and that it derives its whole consequence merely from being the giver of places and pensions, is self-evident, wherefore, though we have been wise enough to shut and lock a door against absolute monarchy, we at the same time have been foolish enough to put the crown in possession of the key.

The prejudice of Englishmen in favour of their own government by king, lords and commons, arises as much or more from national pride than reason. Individuals are undoubtedly safer in England than in some other countries, but the *will* of the king is as much the *law* of the land in Britain as in France, with this difference, that instead of proceeding directly from his mouth, it is handed to the people under the more formidable shape of an act of parliament. For the fate of Charles the First hath only made kings more subtle—not more just.

Wherefore, laying aside all national pride and prejudice in favour of modes and forms, the plain truth is, that *it is wholly owing to the constitution of the people, and not to the constitution of the government,* that the crown is not as oppressive in England as in Turkey.

An inquiry into the *constitutional errors* in the English form of government is at this time highly necessary; for as we are never in a proper condition of doing justice to others, while we continue under the influence of some leading partiality, so neither are we capable of doing it to ourselves while we remain fettered by any obstinate prejudice. And as a man, who is attached to a prostitute, is unfitted to choose or judge a wife, so any prepossession in favour of a rotten constitution of government will disable us from discerning a good one.

Of monarchy and hereditary succession

Mankind being originally equals in the order of creation, the equality could only be destroyed by some subsequent circumstance; the distinctions of rich, and poor, may in a great measure be accounted for, and that without having recourse to the harsh, ill-sounding names of oppression and avarice. Oppression is often the *consequence*, but seldom or never the *means* of riches; and though avarice will preserve a man from being necessitously poor, it generally makes him too timorous to be wealthy.

But there is another and greater distinction, for which no truly natural or religious reason can be assigned, and that is, the distinction of men into KINGS and SUBJECTS. Male and female are the distinctions of nature, good and bad are distinctions of heaven; but how a race of men came into the world so exalted above the rest, and distinguished like some new species, is worth inquiring into, and whether they are the means of happiness or of misery to mankind.

In the early ages of the world, according to the

scripture chronology, there were no kings; the consequence of which was, there were no wars; it is the pride of kings which throw mankind into confusion. Holland without a king hath enjoyed more peace for this last century than any of the monarchical governments in Europe. Antiquity favours the same remark; for the quiet and rural lives of the first patriarchs hath a happy something in them, which vanishes away when we come to the history of Jewish royalty.

Government by kings was first introduced into the world by the Heathens, from whom the children of Israel copied the custom. It was the most prosperous invention the Devil ever set on foot for the promotion of idolatry. The Heathens paid divine honors to their deceased kings, and the Christian world hath improved on the plan, by doing the same to their living ones. How impious is the title of sacred majesty applied to a worm, who in the midst of his splendor is crumbling into dust!

As the exalting one man so greatly above the rest cannot be justified on the equal rights of nature, so neither can it be defended on the authority of scripture; for the will of the Almighty, as declared by Gideon and the prophet Samuel, expressly disapproves of government by kings. All antimonarchical parts of scripture have been very smoothly glossed over in monarchical governments, but they undoubtedly merit the attention of countries which have their governments yet to form. *"Render unto Caesar the things which are Caesar's"* is the scripture doctrine of courts, yet it is no support of monarchical government, for the Jews at that time were without a king, and in a state of vassalage to the Romans.

Near three thousand years passed away from the Mosaic account of the creation, till the Jews under a national delusion requested a king. Till then their form of government (except in extraordinary cases, where the Almighty interposed) was a kind of republic administered by a judge and the elders of the tribes. Kings they had none, and it was held sinful to acknowledge any being under that title but the Lord of Hosts. And when a man seriously reflects on the idolatrous homage which is paid to the persons of kings, he need not wonder that the Almighty, ever jealous of his honor, should disapprove of a form of government which so impiously invades the prerogative of heaven.

Monarchy is ranked in scripture as one of the sins of the Jews, for which a curse in reserve is denounced against them. The history of that transaction is worth attending to.

The children of Israel being oppressed by the Midianites, Gideon marched against them with a small army, and victory, thro' the divine interposition, decided in his favour. The Jews, elate with success, and attributing it to the generalship of Gideon, proposed making him a king, saying, *Rule thou over us, thou and thy son and thy son's son.* Here was temptation in its fullest extent; not a kingdom only, but an hereditary one, but Gideon in the piety of his soul replied, *I will not rule over you, neither shall my son rule over you,* THE LORD SHALL RULE OVER YOU. Words need not be more explicit; Gideon doth not decline the honor, but denieth their right to give it; neither doth he compliment them with invented declarations of his thanks, but in the positive stile of a prophet charges them with disaffection to their proper Sovereign, the King of heaven.

About one hundred and thirty years after this, they fell again into the same error. The hankering which the Jews had for the idolatrous customs of the Heathens, is something exceedingly unaccountable; but so it was, that laying hold of the misconduct of Samuel's two sons, who were entrusted with some secular concerns, they came in an abrupt and clamorous manner to Samuel, saying, *Behold thou art old, and thy sons walk not in thy ways, now make us a king to judge us, like all the other nations.* And here we cannot but observe that their motives were bad, viz. that they might be *like* unto other nations, i.e. the Heathens, whereas their true glory laid in being as much *unlike* them as possible. *But the thing displeased Samuel when they said, Give us a king to judge us; and Samuel prayed unto the Lord, and the Lord said unto Samuel, Hearken unto the voice of the people in all that they say unto thee, for they have not rejected thee, but they have rejected me,* THAT I SHOULD NOT REIGN OVER THEM. *According to all the works which they have done since the day that I brought them up out of Egypt, even unto this day; wherewith they have forsaken me and served other Gods; so do they also unto thee. Now therefore hearken unto their voice, howbeit, protest solemnly unto them and shew them the manner of the king that shall reign over them, i.e.* not of any particular king, but the general manner of the kings of the earth, whom Israel was so eagerly copying after. And notwithstanding the great distance of time and difference of manners, the character is still in fashion. *And Samuel told all the words of the Lord unto the people, that asked of him a king. And he said, This shall be the manner of the king that shall reign over you: he will take your sons and appoint them for himself, for his chariots, and to be his horsemen, and some shall run before his chariots* (this description agrees with the present mode of impressing men) *and he will appoint him captains over thousands and captains over fifties, and will set them to ear his ground and to reap his harvest, and to make his instruments of war, and instruments of his chariots; and he will take your daughters to be confectionaries, and to be cooks and to be bakers* (this describes the expence and luxury as well as the oppression of kings) *and he will take your fields and your olive yards, even the best of them, and give them to his servants; and he will take the tenth of your seed, and of your vineyards, and give them to his officers and to his servants* (by which we see that bribery, corruption and favouritism are the standing vices of kings) *and he will take the tenth of your men servants, and your maid servants, and your goodliest young men and your asses, and put them to his work; and he will take the tenth of your sheep, and ye shall be his servants, and ye shall cry out in that day because of your king which ye shall have chosen,* AND THE LORD WILL NOT HEAR YOU IN THAT DAY. This accounts for the continuation of monarchy; neither do the characters of the few good kings which have lived since, either sanctify the title, or blot out the sinfulness of the origin; the high encomium given of David takes no notice of him *officially as a king,* but only as a *man* after God's own heart. *Nevertheless the people refused to obey the voice of Samuel, and they said, Nay, but we will have a king over us, that we may be like all the nations, and that our king may judge us, and go out before us, and fight our battles.* Samuel continued to reason with them, but to no purpose; he set before them their ingratitude, but all would not avail; and seeing them bent on their folly, he cried out, *I will call unto the Lord, and he shall send thunder and rain* (which then was a punishment, being in the time of wheat harvest) *that ye may perceive and see that your wickedness is great which ye have done in the sight of the Lord,* IN ASKING YOU A KING. *So Samuel called unto the Lord, and the Lord sent thunder and rain that day, and all the people greatly feared the Lord and Samuel. And all the people said unto Samuel, pray for thy servants unto the Lord thy God that we die not, for* WE HAVE ADDED UNTO OUR SINS THIS EVIL, TO ASK A KING. These portions of scripture are direct and positive. They admit of no equivocal construction. That the Almighty hath here entered his protest against monarchical government, is true, or the scripture is false. And a man hath good reason to believe that there is as much of king-craft, as priest-craft, in withholding the scripture from the public in Popish countries. For monarchy in every instance is the Popery of government.

To the evil of monarchy we have added that of hereditary succession; and as the first is a degradation and lessening of ourselves, so the second, claimed as a matter of right, is an insult and an imposition on posterity. For all men being originally equals, no *one* by *birth* could have a right to set up his own family in perpetual preference to all others for ever, and though himself might deserve *some* decent degree of honors of his contemporaries, yet his descendants might be far too unworthy to inherit them. One of the strongest *natural* proofs of the folly of hereditary right in kings, is, that nature disapproves it, otherwise she would not so frequently turn it into ridicule by giving mankind an *Ass for a Lion*.

Secondly, as no man at first could possess any other public honors than were bestowed upon him, so the givers of those honors could have no power to give away the right of posterity. And though they might say, "We choose you for *our* head," they could not, without manifest injustice to their children, say "that your children and your children's children shall reign over *ours* for ever." Because such an unwise, unjust, unnatural compact might (perhaps) in the next succession put them under the government of a rogue or a fool. Most wise men, in their private sentiments, have ever treated hereditary right with contempt; yet it is one of those evils, which when once established is not easily removed; many submit from fear, others from superstition, and the more powerful part shares with the king the plunder of the rest.

This is supposing the present race of kings in the world to have had an honorable origin; whereas it is more than probable, that could we take off the dark covering of antiquity, and trace them to their first rise, that we should find the first of them nothing better than the principal ruffian of some restless gang, whose savage manners or pre-eminence in subtilty obtained him the title of chief among plunderers; and who by increasing in power, and extending his depredations, overawed the quiet and defenceless to purchase their safety by frequent contributions. Yet his electors could have no idea of giving hereditary right to his descendants, because such a perpetual exclusion of themselves was incompatible with the free and unrestrained principles they professed to live by. Wherefore, hereditary succession in the early ages of monarchy could not take place as a matter of claim, but as something casual or complimental; but as few or no records were extant in those days, and traditionary history stuffed with fables, it was very easy, after the lapse of a few generations, to trump up some superstitious tale, conveniently timed, Mahomet like, to cram hereditary right down the throats of the vulgar. Perhaps the disorders which threatened, or seemed to threaten, on the decease of a leader and the choice of a new one (for elections among ruffians could not be very orderly) induced many at first to favor hereditary pretensions; by which means it happened, as it hath happened since, that what at first was submitted to as a convenience, was afterwards claimed as a right.

England, since the conquest, hath known some few good monarchs, but groaned beneath a much larger number of bad ones; yet no man in his senses can say that their claim under William the Conqueror is a very honorable one. A French bastard landing with an armed banditti, and establishing himself king of England against the consent of the natives, is in plain terms a very paltry rascally original.—It certainly hath no divinity in it. However, it is needless to spend much time in exposing the folly of hereditary right; if there are any so weak as to believe it, let them promiscuously worship the ass and lion, and welcome. I shall neither copy their humility, nor disturb their devotion.

Yet I should be glad to ask how they suppose kings came at first? The question admits but of three answers, viz. either by lot, by election, or by usurpation. If the first king was taken by lot, it establishes a precedent for the next, which excludes hereditary succession. Saul was by lot, yet the succession was not hereditary, neither does it appear from that transaction there was any intention it ever should. If the first king of any country was by election, that likewise establishes a precedent for the next; for to say, that the *right* of all future generations is taken away, by the act of the first electors, in their choice not only of a king, but of a family of kings for ever, hath no parallel in or out of scripture but the doctrine of original sin, which supposes the free will of all men lost in Adam; and from such comparison, and it will admit of no other, hereditary succession can derive no glory. For as in Adam all sinned, and as in the first electors all men obeyed; as in the one all mankind were subjected to Satan, and in the other to Sovereignty; as our innocence was lost in the first, and our authority in the last; and as both disable us from reassuming some former state and privilege, it unanswerably follows that original sin and hereditary succession are parallels. Dishonorable rank! Inglorious connexion! Yet the most subtile sophist cannot produce a juster simile.

As to usurpation, no man will be so hardy as to defend it; and that William the Conqueror was an usurper is a fact not to be contradicted. The plain truth is, that the antiquity of English monarchy will not bear looking into.

But it is not so much the absurdity as the evil of hereditary succession which concerns mankind. Did it ensure a race of good and wise men it would have the seal of divine authority, but as it opens a door to the *foolish,* the *wicked,* and the *improper,* it hath in it the nature of oppression. Men who look upon themselves born to reign, and others to obey, soon grow insolent; selected from the rest of mankind their minds are early poisoned by importance; and the world they act in differs so materially from the world at large, that they have but little opportunity of knowing its true interests, and when they succeed to the government are frequently the most ignorant and unfit of any throughout the dominions.

Another evil which attends hereditary succession is, that the throne is subject to be possessed by a minor at any age; all which time the regency, acting under the cover of a king, have every opportunity and inducement to betray their trust. The same national misfortune happens, when a king, worn out with age and infirmity, enters the last stage of human weakness. In both these cases the public becomes a prey to every miscreant, who can tamper successfully with the follies · either of age or infancy.

The most plausible plea, which hath ever been offered in favour of hereditary succession, is, that it preserves a nation from civil wars; and were this true, it would be weighty; whereas, it is the most barefaced falsity ever imposed upon mankind. The whole history of England disowns the fact. Thirty kings and two minors have reigned in that distracted kingdom since the conquest, in which time there have been (including the Revolution) no less than eight civil wars and nineteen rebellions. Wherefore instead of making for peace, it makes against it, and destroys the very foundation it seems to stand on.

The contest for monarchy and succession, between the houses of York and Lancaster, laid England in a scene of blood for many years. Twelve pitched battles, besides skirmishes and sieges, were fought between Henry and Edward. Twice was Henry prisoner to Edward, who in his turn was prisoner to Henry. And so uncertain is the fate of war and the temper of a nation, when nothing but personal matters are the ground of a quarrel, that Henry was taken in triumph from a prison to a palace, and Edward obliged to fly from a palace to a foreign land; yet, as sudden transitions of temper are seldom lasting, Henry in his turn was driven from the throne, and Edward recalled to succeed him. The parliament always following the strongest side.

This contest began in the reign of Henry the Sixth, and was not entirely extinguished till Henry the Seventh, in whom the families were united. Including a period of 67 years, viz. from 1422 to 1489.

In short, monarchy and succession have laid (not this or that kingdom only) but the world in blood and ashes. 'Tis a form of government which the word of God bears testimony against, and blood will attend it.

If we inquire into the business of a king, we shall find that in some countries they have none; and after sauntering away their lives without pleasure to themselves or advantage to the nation, withdraw from the scene, and leave their successors to tread the same idle ground. In absolute monarchies the whole weight of business, civil and military, lies on the king; the children of Israel in their request for a king, urged this plea "that he may judge us, and go out before us and fight our battles." But in countries where he is neither a judge nor a general, as in England, a man would be puzzled to know what *is* his business.

The nearer any government approaches to a republic the less business there is for a king. It is somewhat difficult to find a proper name for the government of England. Sir William Meredith calls it a republic; but in its present state it is unworthy of the name, because the corrupt influence of the crown, by having all the places in its disposal, hath so effectually swallowed up the power, and eaten out the virtue of the house of commons (the republican part in the constitution) that the government of England is nearly as monarchical as that of France or Spain. Men fall out with names without understanding them. For it is the republican and not the monarchical part of the constitution of England which Englishmen glory in, viz. the liberty of choosing an house of commons from out of their own body—and it is easy to see that when republican virtue fails, slavery ensues. Why is the constitution of England sickly, but because monarchy hath poisoned the republic, the crown hath engrossed the commons?

In England a king hath little more to do than to make war and give away places; which in plain terms, is to impoverish the nation and set it together by the ears. A pretty business indeed for a man to be allowed eight hundred thousand sterling for a year, and worshipped into the bargain! Of more worth is one honest man to society and in the sight of God, than all the crowned ruffians that ever lived.

Thoughts on the present state of American affairs

In the following pages I offer nothing more than simple facts, plain arguments, and common sense; and have no other preliminaries to settle with the reader, than that he will divest himself of prejudice and prepossession, and suffer his reason and his feelings to determine for themselves; that he will put *on,* or rather that he will not put *off* the true character of a man, and generously enlarge his views beyond the present day.

Volumes have been written on the subject of the struggle between England and America. Men of all ranks have embarked in the controversy, from different motives, and with various designs; but all have been ineffectual, and the period of debate is closed. Arms, as the last resource, decide the contest; the appeal was the choice of the king, and the continent hath accepted the challenge.

It hath been reported of the late Mr. Pelham (who tho' an able minister was not without his faults) that on his being attacked in the house of commons, on the score, that his measures were only of a temporary kind, replied *"they will last my time."* Should a thought so fatal and unmanly possess the colonies in the present contest, the name of ancestors will be remembered by future generations with detestation.

The sun never shined on a cause of greater worth. 'Tis not the affair of a city, a county, a province, or a kingdom, but of a continent—of at least one eighth part of the habitable globe. 'Tis not the concern of a day, a year, or an age; posterity are virtually involved in the contest, and will be more or less affected, even to the end of time, by the proceedings now. Now is the seed-time of continental union, faith and honor. The least fracture now will be like a name engraved with the point of a pin on the tender rind of a young oak; the wound will enlarge with the tree, and posterity read it in full grown characters.

By referring the matter from argument to arms, a new aera for politics is struck; a new method of thinking hath arisen. All plans, proposals, &c. prior to the nineteenth of April, *i.e.* to the commencement of hostilities, are like the almanacks of the last year; which, though proper then are superseded and useless now. Whatever was advanced by the advocates on either side of the question then, terminated in one and the same point, viz. a union with Great-Britain; the only difference between the parties was the method of effecting it; the one proposing force, the other friendship; but it hath so far happened that the first hath failed, and the second hath withdrawn her influence.

As much hath been said of the advantages of reconciliation, which, like an agreeable dream, hath passed away and left us as we were, it is but right, that we should examine the contrary side of the argument, and inquire into some of the many material injuries which these colonies sustain, and always will sustain, by being connected with, and dependant on Great-Britain: To examine that connexion and dependance, on the principles of nature and common sense, to see what we have to trust to, if separated, and what we are to expect, if dependant.

I have heard it asserted by some, that as America hath flourished under her former connexion with Great-Britain, that the same connexion is necessary towards her future happiness, and will always have the same effect. Nothing can be more fallacious than this kind of argument. We may as well assert that because a child has thrived upon milk, that it is never to have meat, or that the first twenty years of our lives is to become a precedent for the next twenty. But even this is admitting more than is true, for I answer roundly, that America would have flourished as much, and probably much more, had no European power had any thing to do with her. The commerce, by which she hath enriched herself, are the necessaries of life, and will always have a market while eating is the custom of Europe.

But she has protected us, say some. That she has engrossed us is true, and defended the continent at our expence as well as her own is admitted, and she would have defended Turkey from the same motive, viz. the sake of trade and dominion.

Alas, we have been long led away by ancient prejudices, and made large sacrifices to superstition. We have boasted the protection of Great-Britain, without considering, that her motive was *interest* not *attachment;* that she did not protect us from *our enemies* on *our account,* but from *her enemies* on *her own account,* from those who had no quarrel with us on any *other account,* and who will always be our enemies on the *same account.* Let Britain waive her pretensions to the continent, or the continent throw off the dependance, and we should be at peace with France and Spain were they at war with Britain. The miseries of Hanover last war ought to warn us against connexions.

It has lately been asserted in parliament, that the colonies have no relation to each other but through the parent country, *i.e.* that Pennsylvania and the Jerseys, and so on for the rest, are sister colonies by the way of England; this is certainly a very round-about way of proving relationship, but it is the nearest and only true way of proving enemyship, if I may so call it. France and Spain never were, nor perhaps ever will be our enemies as *Americans,* but as our being the *subjects of Great-Britain.*

But Britain is the parent country, say some. Then the more shame upon her conduct. Even brutes do not devour their young, nor savages make war upon their families; wherefore the assertion, if true, turns to her reproach; but it happens not to be true, or only partly so, and the phrase *parent* or *mother country* hath been jesuitically adopted by the king and his parasites, with a low papistical design of gaining an unfair bias on the credulous weakness of our minds. Europe, and not England, is the parent country of America. This new world hath been the asylum for the persecuted lovers of civil and religious liberty from *every part* of Europe. Hither have they fled, not from the tender embraces of the mother, but from the cruelty of the monster; and it is so far true of England, that the same tyranny which drove the first emigrants from home, pursues their descendants still.

In this extensive quarter of the globe, we forget the narrow limits of three hundred and sixty miles (the extent of England) and carry our friendship on a larger scale; we claim brotherhood with every European Christian, and triumph in the generosity of the sentiment.

It is pleasant to observe by what regular gradations

we surmount the force of local prejudice, as we enlarge our acquaintance with the world. A man born
in any town in England divided into parishes, will naturally associate most with his fellow-parishioners (because their interests in many cases will be common)
and distinguish him by the name of *neighbour;* if he
meet him but a few miles from home, he drops the
narrow idea of a street, and salutes him by the name
of *townsman;* if he travel out of the county, and meet
him in any other, he forgets the minor divisions of
street and town, and calls him *countryman,* i.e. *coun-
tyman;* but if in their foreign excursions they should
associate in France or any other part of *Europe,* their
local remembrance would be enlarged into that of *Englishmen.* And by a just parity of reasoning, all Euro-
peans meeting in America, or any other quarter of the
globe, are *countrymen;* for England, Holland, Germany, or Sweden, when compared with the whole,
stand in the same places on the larger scale, which the
divisions of street, town, and county do on the smaller
ones; distinctions too limited for continental minds.
Not one third of the inhabitants, even of this province,
are of English descent. Wherefore I reprobate the
phrase of parent or mother country applied to England only, as being false, selfish, narrow and un-
generous.

But admitting, that we were all of English descent,
what does it amount to? Nothing. Britain, being now
an open enemy, extinguishes every other name and
title: And to say that reconciliation is our duty, is truly
farcical. The first king of England, of the present line
(William the Conqueror) was a Frenchman, and half
the Peers of England are descendants from the same
country; wherefore, by the same method of reasoning,
England ought to be governed by France.

Much hath been said of the united strength of Britain and the colonies, that in conjunction they might
bid defiance to the world. But this is mere presump-

tion; the fate of war is uncertain, neither do the expressions mean any thing; for this continent would never suffer itself to be drained of inhabitants, to support the British arms in either Asia, Africa, or Europe.

Besides what have we to do with setting the world at defiance? Our plan is commerce, and that, well attended to, will secure us the peace and friendship of all Europe; because, it is the interest of all Europe to have America a *free port*. Her trade will always be a protection, and her barrenness of gold and silver secure her from invaders.

I challenge the warmest advocate for reconciliation, to shew, a single advantage that this continent can reap, by being connected with Great-Britain. I repeat the challenge, not a single advantage is derived. Our corn will fetch its price in any market in Europe, and our imported goods must be paid for, buy them where we will.

But the injuries and disadvantages we sustain by that connexion, are without number; and our duty to mankind at large, as well as to ourselves, instruct us to renounce the alliance: Because, any submission to, or dependance on Great-Britain, tends directly to involve this continent in European wars and quarrels; and sets us at variance with nations, who would otherwise seek our friendship, and against whom, we have neither anger nor complaint. As Europe is our market for trade, we ought to form no partial connexion with any part of it. It is the true interest of America to steer clear of European contentions, which she never can do, while by her dependance on Britain, she is made the make-weight in the scale of British politics.

Europe is too thickly planted with kingdoms to be long at peace, and whenever a war breaks out between England and any foreign power, the trade of America goes to ruin, *because of her connexion with Britain.* The next war may not turn out like the last, and should it not, the advocates for reconciliation now, will be wishing for separation then, because, neutrality in that case, would be a safer convoy than a man of war. Every thing that is right or natural pleads for separation. The blood of the slain, the weeping voice of nature cries, 'TIS TIME TO PART. Even the distance at which the Almighty hath placed England and America, is a strong and natural proof, that the authority of the one, over the other, was never the design of Heaven. The time likewise at which the continent was discovered, adds weight to the argument, and the manner in which it was peopled increases the force of it. The reformation was preceded by the discovery of America, as if the Almighty graciously meant to open a sanctuary to the persecuted in future years, when home should afford neither friendship nor safety.

The authority of Great-Britain over this continent, is a form of government, which sooner or later must have an end: And a serious mind can draw no true pleasure by looking forward, under the painful and positive conviction, that what he calls "the present constitution" is merely temporary. As parents, we can have no joy, knowing that *this government* is not sufficiently lasting to ensure any thing which we may bequeath to posterity: And by a plain method of argument, as we are running the next generation into debt, we ought to do the work of it, otherwise we use them meanly and pitifully. In order to discover the line of our duty rightly, we should take our children in our hand, and fix our station a few years farther into life; that eminence will present a prospect, which a few present fears and prejudices conceal from our sight.

Though I would carefully avoid giving unnecessary offence, yet I am inclined to believe, that all those who espouse the doctrine of reconciliation, may be included within the following descriptions. Interested men, who are not to be trusted; weak men, who *cannot* see; prejudiced men, who *will not* see; and a certain set of moderate men, who think better of the European world than it deserves; and this last class, by an ill-judged deliberation, will be the cause of more calamities to this continent, than all the other three.

It is the good fortune of many to live distant from the scene of sorrow; the evil is not sufficient brought to *their* doors to make *them* feel the precariousness with which all American property is possessed. But let our imaginations transport us for a few moments to Boston, that seat of wretchedness will teach us wisdom, and instruct us for ever to renounce a power in whom we can have no trust. The inhabitants of that unfortunate city, who but a few months ago were in ease and affluence, have now, no other alternative than to stay and starve, or turn out to beg. Endangered by the fire of their friends if they continue within the city, and plundered by the soldiery if they leave it. In their present condition they are prisoners without the hope of redemption, and in a general attack for their relief, they would be exposed to the fury of both armies.

Men of passive tempers look somewhat lightly over the offences of Britain, and, still hoping for the best, are apt to call out, *"Come, come, we shall be friends again, for all this."* But examine the passions and feelings of mankind, bring the doctrine of reconciliation to the touchstone of nature, and then tell me, whether you can hereafter love, honor, and faithfully serve the power that hath carried fire and sword into your land? If you cannot do all these, then are you only deceiving yourselves, and by your delay bringing ruin upon posterity. Your future connexion with Britain, whom you can neither love nor honor, will be forced and unnatural, and being formed only on the plan of present convenience, will in a little time fall into a relapse more wretched than the first. But if you say, you can still pass the violations over, then I ask, Hath your house been burnt? Hath your property been destroyed before your face? Are your wife and children destitute of a bed to lie on, or bread to live on? Have you lost a parent or a child by their hands, and yourself the ruined and wretched survivor? If you have not, then are you not a judge of those who have. But if you have, and still can shake hands with the murderers, then you are unworthy the name of husband, father, friend, or lover, and whatever may be your rank or title in life, you have the heart of a coward, and the spirit of a sycophant.

This is not inflaming or exaggerating matters, but trying them by those feelings and affections which nature justifies, and without which, we should be incapable of discharging the social duties of life, or enjoying the felicities of it. I mean not to exhibit horror for the purpose of provoking revenge, but to awaken us from fatal and unmanly slumbers, that we may pursue determinately some fixed object. It is not in the power of Britain or of Europe to conquer America, if she do not conquer herself by *delay* and *timidity*. The present winter is worth an age if rightly employed, but if lost or neglected, the whole continent will partake of the misfortune; and there is no punishment which that man will not deserve, be he who, or what, or where he will, that may be the means of sacrificing a season so precious and useful.

It is repugnant to reason, to the universal order of things, to all examples from former ages, to suppose, that this continent can longer remain subject to any external power. The most sanguine in Britain does not think so. The utmost stretch of human wisdom cannot, at this time, compass a plan short of separation, which can promise the continent even a year's security. Reconciliation is *now* a fallacious dream. Nature hath deserted the connexion, and Art cannot supply her place.

For, as Milton wisely expresses, "never can true reconcilement grow, where wounds of deadly hate have pierc'd so deep."

Every quiet method for peace hath been ineffectual. Our prayers have been rejected with disdain; and only tended to convince us, that nothing flatters vanity, or confirms obstinacy in Kings more than repeated petitioning—and nothing hath contributed more than that very measure to make the Kings of Europe absolute: Witness Denmark and Sweden. Wherefore, since nothing but blows will do, for God's sake, let us come to a final separation, and not leave the next generation to be cutting throats, under the violated unmeaning names of parent and child.

To say, they will never attempt it again is idle and visionary, we thought so at the repeal of the stampact, yet a year or two undeceived us; as well may we suppose that nations, which have been once defeated, will never renew the quarrel.

As to government matters, it is not in the power of Britain to do this continent justice: The business of it will soon be too weighty, and intricate, to be managed with any tolerable degree of convenience, by a power so distant from us, and so very ignorant of us; for if they cannot conquer us, they cannot govern us. To be always running three or four thousand miles with a tale or a petition, waiting four or five months for an answer, which when obtained requires five or six more to explain it in, will in a few years be looked upon as folly and childishness—There was a time when it was proper, and there is a proper time for it to cease.

Small islands not capable of protecting themselves, are the proper objects for kingdoms to take under their care; but there is something very absurd, in supposing a continent to be perpetually governed by an island. In no instance hath nature made the satellite larger than its primary planet, and as England and America, with respect to each other, reverses the common order of nature, it is evident they belong to different systems; England to Europe, America to itself.

I am not induced by motives of pride, party, or resentment to espouse the doctrine of separation and independance; I am clearly, positively, and conscientiously persuaded that it is the true interest of this continent to be so; that every thing short of *that* is mere patchwork, that it can afford no lasting felicity,—that it is leaving the sword to our children, and shrinking back at a time, when, a little more, a little farther, would have rendered this continent the glory of the earth.

As Britain hath not manifested the least inclination towards a compromise, we may be assured that no terms can be obtained worthy the acceptance of the continent, or any ways equal to the expence of blood and treasure we have been already put to.

The object, contended for, ought always to bear some just proportion to the expence. The removal of North, or the whole detestable junto, is a matter un worthy the millions we have expended. A temporary stoppage of trade, was an inconvenience, which would have sufficiently balanced the repeal of all the acts complained of, had such repeals been obtained; but if the whole continent must take up arms, if every man must be a soldier, it is scarcely worth our while to fight against a contemptible ministry only. Dearly, dearly, do we pay for the repeal of the acts, if that is all we fight for; for in a just estimation, it is as great a folly to pay a Bunker-hill price for law, as for land. As I have always considered the independancy of this continent, as an event, which sooner or later must arrive, so from the late rapid progress of the continent to maturity, the event could not be far off. Wherefore, on the breaking out of hostilities, it was not worth while to have disputed a matter, which time would have finally redressed, unless we meant to be in earnest; otherwise, it is like wasting an estate on a suit at law, to regulate the trespasses of a tenant, whose

lease is just expiring. No man was a warmer wisher for
reconciliation than myself, before the fatal nineteenth of
April 1775 ,* but the moment the event of that day was
made known, I rejected the hardened, sullen tempered
Pharaoh of England for ever; and disdain the wretch,
that with the pretended title of FATHER OF HIS PEOPLE
can unfeelingly hear of their slaughter, and composedly
sleep with their blood upon his soul.

But admitting that matters were now made up, what
would be the event? I answer, the ruin of the continent. And that for several reasons.

First. The powers of governing still remaining in the
hands of the king, he will have a negative over the
whole legislation of this continent. And as he hath
shewn himself such an inveterate enemy to liberty,
and discovered such a thirst for arbitrary power; is he,
or is he not, a proper man to say to these colonies,
"You shall make no laws but what I please." And is
there any inhabitant in America so ignorant, as not
to know, that according to what is called the *present
constitution,* that this continent can make no laws but
what the king gives leave to; and is there any man
so unwise, as not to see, that (considering what has
happened) he will suffer no law to be made here, but
such as suit *his* purpose. We may be as effectually
enslaved by the want of laws in America as by submitting to laws made for us in England. After matters
are made up (as it is called) can there be any doubt,
but the whole power of the crown will be exerted, to
keep this continent as low and humble as possible?
Instead of going forward we shall go backward, or be
perpetually quarrelling or ridiculously petitioning.—
We are already greater than the king wishes us to be,
and will he not hereafter endeavour to make us less?
To bring the matter to one point. Is the power who
is jealous of our prosperity, a proper power to govern

* Massacre at Lexington.

us? Whoever says *No* to this question, is an *independent,* for independancy means no more, than, whether we shall make our own laws, or whether the king, the greatest enemy this continent hath, or can have, shall tell us *"there shall be no laws but such as I like."*

But the king you will say has a negative in England; the people there can make no laws without his consent. In point of right and good order, there is something very ridiculous, that a youth of twenty-one (which hath often happened) shall say to several millions of people, older and wiser than himself, I forbid this or that act of yours to be law. But in this place I decline this sort of reply, though I will never cease to expose the absurdity of it, and only answer, that England being the King's residence, and America not so, makes quite another case. The king's negative *here* is ten times more dangerous and fatal than it can be in England, for *there* he will scarcely refuse his consent to a bill for putting England into as strong a state of defence as possible, and in America he would never suffer such a bill to be passed.

America is only a secondary object in the system of British politics, England consults the good of *this* country, no farther than it answers her *own* purpose. Wherefore, her own interest leads her to suppress the growth of *ours* in every case which doth not promote her advantage, or in the least interferes with it. A pretty state we should soon be in under such a second-hand government, considering what has happened! Men do not change from enemies to friends by the alteration of a name: And in order to shew that reconciliation *now* is a dangerous doctrine, I affirm, *that it would be policy in the king at this time, to repeal the acts for the sake of reinstating himself in the government of the provinces;* in order, that HE MAY ACCOMPLISH BY CRAFT AND SUBTILTY, IN THE LONG RUN, WHAT HE CANNOT DO BY FORCE AND VIOLENCE IN THE SHORT ONE. Reconciliation and ruin are nearly related.

Secondly. That as even the best terms, which we

can expect to obtain, can amount to no more than a temporary expedient, or a kind of government by guardianship, which can last no longer than till the colonies come of age, so the general face and state of things, in the interim, will be unsettled and unpromising. Emigrants of property will not choose to come to a country whose form of government hangs but by a thread, and who is every day tottering on the brink of commotion and disturbance; and numbers of the present inhabitants would lay hold of the interval, to dispose of their effects, and quit the continent.

But the most powerful of all arguments, is, that nothing but independance, i.e. a continental form of government, can keep the peace of the continent and preserve it inviolate from civil wars. I dread the event of a reconciliation with Britain now, as it is more than probable, that it will be followed by a revolt somewhere or other, the consequences of which may be far more fatal than all the malice of Britain.

Thousands are already ruined by British barbarity; (thousands more will probably suffer the same fate). Those men have other feelings than us who have nothing suffered. All they *now* possess is liberty, what they before enjoyed is sacrificed to its service, and having nothing more to lose, they disdain submission. Besides, the general temper of the colonies, towards a British government, will be like that of a youth, who is nearly out of his time; they will care very little about her. And a government which cannot preserve the peace, is no government at all, and in that case we pay our money for nothing; and pray what is it that Britain can do whose power will be wholly on paper, should a civil tumult break out the very day after reconciliation? I have heard some men say, many of whom I believe spoke without thinking, that they dreaded an independance, fearing that it would produce civil wars. It is but seldom that our first thoughts are truly correct, and that is the case here; for there are ten times more to dread from a patched up connexion than from independance. I make the sufferers case my own, and I protest, that were I driven from house and home, my property destroyed, and my circumstances ruined, that as man, sensible of injuries, I could never relish the doctrine of reconciliation, or consider myself bound thereby.

The colonies have manifested such a spirit of good order and obedience to continental government, as is sufficient to make every reasonable person easy and happy on that head. No man can assign the least pretence for his fears, on any other grounds, than such as are truly childish and ridiculous, viz. that one colony will be striving for superiority over another.

Where there are no distinctions there can be no superiority, perfect equality affords no temptation. The republics of Europe are all (and we may say always) in peace. Holland and Swisserland are without wars, foreign or domestic: Monarchical governments, it is true, are never long at rest; the crown itself is a temptation to enterprizing ruffians at *home;* and that degree of pride and insolence ever attendant on regal authority, swells into a rupture with foreign powers, in instances, where a republican government, by being formed on more natural principles, would negotiate the mistake.

If there is any true cause of fear respecting independance, it is because no plan is yet laid down. Men do not see their way out—Wherefore, as an opening into that business, I offer the following hints; at the same time modestly affirming, that I have no other opinion of them myself, than that they may be the means of giving rise to something better. Could the straggling thoughts of individuals be collected, they would frequently form materials for wise and able men to improve into useful matter.

LET the assemblies be annual, with a President only. The representation more equal. Their business wholly domestic, and subject to the authority of a Continental Congress.

Let each colony be divided into six, eight, or ten, convenient districts, each district to send a proper number of delegates to Congress, so that each colony send at least thirty. The whole number in Congress will be at least 390. Each Congress to sit and to choose a president by the following method. When the delegates are met, let a colony be taken from the whole thirteen colonies by lot, after which, let the whole Congress choose (by ballot) a president from out of the delegates of *that* province. In the next Congress, let a colony be taken by lot from twelve only, omitting that colony from which the president was taken in the former Congress, and so proceeding on till the whole thirteen shall have had their proper rotation. And in order that nothing may pass into a law but what is satisfactorily just, not less than three fifths of the Congress to be called a majority—He that will promote discord, under a government so equally formed as this, would have joined Lucifer in his revolt.

But as there is a peculiar delicacy, from whom, or in what manner, this business must first arise, and as it seems most agreeable and consistent, that it should come from some intermediate body between the governed and the governors, that is, between the Congress and the people, let a CONTINENTAL CONFERENCE be held, in the following manner, and for the following purpose.

A committee of twenty-six members of Congress, viz. two for each colony. Two Members from each House of Assembly, or Provincial Convention; and five representatives of the people at large, to be chosen in the capital city or town of each province, for and in behalf of the whole province, by as many qualified voters as shall think proper to attend from all parts of the province for that purpose; or, if more convenient, the representatives may be chosen in two or three of the most populous parts thereof. In this conference, thus assembled, will be united, the two grand principles of business *knowledge* and *power*. The members of Congress, Assemblies, or Conventions, by having had experience in national concerns, will be able and useful counsellors, and the whole, being empowered by the people, will have a truly legal authority.

The conferring members being met, let their business be to frame a CONTINENTAL CHARTER, or Charter of the United Colonies; (answering to what is called the Magna Charta of England) fixing the number and manner of choosing members of Congress, members of Assembly, with their date of sitting, and drawing the line of business and jurisdiction between them: (Always remembering, that our strength is continental, not provincial:) Securing freedom and property to all men, and above all things, the free exercise of religion, according to the dictates of conscience; with such other matter as is necessary for a charter to contain. Immediately after which, the said Conference to dissolve, and the bodies which shall be chosen conformable to the said charter, to be the legislators and governors of this continent for the time being: Whose peace and happiness may God preserve, Amen.

· Should any body of men be hereafter delegated for this or some similar purpose, I offer them the following extracts from that wise observer on governments *Dragonetti*. "The science" says he "of the politician consists in fixing the true point of happiness and freedom. Those men would deserve the gratitude of ages, who should discover a mode of government that contained the greatest sum of individual happiness, with the least national expence.

Dragonetti on virtue and rewards."

But where, says some, is the King of America? I'll tell you. Friend, he reigns above, and doth not make havoc of mankind like the Royal Brute of Britain. Yet that we may not appear to be defective even in earthly honors, let a day be solemnly set apart for proclaiming the charter; let it be brought forth placed on the divine law, the word of God; let a crown be placed thereon, by which the world may know, that so far we approve of monarchy, that in America THE LAW IS KING. For as in absolute governments the King is law, so in free countries the law *ought* to be King; and there ought to be no other. But lest any ill use should afterwards arise, let the crown at the conclusion of the ceremony, be demolished, and scattered among the people whose right it is.

A government of our own is our natural right: And when a man seriously reflects on the precariousness of human affairs, he will become convinced, that it is infinitely wiser and safer, to form a constitution of our own in a cool deliberate manner, while we have it in our power, than to trust such an interesting event to time and chance. If we omit it now, some* Massanello may hereafter arise, who laying hold of popular disquietudes, may collect together the desperate and the discontented, and by assuming to themselves the powers of government, may sweep away the liberties of the continent like a deluge. Should the government of America return again into the hands of Britain, the tottering situation of things will be a temptation for some desperate adventurer to try his fortune; and in such a case, what relief can Britain give? Ere she could hear the news, the fatal business might be done; and ourselves suffering like the wretched Britons under the oppression of the Conqueror. Ye that oppose independance now, ye know not what ye do; ye are opening a door to eternal tyranny, by keeping vacant the seat of government. There are thousands, and tens of thousands, who would think it glorious to expel

* Thomas Anello otherwise Massanello a fisherman of Naples, who after spiriting up his countrymen in the public market-place, against the oppressions of the Spaniards, to whom the place was then subject prompted them to revolt, and in the space of a day became king.

from the continent that barbarous and hellish power, which hath stirred up the Indians and Negroes to destroy us; the cruelty hath a double guilt, it is dealing brutally by us, and treacherously by them.

To talk of friendship with those in whom our reason forbids us to have faith, and our affections wounded through a thousand pores instruct us to detest, is madness and folly. Every day wears out the little remains of kindred between us and them, and can there be any reason to hope, that as the relationship expires, the affection will increase, or that we shall agree better, when we have ten times more and greater concerns to quarrel over than ever?

Ye that tell us of harmony and reconciliation, can ye restore to us the time that is past? Can ye give to prostitution its former innocence? Neither can ye reconcile Britain and America. The last cord now is broken, the people of England are presenting addresses against us. There are injuries which nature cannot forgive; she would cease to be nature if she did. As well can the lover forgive the ravisher of his mistress, as the continent forgive the murders of Britain. The Almighty hath implanted in us these inextinguishable feelings for good and wise purposes. They are the guardians of his image in our hearts. They distinguish us from the herd of common animals. The social compact would dissolve, and justice be extirpated the earth, or have only a casual existence were we callous to the touches of affection. The robber, and the murderer, would often escape unpunished, did not the injuries which our tempers sustain, provoke us into justice.

O ye that love mankind! Ye that dare oppose, not only the tyranny, but the tyrant, stand forth! Every spot of the old world is overrun with oppression. Freedom hath been hunted round the globe. Asia, and Africa, have long expelled her—Europe regards her like a stranger, and England hath given her warning to depart. O! receive the fugitive, and prepare in time an asylum for mankind.

Of the present ABILITY of AMERICA, with some miscellaneous REFLEXIONS

I have never met with a man, either in England or America, who hath not confessed his opinion, that a separation between the countries, would take place one time or other: And there is no instance, in which we have shewn less judgment, than in endeavouring to describe, what we call the ripeness or fitness of the Continent for independance.

As all men allow the measure, and vary only in their opinion of the time, let us, in order to remove mistakes, take a general survey of things, and endeavour, if possible, to find out the *very* time. But we need not go far, the inquiry ceases at once, for, the *time hath found us*. The general concurrence, the glorious union of all things prove the fact.

It is not in numbers, but in unity, that our great strength lies; yet our present numbers are sufficient to repel the force of all the world. The Continent hath, at this time, the largest body of armed and disciplined men of any power under Heaven; and is just arrived at that pitch of strength, in which no single colony is able to support itself, and the whole, when united, can accomplish the matter, and either more, or, less than this, might be fatal in its effects. Our land force is already sufficient, and as to naval affairs, we cannot be insensible, that Britain would never suffer an American man of war to be built, while the continent remained in her hands. Wherefore, we should be no forwarder an hundred years hence in that branch, than we are now; but the truth is, we should be less so, because the timber of the country is every day diminishing, and that, which will remain at last, will be far off and difficult to procure.

Were the continent crowded with inhabitants, her sufferings under the present circumstances would be intolerable. The more seaport towns we had, the more should we have both to defend and to lose. Our present numbers are so happily proportioned to our wants, that no man need be idle. The diminution of trade affords an army, and the necessities of an army create a new trade.

Debts we have none; and whatever we may contract on this account will serve as a glorious memento of our virtue. Can we but leave posterity with a settled form of government, an independant constitution of its own, the purchase at any price will be cheap. But to expend millions for the sake of getting a few vile acts repealed, and routing the present ministry only, is unworthy the charge, and is using posterity with the utmost cruelty; because it is leaving them the great work to do, and a debt upon their backs, from which they derive no advantage. Such a thought is unworthy a man of honor, and is the true characteristic of a narrow heart and a peddling politician.

The debt we may contract doth not deserve our regard, if the work be but accomplished. No nation ought to be without a debt. A national debt is a national bond; and when it bears no interest, is in no case a grievance. Britain is oppressed with a debt of upwards of one hundred and forty millions sterling, for which she pays upwards of four millions interest. And as a compensation for her debt, she has a large navy; America is without a debt, and without a navy; yet for the twentieth part of the English national debt, could have a navy as large again. The navy of England is not worth, at this time, more than three millions and an half sterling.

The first and second editions of this pamphlet were published without the following calculations, which are now given as a proof that the above estimation of the navy is a just one. *See Entic's naval history, intro.* page 56.

The charge of building a ship of each rate, and furnishing her with masts, yards, sails and rigging, together with a proportion of eight months boatswain's and carpenter's sea-stores, as calculated by Mr. Burchett, Secretary to the navy.

		£
For a ship of a 100 guns	—	35,553
90	— —	29,886
80	— —	23,638
70	— —	17,785
60	— —	14,197
50	— —	10,606
40	— —	7,558
30	— —	5,846
20	— —	3,710

And from hence it is easy to sum up the value, or cost rather, of the whole British navy, which in the year 1757, when it was at its greatest glory consisted of the following ships and guns:

Ships	Guns	Cost of one.		Cost of all.
6 —	100 —	35,553*l.*	———	213,318*l.*
12 —	90 —	29,886	———	358,632
12 —	80 —	23,638	———	283,656
43 —	70 —	17,785	———	764,755
35 —	60 —	14,197	———	496,895
40 —	50 —	10,606	———	424,240
45 —	40 —	7,558	———	340,110
58 —	20 —	3,710	———	215,180
85 Sloops, bombs, and fireships, one with another,		} 2,000		170,000
			Cost	3,266,786
Remains for guns,		———		233,214
				3,500,000

No country on the globe is so happily situated, or so internally capable of raising a fleet as America. Tar, timber, iron, and cordage are her natural produce. We need go abroad for nothing. Whereas the Dutch, who make large profits by hiring out their ships of war to the Spaniards and Portuguese, are obliged to import most of their materials they use. We ought to view the building a fleet as an article of commerce, it being the natural manufactory of this country. It is the best money we can lay out. A navy when finished is worth more than it cost. And is that nice point in national policy, in which commerce and protection are united. Let us build; if we want them not, we can sell; and by that means replace our paper currency with ready gold and silver.

In point of manning a fleet, people in general run into great errors; it is not necessary that one fourth part should be sailors. The *Terrible* privateer, Captain Death, stood the hottest engagement of any ship last war, yet had not twenty sailors on board, though her complement of men was upwards of two hundred. A few able and social sailors will soon instruct a sufficient number of active landmen in the common work of a ship. Wherefore, we never can be more capable to begin on maritime matters than now, while our timber is standing, our fisheries blocked up, and our sailors and shipwrights out of employ. Men of war of seventy and eighty guns were built forty years ago in New-England, and why not the same now? Shipbuilding is America's greatest pride, and in which she will in time excel the whole world. The great empires of the east are mostly inland, and consequently excluded from the possibility of rivalling her. Africa is in a state of barbarism; and no power in Europe hath either such an extent of coast, or such an internal supply of materials. Where nature hath given the one, she has withheld the other; to America only hath she been liberal of both. The vast empire of Russia is almost shut out from the sea: wherefore, her boundless forests, her tar, iron, and cordage are only articles of commerce.

In point of safety, ought we to be without a fleet? We are not the little people now, which we were sixty years ago; at that time we might have trusted our property in the streets, or fields rather; and slept securely without locks or bolts to our doors or windows. The case now is altered, and our methods of defence ought to improve with our increase of property. A common pirate, twelve months ago, might have come up the Delaware, and laid the city of Philadelphia under instant contribution, for what sum he pleased; and the same might have happened to other places. Nay, any daring fellow, in a brig of fourteen or sixteen guns might have robbed the whole continent, and carried off half a million of money. These are circumstances which demand our attention, and point out the necessity of naval protection.

Some, perhaps, will say, that after we have made it up with Britain, she will protect us. Can we be so unwise as to mean, that she shall keep a navy in our harbours for that purpose? Common sense will tell us, that the power which hath endeavoured to subdue us, is of all others the most improper to defend us. Conquest may be effected under the pretence of friendship; and ourselves after a long and brave resistance, be at last cheated into slavery. And if her ships are not to be admitted into our harbours, I would ask, how is she to protect us? A navy three or four thousand miles off can be of little use, and on sudden emergencies, none at all. Wherefore, if we must hereafter protect ourselves, why not do it for ourselves? Why do it for another?

The English list of ships of war, is long and formidable, but not a tenth part of them are at any one time fit for service, numbers of them not in being; yet their names are pompously continued in the list, if only a

plank be left of the ship: and not a fifth part of such
as are fit for service, can be spared on any one station
at one time. The East and West Indies, Mediterranean, Africa, and other parts over which Britain extends her claim, make large demands upon her navy.
From a mixture of prejudice and inattention, we have
contracted a false notion respecting the navy of England, and have talked as if we should have the show
of it to encounter at once, and for that reason, supposed, that we must have one as large; which not
being instantly practicable, have been made use of by
a set of disguised Tories to discourage our beginning
thereon. Nothing can be farther from truth than this;
for if America had only a twentieth part of the naval
force of Britain, she would be by far an overmatch for her;
because, as we neither have, nor claim any foreign
dominion, our whole force would be employed on our
own coast, where we should, in the long run, have two
to one the advantage of those who had three or four
thousand miles to sail over, before they could attack
us, and the same distance to return in order to refit
and recruit. And although Britain, by her fleet, hath
a check over our trade to Europe, we have as large a
one over her trade to the West Indies, which, by laying
in the neighbourhood of the continent, is entirely at
its mercy.

Some method might be fallen on to keep up a naval
force in time of peace, if we should not judge it necessary to support a constant navy. If premiums were to
be given to merchants, to build and employ in their
service ships mounted with twenty, thirty, forty or fifty
guns, (the premiums to be in proportion to the loss
of bulk to the merchants) fifty or sixty of those ships,
with a few guardships on constant duty, would keep
up a sufficient navy, and that without burdening ourselves with the evil so loudly complained of in England, of suffering their fleet, in time of peace to lie
rotting in the docks. To unite the sinews of commerce

and defence is sound policy; for when our strength and our riches play into each other's hand, we need fear no external enemy.

In almost every article of defence we abound. Hemp flourishes even to rankness, so that we need not want cordage. Our iron is superior to that of other countries. Our small arms equal to any in the world. Cannon we can cast at pleasure. Saltpetre and gunpowder we are every day producing. Our knowledge is hourly improving. Resolution is our inherent character, and courage hath never yet forsaken us. Wherefore, what is it that we want? Why is it that we hesitate? From Britain we can expect nothing but ruin. If she is once admitted to the government of America again, this Continent will not be worth living in. Jealousies will be always arising; insurrections will be constantly happening; and who will go forth to quell them? Who will venture his life to reduce his own countrymen to a foreign obedience? The difference between Pennsylvania and Connecticut, respecting some unlocated lands, shews the insignificance of a British government, and fully proves, that nothing but Continental authority can regulate Continental matters.

Another reason why the present time is preferable to all others, is, that the fewer our numbers are, the more land there is yet unoccupied, which instead of being lavished by the king on his worthless dependants, may be hereafter applied, not only to the discharge of the present debt, but to the constant support of government. No nation under heaven hath such an advantage as this.

The infant state of the Colonies, as it is called, so far from being against, is an argument in favor of independence. We are sufficiently numerous, and were we more so, we might be less united. It is a matter worthy of observation, that the more a country is peopled, the smaller their armies are. In military numbers, the ancients far exceeded the moderns: and the reason is evident, for trade being the consequence of population, men become too much absorbed thereby to attend to anything else. Commerce diminishes the spirit, both of patriotism and military defence. And history sufficiently informs us, that the bravest achievements were always accomplished in the non-age of a nation. With the increase of commerce, England hath lost its spirit. The city of London, notwithstanding its numbers, submits to continued insults with the patience of a coward. The more men have to lose, the less willing are they to venture. The rich are in general slaves to fear, and submit to courtly power with the trembling duplicity of a Spaniel.

Youth is the seed time of good habits, as well in nations as in individuals. It might be difficult, if not impossible, to form the Continent into one government half a century hence. The vast variety of interests, occasioned by an increase of trade and population, would create confusion. Colony would be against colony. Each being able might scorn each other's assistance: and while the proud and foolish gloried in their little distinctions, the wise would lament, that the union had not been formed before. Wherefore, the *present time* is the *true time* for establishing it. The intimacy which is contracted in infancy, and the friendship which is formed in misfortune, are, of all others, the most lasting and unalterable. Our present union is marked with both these characters: we are young, and we have been distressed; but our concord hath withstood our troubles, and fixes a memorable aera for posterity to glory in.

The present time, likewise, is that peculiar time, which never happens to a nation but once, *viz.* the time of forming itself into a government. Most nations have let slip the opportunity, and by that means have been compelled to receive laws from their conquerors, instead of making laws for themselves. First, they had a king, and then a form of government; whereas, the

articles or charter of government, should be formed
first, and men delegated to execute them afterward:
but from the errors of other nations, let us learn wisdom, and lay hold of the present opportunity——*To
begin government at the right end.*

When William the Conqueror subdued England, he
gave them law at the point of the sword; and until we
consent, that the seat of government, in America, be
legally and authoritatively occupied, we shall be in
danger of having it filled by some fortunate ruffian,
who may treat us in the same manner, and then, where
will be our freedom? where our property?

As to religion, I hold it to be the indispensable duty
of all government, to protect all conscientious profes-
sors thereof, and I know of no other business which
government hath to do therewith. Let a man throw
aside that narrowness of soul, that selfishness of principle, which the niggards of all professions are so unwilling to part with, and he will be at once delivered of
his fears on that head. Suspicion is the companion of
mean souls, and the bane of all good society. For myself, I fully and conscientiously believe, that it is the
will of the Almighty, that there should be diversity of
religious opinions among us: It affords a large field
for our Christian kindness. Were we all of one way of
thinking, our religious dispositions would want matter
for probation; and on this liberal principle, I look on
the various denominations among us, to be like children of the same family, differing only, in what is
called, their Christian names.

In page thirty-seven I threw out a few thoughts on
the propriety of a Continental Charter, (for I only
presume to offer hints, not plans) and in this place, I
take the liberty of rementioning the subject, by observing, that a charter is to be understood as a bond
of solemn obligation, which the whole enters into, to
support the right of every separate part, whether of

religion, personal freedom, or property. A firm bargain and a right reckoning make long friends.

In a former page I likewise mentioned the necessity of a large and equal representation; and there is no political matter which more deserves our attention. A small number of electors, or a small number of representatives, are equally dangerous. But if the number of the representatives be not only small, but unequal, the danger is increased. As an instance of this, I mention the following; when the Associators petition was before the House of Assembly of Pennsylvania; twenty-eight members only were present, all the Bucks county members, being eight, voted against it, and had seven of the Chester members done the same, this whole province had been governed by two counties only, and this danger it is always exposed to. The unwarrantable stretch likewise, which that house made in their last sitting, to gain an undue authority over the Delegates of that province, ought to warn the people at large, how they trust power out of their own hands. A set of instructions for the Delegates were put together, which in point of sense and business would have dishonored a schoolboy, and after being approved by a *few,* a *very few* without doors, were carried into the House, and there passed *in behalf of the whole colony;* whereas, did the whole colony know, with what ill-will that House hath entered on some necessary public measures, they would not hesitate a moment to think them unworthy of such a trust.

Immediate necessity makes many things convenient, which if continued would grow into oppressions. Expedience and right are different things. When the calamities of America required a consultation, there was no method so ready, or at that time so proper, as to appoint persons from the several Houses of Assembly for that purpose; and the wisdom with which they have proceeded hath preserved this continent from ruin.

But as it is more than probable that we shall never be without a CONGRESS, every well wisher to good order, must own, that the mode for choosing members of that body, deserves consideration. And I put it as a question to those, who make a study of mankind, whether *representation and election* is not too great a power for one and the same body of men to possess? When we are planning for posterity, we ought to remember, that virtue is not hereditary.

It is from our enemies that we often gain excellent maxims, and are frequently surprised into reason by their mistakes. Mr. Cornwall (one of the Lords of the Treasury) treated the petition of the New-York Assembly with contempt, because *that* House, he said, consisted but of twenty-six members, which trifling number, he argued, could not with decency be put for the whole. We thank him for his involuntary honesty.*

To CONCLUDE, however strange it may appear to some, or however unwilling they may be to think so, matters not, but many strong and striking reasons may be given, to shew, that nothing can settle our affairs so expeditiously as an open and determined declaration for independance. Some of which are,

First.—It is the custom of nations, when any two are at war, for some other powers, not engaged in the quarrel, to step in as mediators, and bring about the preliminaries of a peace: but while America calls herself the Subject of Great-Britain, no power, however well disposed she may be, can offer her mediation. Wherefore, in our present state we may quarrel on for ever.

Secondly.—It is unreasonable to suppose, that France or Spain will give us any kind of assistance, if

* Those who would fully understand of what great consequence a large and equal representation is to a state, should read Burgh's political Disquisitions.

we mean only, to make use of that assistance for the purpose of repairing the breach, and strengthening the connexion between Britain and America; because, those powers would be sufferers by the consequences.

Thirdly.—While we profess ourselves the subjects of Britain, we must, in the eye of foreign nations, be considered as rebels. The precedent is somewhat dangerous to *their peace,* for men to be in arms under the name of subjects; we, on the spot, can solve the paradox: but to unite resistance and subjection, requires an idea much too refined for common understanding.

Fourthly.—Were a manifesto to be published, and despatched to foreign courts, setting forth the miseries we have endured, and the peaceable methods we have ineffectually used for redress; declaring, at the same time, that not being able, any longer, to live happily or safely under the cruel disposition of the British court, we had been driven to the necessity of breaking off all connexions with her; at the same time, assuring all such courts of our peaceable disposition towards them, and of our desire of entering into trade with them: Such a memorial would produce more good effects to this Continent, than if a ship were freighted with petitions to Britain.

Under our present denomination of British subjects, we can neither be received nor heard abroad: The custom of all courts is against us, and will be so, until, by an independance, we take rank with other nations.

These proceedings may at first appear strange and difficult; but, like all other steps which we have already passed over, will in a little time become familiar and agreeable; and, until an independance is declared, the Continent will feel itself like a man who continues putting off some unpleasant business from day to day, yet knows it must be done, hates to set about it, wishes it over, and is continually haunted with the thoughts of its necessity.

APPENDIX

Since the publication of the first edition of this pamphlet, or rather, on the same day on which it came out, the King's Speech made its appearance in this city. Had the spirit of prophecy directed the birth of this production, it could not have brought it forth, at a more seasonable juncture, or a more necessary time. The bloody mindedness of the one, shew the necessity of pursuing the doctrine of the other. Men read by way of revenge. And the Speech, instead of terrifying, prepared a way for the manly principles of Independance.

Ceremony, and even, silence, from whatever motive they may arise, have a hurtful tendency, when they give the least degree of countenance to base and wicked performances; wherefore, if this maxim be admitted, it naturally follows, that the King's Speech, as being a piece of finished villainy, deserved, and still deserves, a general execration both by the Congress and the people. Yet, as the domestic tranquillity of a nation, depends greatly, on the *chastity* of what may properly be called NATIONAL MANNERS, it is often better, to pass some things over in silent disdain, than to make use of such new methods of dislike, as might introduce the least innovation, on that guardian of our peace and safety. And, perhaps, it is chiefly owing to this prudent delicacy, that the King's Speech, hath not, before now, suffered a public execution. The Speech if it may be called one, is nothing better than a wilful audacious libel against the truth, the common good, and the existence of mankind; and is a formal and pompous method of offering up human sacrifices to the pride of tyrants. But this general massacre of mankind, is one of the privileges, and the certain consequence of Kings; for as nature knows them *not,* they know *not her,* and although they are beings of our *own* creating, they know not *us,* and are become the gods of their creators. The Speech hath one good quality, which is, that it is not calculated to deceive, neither can we, even if we would, be deceived by it. Brutality and tyranny appear on the face of it. It leaves us at no loss: And every line convinces, even in the moment of reading, that He, who hunts the woods for prey, the naked and untutored Indian, is less a Savage than the King of Britain.

Sir John Dalrymple, the putative father of a whining Jesuitical piece, fallaciously called, *"The Address of the people of* ENGLAND *to the inhabitants of* AMERICA,*"* hath, perhaps from a vain supposition, that the people *here* were to be frightened at the pomp and description of a king, given, (though very unwisely on his part) the real character of the present one: "But," says this writer, "if you are inclined to pay compliments to an administration, which we do not complain of," (meaning the Marquis of Rockingham's at the repeal of the Stamp Act) "it is very unfair in you to withhold them from that prince, *by whose* NOD ALONE *they were permitted to do anything."* This is toryism with a witness! Here is idolatry even without a mask: And he who can calmly hear, and digest such doctrine, hath forfeited his claim to rationality—an apostate from the order of manhood; and ought to be considered—as one, who hath not only given up the proper dignity of man, but sunk himself beneath the rank of animals, and contemptibly crawl through the world like a worm.

However, it matters very little now, what the king of England either says or does; he hath wickedly broken through every moral and human obligation, trampled nature and conscience beneath his feet; and by a steady and constitutional spirit of insolence and cruelty, procured for himself an universal hatred. It is *now* the interest of America to provide for herself. She hath already a large and young family, whom it is more her duty to take care of, than to be granting away her property, to support a power who is become a reproach to the names of men and Christians—YE, whose office it is to watch over the morals of a nation, of whatsoever sect or denomination ye are of, as well as ye, who, are more immediately the guardians of the public liberty, if ye wish to preserve your native country uncontaminated by European corruption, ye must in secret wish a separation—But leaving the moral part to private reflection, I shall chiefly confine my farther remarks to the following heads.

First. That it is the interest of America to be separated from Britain.

Secondly. Which is the easiest and most practicable plan, RECONCILIATION OR INDEPENDENCE? with some occasional remarks.

In support of the first, I could, if I judged it proper, produce the opinion of some of the ablest and most experienced men on this continent; and whose sentiments, on that head, are not yet publicly known. It is in reality a self-evident position: For no nation in a state of foreign dependence, limited in its commerce, and cramped and fettered in its legislative powers, can ever arrive at any material eminence. America doth not yet know what opulence is; and although the progress which she hath made stands unparalleled in the history of other nations, it is but childhood, compared with what she would be capable of arriving at, had she, as she ought to have, the legislative powers in her own hands. England is, at this time, proudly coveting

what would do her no good, were she to accomplish
it; and the Continent hesitating on a matter, which
will be her final ruin if neglected. It is the commerce
and not the conquest of America, by which England
is to be benefited, and that would in a great measure
continue, were the countries as independant of each
other as France and Spain; because in many articles,
neither can go to a better market. But it is the independence of this country on Britain or any other,
which is now the main and only object worthy of contention, and which, like all other truths discovered by
necessity, will appear clearer and stronger every day.

First. Because it will come to that one time or other.

Secondly. Because, the longer it is delayed the harder
it will be to accomplish.

I have frequently amused myself both in public and
private companies, with silently remarking, the specious errors of those who speak without reflecting.
And among the many which I have heard, the following seems the most general, viz. that had this rupture
happened forty or fifty years hence, instead of *now*,
the Continent would have been more able to have
shaken off the dependance. To which I reply, that our
military ability, *at this time,* arises from the experience
gained in the last war, and which in forty or fifty years
time, would have been totally extinct. The Continent,
would not, by that time, have had a General, or even
a military officer left; and we, or those who may succeed us, would have been as ignorant of martial matters as the ancient Indians: And this single position,
closely attended to, will unanswerably prove, that the
present time is preferable to all others. The argument
turns thus—at the conclusion of the last war, we had
experience, but wanted numbers; and forty or fifty
years hence, we should have numbers, without experi-

ence; wherefore, the proper point of time, must be some particular point between the two extremes, in which a sufficiency of the former remains, and a proper increase of the latter is obtained: And that point of time is the present time.

The reader will pardon this digression, as it does not properly come under the head I first set out with, and to which I again return by the following position, viz.

Should affairs be patched up with Britain, and she to remain the governing and sovereign power of America, (which, as matters are now circumstanced, is giving up the point entirely) we shall deprive ourselves of the very means of sinking the debt we have, or may contract. The value of the back lands which some of the provinces are clandestinely deprived of, by the unjust extension of the limits of Canada, valued only at five pounds sterling per hundred acres, amount to upwards of twenty-five millions, Pennsylvania currency; and the quit-rents at one penny sterling per acre, to two millions yearly.

It is by the sale of those lands that the debt may be sunk, without burthen to any, and the quit-rent reserved thereon, will always lessen, and in time, will wholly support the yearly expence of government. It matters not how long the debt is in paying, so that the lands when sold be applied to the discharge of it, and for the execution of which, the Congress for the time being, will be the continental trustees.

I proceed now to the second head, viz. Which is the easiest and most practicable plan, RECONCILIATION or INDEPENDANCE; with some occasional remarks.

He who takes nature for his guide is not easily beaten out of his argument, and on that ground, I answer generally—That INDEPENDANCE being a SINGLE SIMPLE LINE, contained within ourselves; and reconcilia-

tion, a matter exceedingly perplexed and complicated, and in which, a treacherous capricious court is to inter-fere, gives the answer without a doubt.

The present state of America is truly alarming to every man who is capable of reflexion. Without law, without government, without any other mode of power than what is founded on, and granted by cour-tesy. Held together by an unexampled concurrence of sentiment, which, is nevertheless subject to change, and which, every secret enemy is endeavouring to dis-solve. Our present condition, is, Legislation without law; wisdom without a plan; a constitution without a name; and, what is strangely astonishing, perfect In-depedance contending for dependance. The instance is without a precedent; the case never existed before; and who can tell what may be the event? The property of no man is secure in the present unbraced system of things. The mind of the multitude is left at random, and seeing no fixed object before them, they pursue such as fancy or opinion starts. Nothing is criminal; there is no such thing as treason; wherefore, every one thinks himself at liberty to act as he pleases. The To-ries dared not have assembled offensively, had they known that their lives, by that act, were forfeited to the laws of the state. A line of distinction should be drawn, between, English soldiers taken in battle, and inhabitants of America taken in arms. The first are prisoners, but the latter traitors. The one forfeits his liberty, the other his head.

Notwithstanding our wisdom, there is a visible fee-bleness in some of our proceedings which gives en-couragement to dissensions. The Continental Belt is too loosely buckled. And if something is not done in time, it will be too late to do any thing, and we shall fall into a state, in which, neither *Reconciliation* nor *Independence* will be practicable. The king and his worthless adherents are got at their old game of dividing the Continent, and there are not wanting among us, Printers, who will be busy in spreading specious falsehoods. The artful and hypocritical letter which appeared a few months ago in two of the New-York papers, and likewise in two others, is an evidence that there are men who want either judgment or honesty.

It is easy getting into holes and corners and talking of reconciliation: But do such men seriously consider, how difficult the task is, and how dangerous it may prove, should the Continent divide thereon. Do they take within their view, all the various orders of men whose situation and circumstances, as well as their own, are to be considered therein. Do they put themselves in the place of the sufferer whose *all* is *already* gone, and of the soldier, who hath quitted *all* for the defence of his country. If their ill judged moderation be suited to their own private situations *only,* regardless of others, the event will convince them, that "they are reckoning without their Host."

Put us, says some, on the footing we were on in sixty-three: To which I answer, the request is not *now* in the power of Britain to comply with, neither will she propose it; but if it were, and even should be granted, I ask, as a reasonable question, By what means is such a corrupt and faithless court to be kept to its engagements? Another parliament, nay, even the present, may hereafter repeal the obligation, on the pretence, of its being violently obtained, or unwisely granted; and in that case, Where is our redress?—No going to law with nations; cannon are the barristers of Crowns; and the sword, not of justice, but of war, decides the suit. To be on the footing of sixty-three, it is not sufficient, that the laws only be put on the same state, but, that our circumstances, likewise, be put on the same state; Our burnt and destroyed towns repaired or built up, our private losses made good, our public debts (contracted for defence) discharged; otherwise, we shall be millions worse than we were at that enviable period. Such a request, had it been complied with a year ago, would have won the heart and soul of the Continent—but now it is too late, "The Rubicon is passed."

Besides, the taking up arms, merely to enforce the repeal of a pecuniary law, seems as unwarrantable by the divine law, and as repugnant to human feelings, as the taking up arms to enforce obedience thereto. The object, on either side, doth not justify the means; for the lives of men are too valuable to be cast away on such trifles. It is the violence which is done and threatened to our persons; the destruction of our property by an armed force; the invasion of our country by fire and sword, which conscientiously qualifies the use of arms: And the instant, in which such a mode of defence became necessary, all subjection to Britain ought to have ceased; and the independancy of America, should have been considered, as dating its aera from, and published by, *the first musket that was fired against her.* This line is a line of consistency; neither drawn by caprice, nor extended by ambition; but produced by a chain of events, of which the colonies were not the authors.

I shall conclude these remarks, with the following timely and well intended hints. We ought to reflect, that there are three different ways, by which an independancy may hereafter be effected; and that *one* of those *three,* will one day or other, be the fate of America, viz. By the legal voice of the people in Congress; by a military power; or by a mob: It may not always happen that our soldiers are citizens, and the multitude a body of reasonable men; virtue, as I have already remarked, is not hereditary, neither is it perpetual. Should an independancy be brought about by the first of those means, we have every opportunity and every encouragement before us, to form the noblest purest constitution on the face of the earth. We have it in our power to begin the world over again.

A situation, similar to the present, hath not happened since the days of Noah until now. The birthday of a new world is at hand, and a race of men, perhaps as numerous as all Europe contains, are to receive their portion of freedom from the event of a few months. The Reflexion is awful—and in this point of view, How trifling, how ridiculous, do the little, paltry cavillings, of a few weak or interested men appear, when weighed against the business of a world.

Should we neglect the present favorable and inviting period, and an Independance be hereafter effected by any other means, we must charge the consequence to ourselves, or to those rather, whose narrow and prejudiced souls, are habitually opposing the measure, without either inquiring or reflecting. There are reasons to be given in support of Independance, which men should rather privately think of, than be publicly told of. We ought not now to be debating whether we shall be independant or not, but, anxious to accomplish it on a firm, secure, and honorable basis, and uneasy rather that it is not yet began upon. Every day convinces us of its necessity. Even the Tories (if such beings yet remain among us) should, of all men, be the most solicitous to promote it; for, as the appointment of committees at first, protected them from popular rage, so, a wise and well established form of government, will be the only certain means of continuing it securely to them. *Wherefore,* if they have not virtue enough to be Whigs, they ought to have prudence enough to wish for Independance.

In short, Independance is the only Bond that can tye and keep us together. We shall then see our object, and our ears will be legally shut against the schemes of an intriguing, as well, as a cruel enemy. We shall then too, be on a proper footing, to treat with Britain; for there is reason to conclude, that the pride of that court, will be less hurt by treating with the American states for terms of peace, than with those, whom she denominates, "rebellious subjects," for terms of accommodation. It is our delaying it that encourages her to hope for conquest, and our backwardness tends only to prolong the war. As we have, without any good effect therefrom, withheld our trade to obtain a redress of our grievances, let us *now* try the alternative, by *independently* redressing them ourselves, and then offering to open the trade. The mercantile and reasonable part in England, will be still with us; because, peace *with* trade, is preferable to war *without* it. And if this offer be not accepted, other courts may be applied to.

On these grounds I rest the matter. And as no offer hath yet been made to refute the doctrine contained in the former editions of this pamphlet, it is a negative proof, that either the doctrine cannot be refuted, or, that the party in favour of it are too numerous to be opposed. WHEREFORE, instead of gazing at each other with suspicious or doubtful curiosity, let each of us, hold out to his neighbour the hearty hand of friendship, and unite in drawing a line, which, like an act of oblivion shall bury in forgetfulness every former dissension. Let the names of Whig and Tory be extinct; and let none other be heard among us, than those of a *good citizen, an open and resolute friend, and a virtuous supporter of the* RIGHTS *of* MANKIND *and of the* FREE AND INDEPENDANT STATES OF AMERICA.

To the Representatives of the Religious Society of the People called Quakers, or to so many of them as were concerned in publishing a late piece, entitled "The ANCIENT TESTIMONY *and* PRINCIPLES *of the People called* QUAKERS *renewed, with Respect to the* KING *and* GOVERNMENT, *and touching the* COMMOTIONS *now prevailing in these and other parts of* AMERICA *addressed to the* PEOPLE IN GENERAL."

The Writer of this, is one of those few, who never

dishonors religion either by ridiculing, or cavilling at any denomination whatsoever. To God, and not to man, are all men accountable on the score of religion. Wherefore, this epistle is not so properly addressed to you as a religious, but as a political body, dabbling in matters, which the professed Quietude of your Principles instruct you not to meddle with.

As you have, without a proper authority for so doing, put yourselves in the place of the whole body of the Quakers, so, the writer of this, in order to be on an equal rank with yourselves, is under the necessity, of putting himself in the place of all those, who, approve the very writings and principles, against which, your testimony is directed: And he hath chosen this singular situation, in order, that you might discover in him that presumption of character which you cannot see in yourselves. For neither he nor you can have any claim or title to *Political Representation.*

When men have departed from the right way, it is no wonder that they stumble and fall. And it is evident from the manner in which ye have managed your testimony, that politics, (as a religious body of men) is not your proper Walk; for however well adapted it might appear to you, it is, nevertheless, a jumble of good and bad put unwisely together, and the conclusion drawn therefrom, both unnatural and unjust.

The first two pages, (and the whole doth not make four) we give you credit for, and expect the same civility from you, because the love and desire of peace is not confined to Quakerism, it is the *natural,* as well the religious wish of all denominations of men. And on this ground, as men laboring to establish an Independant Constitution of our own, do we exceed all others in our hope, end, and aim. *Our plan is peace for ever.* We are tired of contention with Britain, and can see no real end to it but in a final separation. We act consistently, because for the sake of introducing an endless and uninterrupted peace, do we bear the evils and burthens of the present day. We are endeavoring, and will steadily continue to endeavor, to separate and dissolve a connexion which hath already filled our land with blood; and which, while the name of it remains, will be the fatal cause of future mischiefs to both countries.

We fight neither for revenge nor conquest; neither from pride nor passion; we are not insulting the world with our fleets and armies, nor ravaging the globe for plunder. Beneath the shade of our own vines are we attacked; in our own houses, and on our own lands, is the violence committed against us. We view our enemies in the character of Highwaymen and Housebreakers, and having no defence for ourselves in the civil law, are obliged to punish them by the military one, and apply the sword, in the very case, where you have before now, applied the halter————Perhaps we feel for the ruined and insulted sufferers in all and every part of the continent, with a degree of tenderness which hath not yet made its way into some of your bosoms. But be ye sure that ye mistake not the cause and ground of your Testimony. Call not coldness of soul, religion; nor put the *Bigot* in the place of the *Christian.*

O ye partial ministers of your own acknowledged principles. If the bearing arms be sinful, the first going to war must be more so, by all the difference between wilful attack and unavoidable defence. Wherefore, if ye really preach from conscience, and mean not to make a political hobbyhorse of your religion, convince the world thereof, by proclaiming your doctrine to our enemies, *for they likewise bear* ARMS. Give us proof of your sincerity by publishing it at St. James's, to the commanders in chief at Boston, to the Admirals and Captains who are piratically ravaging our coasts, and to all the murdering miscreants who are acting in authority under HIM whom ye profess to serve. Had ye the honest soul of *Barclay*** ye would preach repentance to *your* king; Ye would tell the Royal Wretch his sins, and warn him of eternal ruin. Ye would not spend your partial invectives against the injured and the insulted only, but, like faithful ministers, would cry aloud and *spare none.* Say not that ye are persecuted, neither endeavour to make us the authors of that reproach, which, ye are bringing upon yourselves; for we testify unto all men, that we do not complain against you because ye are *Quakers,* but because ye pretend to *be* and are NOT Quakers.

Alas! it seems by the particular tendency of some part of your testimony, and other parts of your conduct, as if, all sin was reduced to, and comprehended in, *the act of bearing arms,* and that by the *people only.* Ye appear to us, to have mistaken party for conscience; because, the general tenor of your actions wants uniformity: And it is exceedingly difficult to us to give credit to many of your pretended scruples; because, we see them made by the same men, who, in the very instant that they are exclaiming against the mammon of this world, are nevertheless, hunting after it with a step as steady as Time, and an appetite as keen as Death.

---

* "Thou hast tasted of prosperity and adversity; thou knowest what it is to be banished thy native country, to be over-ruled as well as to rule, and set upon the throne; and being *oppressed* thou hast reason to know how *hateful* the *oppressor* is both to God and man: If after all these warnings and advertisements, thou dost not turn unto the Lord with all thy heart, but forget him who remembered thee in thy distress, and give up thyself to follow lust and vanity, surely great will be thy condemnation.—Against which snare, as well as the temptation of those who may or do feed thee, and prompt thee to evil, the most excellent and prevalent remedy will be, to apply thyself to that light of Christ which shineth in thy conscience, and which neither can, nor will flatter thee, nor suffer thee to be at ease in thy sins."

Barclay's Address to Charles II.

The quotation which ye have made from Proverbs, in the third page of your testimony, that, "when a man's ways please the Lord, he maketh even his enemies to be at peace with him"; is very unwisely chosen on your part; because, it amounts to a proof, that the king's ways (whom ye are so desirous of supporting) do *not* please the Lord, otherwise, his reign would be in peace.

I now proceed to the latter part of your testimony, and that, for which all the foregoing seems only an introduction, viz.

"It hath ever been our judgment and principle, since we were called to profess the light of Christ Jesus, manifested in our consciences unto this day, that the setting up and putting down kings and governments, is God's peculiar prerogative; for causes best known to himself: And that it is not our business to have any hand or contrivance therein; nor to be busy bodies above our station, much less to plot and contrive the ruin, or overturn of any of them, but to pray for the king, and safety of our nation, and good of all men: That we may live a peaceable and quiet life, in all godliness and honesty; *under the government which God is pleased to set over us.*"—If these are *really* your principles why do ye not abide by them? Why do ye not leave that, which ye call God's Work, to be managed by himself? These very principles instruct you to wait with patience and humility, for the event of all public measures, and to receive *that event* as the divine will towards you. *Wherefore,* what occasion is there for your *political testimony* if you fully believe what it contains? And the very publishing it proves, that either, ye do not believe what ye profess, or have not virtue enough to practise what ye believe.

The principles of Quakerism have a direct tendency to make a man the quiet and inoffensive subject of any, and every government *which is set over him.* And if the setting up and putting down of kings and governments is God's peculiar prerogative, he most certainly will not be robbed thereof by us; wherefore, the principle itself leads you to approve of every thing, which ever happened, or may happen to kings as being his work. OLIVER CROMWELL thanks you. CHARLES, then, died not by the hands of man; and should the present Proud Imitator of him, come to the same untimely end, the writers and publishers of the Testimony, are bound, by the doctrine it contains, to applaud the fact. Kings are not taken away by miracles, neither are changes in governments brought about by any other means than such as are common and human; and such as we are now using. Even the dispersion of the Jews, though foretold by our Saviour, was effected by arms. Wherefore, as ye refuse to be the means on one side, ye ought not to be meddlers on the other; but to wait the issue in silence; and unless ye can produce divine authority, to prove, that the Almighty who hath created and placed this *new* world, at the greatest distance it could possibly stand, east and west, from every part of the old, doth, nevertheless, disapprove of its being independent of the corrupt and abandoned court of Britain, unless I say, ye can shew this, how can ye on the ground of your principles, justify the exciting and stirring up the people "firmly to unite in the *abhorrence* of all such *writings,* and *measures,* as evidence a desire and design to break off the *happy* connexion we have hitherto enjoyed, with the kingdom of Great-Britain, and our just and necessary subordination to the king, and those who are lawfully placed in authority under him." What a slap of the face is here! The men, who in the very paragraph before, have quietly and passively resigned up the ordering, altering, and disposal of kings and governments, into the hands of God, are now, recalling their principles, and putting in for a share of the business. Is it possible, that the conclusion, which is here justly quoted, can any ways follow from the doctrine laid down? The inconsistency is too glaring not to be seen; the absurdity too great not to be laughed at; and such as could only have been made by those, whose understandings were darkened by the narrow and crabby spirit of a despairing political party; for ye are not to be considered as the whole body of the Quakers but only as a factional and fractional part thereof.

Here ends the examination of your testimony; (which I call upon no man to abhor, as ye have done, but only to read and judge of fairly;) to which I subjoin the following remark; "That the setting up and putting down of kings," most certainly mean, the making him a king, who is yet not so, and the making him no king who is already one. And pray what hath this to do in the present case? We neither mean to *set up* nor to *put down,* neither to *make* nor to *unmake,* but to have nothing to *do* with them. Wherefore, your testimony in whatever light it is viewed serves only to dishonor your judgment, and for many other reasons had better have been let alone than published.

First, Because it tends to the decrease and reproach of all religion whatever, and is of the utmost danger to society, to make it a party in political disputes.

Secondly, Because it exhibits a body of men, numbers of whom disavow the publishing political testimonies, as being concerned therein and approvers thereof.

Thirdly, Because it hath a tendency to undo that continental harmony and friendship which yourselves by your late liberal and charitable donations hath lent a hand to establish; and the preservation of which, is of the utmost consequence to us all.

And here without anger or resentment I bid you farewel. Sincerely wishing, that as men and Christians, ye may always fully and uninterruptedly enjoy every civil and religious right; and be, in your turn, the means of securing it to others; but that the example which ye have unwisely set, of mingling religion with politics, *may be disavowed and reprobated by every inhabitant of* AMERICA.

FINIS.

THE CRISIS

1776–83

NUMBER I

December 23, 1776

These are the times that try men's souls: The summer soldier and the sunshine patriot will, in this crisis, shrink from the service of his country; but he that stands it NOW, deserves the love and thanks of man and woman. Tyranny, like hell, is not easily conquered; yet we have this consolation with us, that the harder the conflict, the more glorious the triumph. What we obtain too cheap, we esteem too lightly: 'Tis dearness only that gives every thing its value. Heaven knows how to put a proper price upon its goods; and it would be strange indeed, if so celestial an article as FREEDOM should not be highly rated. Britain, with an army to enforce her tyranny, has declared that she has a right (*not only to* TAX) but "*to* BIND *us in* ALL CASES WHATSOEVER," and if being *bound in that manner,* is not slavery, then is there not such a thing as slavery upon earth. Even the expression is impious, for so unlimited a power can belong only to GOD.

Whether the independence of the continent was declared too soon, or delayed too long, I will not now enter into as an argument; my own simple opinion is, that had it been eight months earlier, it would have been much better. We did not make a proper use of last winter, neither could we, while we were in a dependant state. However, the fault, if it were one, was all our own; we have none to blame but ourselves. But no great deal is lost yet; all that Howe has been doing for this month past is rather a ravage than a conquest, which the spirit of the Jerseys a year ago would have quickly repulsed, and which time and a little resolution will soon recover.

I have as little superstition in me as any man living, but my secret opinion has ever been, and still is, that God Almighty will not give up a people to military destruction, or leave them unsupportedly to perish, who had so earnestly and so repeatedly sought to avoid the calamities of war, by every decent method which wisdom could invent. Neither have I so much of the infidel in me, as to suppose that HE has relinquished the government of the world, and given us up to the care of devils; and as I do not, I cannot see on what grounds the king of Britain can look up to Heaven for help against us: A common murderer, a highwayman, or a house-breaker has as good a pretence as he.

'Tis surprising to see how rapidly a panic will sometimes run through a country. All nations and ages have been subject to them: Britain has trembled like an ague at the report of a French fleet of flat bottomed boats; and in the fourteenth century the whole English army, after ravaging the kingdom of France, was driven back like men petrified with fear; and this brave exploit was performed by a few broken forces collected and headed by a woman, Joan of Arc. Would, that Heaven might inspire some Jersey maid to spirit up her countrymen, and save her fair fellow sufferers from ravage and ravishment! Yet panics, in some cases, have their uses, they produce as much good as hurt. Their duration is always short; the mind soon grows through them, and acquires a firmer habit than before. But their peculiar advantage is, that they are the touchstones of sincerity and hypocrisy, and bring things and men to light, which might otherwise have lain for ever undiscovered. In fact, they have the same effect on secret traitors, which an imaginary apparition would have upon a private murderer. They sift out the hidden thoughts of man, and hold them up in public to the world. Many a disguised tory has lately shewn his head, that shall penitentially solemnize with curses the day on which Howe arrived upon the Delaware.

As I was with the troops at Fort-Lee, and marched with them to the edge of Pennsylvania, I am well acquainted with many circumstances, which those, who lived at a distance, know but little or nothing of. Our situation there was exceedingly cramped, the place being on a narrow neck of land between the North-River and the Hackensack. Our force was inconsiderable, being not one fourth so great as Howe could bring against us. We had no army at hand to have relieved the garrison, had we shut ourselves up and stood on the defence. Our ammunition, light artillery, and the best part of our stores, had been removed upon the apprehension that Howe would endeavor to penetrate the Jerseys, in which case Fort-Lee could be of no use to us; for it must occur to every thinking man, whether in the army or not, that these kind of field forts are only for temporary purposes, and last in use no longer than the enemy directs his force against the particular object, which such forts are raised to defend. Such was our situation and condition at Fort-Lee on the morning of the 20th of November, when an officer arrived with information that the enemy with 200 boats had landed about seven or eight miles above: Major General Greene, who commanded the garrison, immediately ordered them under arms, and sent express to his Excellency General Washington at the town of Hackensack, distant by the way of the ferry six miles. Our first object was to secure the bridge over the Hackensack, which laid up the river between the enemy and us, about six miles from us, and three from them. General Washington arrived in about three quarters of an hour, and marched at the head of the troops towards the bridge, which place I expected we should have a brush for; however they did not choose to dispute it with us, and the greatest part of our troops went over the bridge, the rest over the ferry, except some which passed at a mill on a small creek, between the bridge and the ferry, and made their way through some marshy grounds up to the town of Hackensack, and there passed the river. We brought off as much baggage as the waggons could contain, the rest was lost. The simple object was to bring off the garrison, and to march them on till they could be strengthened by the Jersey or Pennsylvania militia, so as to be enabled to make a stand. We staid four days at Newark, collected in our out-posts with some of the Jersey militia, and marched out twice to meet the enemy on information of their being advancing, though our numbers were greatly inferior to theirs. Howe, in my little opinion, committed a great error in generalship in not throwing a body of forces off from Staten-Island through Amboy, by which means he might have seized all our stores at Brunswick, and intercepted our march into Pennsylvania: But if we believe the power of hell to be limited, we must likewise believe that their agents are under some providential controul.

I shall not now attempt to give all the particulars of our retreat to the Delaware; suffice it for the present to say, that both officers and men, though greatly harassed and fatigued, frequently without rest, covering, or provision, the inevitable consequences of a long retreat, bore it with a manly and a martial spirit. All their wishes were one, which was, that the country would turn out and help them to drive the enemy back. Voltaire has remarked that King William never appeared to full advantage but in difficulties and in action; the same remark may be made on General Washington, for the character fits him. There is a natural firmness in some minds which cannot be unlocked by trifles, but which, when unlocked, discovers a cabinet of fortitude; and I reckon it among those kind of public blessings, which we do not immediately see, that GOD hath blest him with uninterrupted health, and given him a mind that can even flourish upon care.

I shall conclude this paper with some miscellaneous remarks on the state of our affairs; and shall begin with asking the following question, Why is it that the enemy have left the New-England provinces, and made these middle ones the seat of war? The answer is easy: New-England is not infested with tories, and we are. I have been tender in raising the cry against these men, and used numberless arguments to shew them their danger, but it will not do to sacrifice a world to either their folly or their baseness. The period is now arrived, in which either they or we must change our sentiments, or one or both must fall. And what is a tory? Good GOD! what is he? I should not be afraid to go with an hundred whigs against a thousand tories, were they to attempt to get into arms. Every tory is a coward, for a servile, slavish, self-interested fear is the foundation of toryism; and a man under such influence, though he may be cruel, never can be brave.

But, before the line of irrecoverable separation be drawn between us, let us reason the matter together: Your conduct is an invitation to the enemy, yet not one in a thousand of you has heart enough to join him. Howe is as much deceived by you as the American cause is injured by you. He expects you will all take up arms, and flock to his standard with muskets on your shoulders. Your opinions are of no use to him, unless you support him personally, for 'tis soldiers, and not tories, that he wants.

I once felt all that kind of anger, which a man ought to feel, against the mean principles that are held by the tories: A noted one, who kept a tavern at Amboy, was standing at his door, with as pretty a child in his hand, about eight or nine years old, as most I ever saw, and after speaking his mind as freely as he thought was prudent, finished with this unfatherly expression, *"Well! give me peace in my day."* Not a man lives on the continent but fully believes that a separation must some time or other finally take place, and a generous parent should have said, *"If there must be trouble, let it be in my day that my child may have peace;"* and this single reflection, well applied, is sufficient to awaken every man to duty. Not a place upon earth might be so happy as America. Her situation is remote from all the wrangling world, and she has nothing to do but to trade with them. A man may easily distinguish in himself between temper and principle, and I am as confident, as I am that GOD governs the world, that America will never be happý till she gets clear of foreign dominion. Wars, without ceasing, will break out till that period arrives, and the continent must in the end be conqueror; for though the flame of liberty may sometimes cease to shine, the coal never can expire.

America did not, nor does not want force; but she wanted a proper application of that force. Wisdom is not the purchase of a day, and it is no wonder that we should err at first setting off. From an excess of tenderness, we were unwilling to raise an army, and trusted our cause to the temporary defence of a well-meaning militia. A summer's experience has now taught us better; yet with those troops, while they were collected, we were able to set bounds to the progress of the enemy, and, thank GOD! they are again assembling. I always considered a militia as the best troops in the world for a sudden exertion, but they will not do for a long campaign. Howe, it is possi-

ble, will make an attempt on this city, should he fail
on this side the Delaware, he is ruined; If he succeeds,
our cause is not ruined. He stakes all on his side
against a part on ours; admitting he succeeds, the consequence will be, that armies from both ends of the
continent will march to assist their suffering friends in
the middle states; for he cannot go every where, it is
impossible. I consider Howe as the greatest enemy the
tories have; he is bringing a war into their country,
which, had it not been for him and partly for themselves, they had been clear of. Should he now be expelled, I wish with all the devotion of a Christian,
that the names of whig and tory may never more be
mentioned; but should the tories give him encouragement to come, or assistance if he come, I as sincerely
wish that our next year's arms may expel them from
the continent, and the congress appropriate their possessions to the relief of those who have suffered in
well-doing. A single successful battle next year will
settle the whole. America could carry on a two years
war by the confiscation of the property of disaffected
persons, and be made happy by their expulsion. Say
not that this is revenge, call it rather the soft resentment of a suffering people, who, having no object in
view but the GOOD of ALL, have staked their OWN
ALL upon a seemingly doubtful event. Yet it is folly
to argue against determined hardness; eloquence may
strike the ear, and the language of sorrow draw forth
the tear of compassion, but nothing can reach the
heart that is steeled with prejudice.

Quitting this class of men, I turn with the warm
ardor of a friend to those who have nobly stood, and
are yet determined to stand the matter out: I call not
upon a few, but upon all; not on THIS state or THAT
state, but on EVERY state; up and help us; lay your
shoulders to the wheel; better have too much force
than too little, when so great an object is at stake. Let
it be told to the future world, that in the depth of

winter, when nothing but hope and virtue could survive, that the city and the country, alarmed at one common danger, came forth to meet and to repulse it. Say not, that thousands are gone, turn out your tens of thousands; throw not the burden of the day upon Providence, but *"shew your faith by your works,"* that God may bless you. It matters not where you live, or what rank of life you hold, the evil or the blessing will reach you all. The far and the near, the home counties and the back, the rich and the poor, will suffer or rejoice alike. The heart that feels not now, is dead: The blood of his children will curse his cowardice, who shrinks back at a time when a little might have saved the whole, and made *them* happy. I love the man that can smile in trouble, that can gather strength from distress, and grow brave by reflection. 'Tis the business of little minds to shrink; but he whose heart is firm, and whose conscience approves his conduct, will pursue his principles unto death. My own line of reasoning is to myself as strait and clear as a ray of light. Not all the treasures of the world, so far as I believe, could have induced me to support an offensive war, for I think it murder; but if a thief break into my house, burn and destroy my property, and kill or threaten to kill me, or those that are in it, and to *"bind me in all cases whatsoever,"* to his absolute will, am I to suffer it? What signifies it to me, whether he who does it, is a king or a common man; my countryman or not my countryman? whether it is done by an individual villain, or an army of them? If we reason to the root of things we shall find no difference; neither can any just cause be assigned why we should punish in the one case and pardon in the other. Let them call me rebel, and welcome, I feel no concern from it; but I should suffer the misery of devils, were I to make a whore of my soul by swearing allegiance to one whose character is that of a sottish, stupid, stubborn, worthless, brutish man. I conceive likewise

a horrid idea in receiving mercy from a being, who at
the last day shall be shrieking to the rocks and moun-
tains to cover him, and fleeing with terror from the
orphan, the widow, and the slain of America.

There are cases which cannot be overdone by language, and this is one. There are persons too who see
not the full extent of the evil which threatens them,
they solace themselves with hopes that the enemy, if
they succeed, will be merciful. It is the madness of
folly to expect mercy from those who have refused to
do justice; and even mercy, where conquest is the object, is only a trick of war: The cunning of the fox is
as murderous as the violence of the wolf; and we
ought to guard equally against both. Howe's first object is partly by threats and partly by promise, to terrify or seduce the people to deliver up their arms, and
receive mercy. The ministry recommended the same
plan to Gage, and this is what the tories call making
their peace; *"a peace which passeth all understanding"*
indeed! A peace which would be the immediate forerunner of a worse ruin than any we have yet thought
of. Ye men of Pennsylvania, do reason upon these
things! Were the back counties to give up their arms,
they would fall an easy prey to the Indians, who are
all alarmed: This perhaps is what some tories would
not be sorry for. Were the home counties to deliver
up their arms, they would be exposed to the resentment of the back counties, who would then have it in
their power to chastise their defection at pleasure.
And were any one state to give up its arms, THAT
state must be garrisoned by all Howe's army of
Britons and Hessians to preserve it from the anger of
the rest. Mutual fear is a principal link in the chain
of mutual love, and woe be to that state that breaks
the compact. Howe is mercifully inviting you to barbarous destruction, and men must be either rogues or
fools that will not see it. I dwell not upon the powers
of imagination; I bring reason to your ears; and in

language as plain as A, B, C, hold up truth to your eyes.

I thank GOD that I fear not. I see no real cause for fear. I know our situation well, and can see the way out of it. While our army was collected, Howe dared not risk a battle, and it is no credit to him that he decamped from the White Plains, and waited a mean opportunity to ravage the defenceless Jerseys; but it is great credit to us, that, with a handful of men, we sustained an orderly retreat for near an hundred miles, brought off our ammunition, all our field-pieces, the greatest part of our stores, and had four rivers to pass. None can say that our retreat was precipitate, for we were near three weeks in performing it, that the country might have time to come in. Twice we marched back to meet the enemy and remained out till dark. The sign of fear was not seen in our camp, and had not some of the cowardly and disaffected inhabitants spread false alarms through the country, the Jerseys had never been ravaged. Once more we are again collected and collecting; our new army at both ends of the continent is recruiting fast, and we shall be able to open the next campaign with sixty thousand men, well armed and cloathed. This is our situation, and who will may know it. By perseverance and fortitude we have the prospect of a glorious issue; by cowardice and submission, the sad choice of a variety of evils—a ravaged country—a depopulated city—habitations without safety, and slavery without hope—our homes turned into barracks and bawdy-houses for Hessians, and a future race to provide for whose fathers we shall doubt of. Look on this picture and weep over it! and if there yet remains one thoughtless wretch who believes it not, let him suffer it unlamented.

NUMBER III (Selections)

Philadelphia, April 19, 1777

. . . after the coolest reflections on the matter, *this must* be allowed, that Britain was too jealous of America, to govern it justly; too ignorant of it, to govern it well; and too distant from it, to govern it at all. . . . All we want to know in America is simply this, who is for independence, and who is not? Those who are for it, will support it, and the remainder will undoubtedly see the reasonableness of their paying the charges; while those who oppose or seek to betray it, must expect the more rigid fate of the gaol and the gibbit. There is a bastard kind of generosity, which, by being extended to all men, is as fatal to society, on one hand, as the want of true generosity is on the other. A lax manner of administering justice, falsely termed moderation, has a tendency both to dispirit public virtue, and promote the growth of public evils.

The necessity of always fitting our internal police to the circumstances of the times we live in, is something so strikingly obvious that no sufficient objection can be made against it. The safety of all societies depend upon it; and where this point is not attended to, the consequences will either be a general languor or a tumult. The encouragement and protection of the good subjects of any state, and the suppression and punishment of bad ones, are the principal objects for which all authority is instituted, and the line in which it ought to operate. We have in this city a strange variety of men and characters, and the circumstances of the times require they should be publicly known; it is not the number of tories that hurt us, so much, as the not finding out who they are; men must now take one side or the other, and abide by the consequences. . . . If Britain cannot conquer us, it proves, that she is neither able to govern or protect us, and our particular situation now is such, that any connection with her would be unwisely exchanging a half defeated enemy for two powerful ones. Europe, by every appearance and information, is now on the eve, nay, on the morning twilight of a war, and any alliance with *George the third* brings *France* and *Spain* upon our backs; a separation from him attach them to our side; therefore, the only road to *peace, honor* and commerce is INDEPENDENCE.

Written this fourth year of the UNION, *which GOD preserve!*

NUMBER IV (Selections)

Philadelphia, Sept. 12, 1777

Those who expect to reap the blessings of freedom, must, like men, undergo the fatigues of supporting it. The event of yesterday is one of those kind alarms which is just sufficient to rouse us to duty, without being of consequence enough to depress our fortitude. It is not a field of a few acres of ground, but a cause that we are defending, and whether we defeat the enemy in one battle, or by degrees, the consequence will be the same.

Look back at the events of last winter and the present year, there you will find that the enemy's successes have always contributed to reduce them. What they have gained in ground, they paid so dearly for in numbers, that their victories have in the end amounted to defeats. We have always been masters at the last push, and always shall while we do our duty. Howe has been once on the banks of the Delaware, and from thence driven back with loss and disgrace; and why not be again driven from the Schuylkill? His condition and ours are very different. He has every body to fight, we have only his *one* army to cope with, and which wastes away at every engagement; we can not only reinforce, but can redouble our numbers; he is cut off from all supplies, and must sooner or later inevitably fall into our hands.

Shall a band of ten or twelve thousand robbers, who are this day fifteen hundred or two thousand men less in strength than they were yesterday, conquer America, or subdue even a single state? The thing cannot be, unless we sit down and suffer them to do it. Another such a brush, notwithstanding we lost the ground, would, by still reducing the enemy, put them in a condition to be afterwards totally defeated.

Could our whole army have come up to the attack at one time, the consequences had probably been otherwise; but our having different parts of the Brandywine-creek to guard, and the uncertainty which road to Philadelphia, the enemy would attempt to take, naturally afforded them an opportunity of passing with their main body at a place where only a part of ours could be posted; for it must strike every thinking man with conviction, that it requires a much greater force to oppose an enemy in several places, than is sufficient to defeat in any one place.

Men who are sincere in defending their freedom, will always feel concern at every circumstance which seems to make against them; it is the natural and honest consequence of all affectionate attachments, and the want of it is a vice. But the dejection lasts only for a moment; they soon rise out of it with additional vigor; the glow of hope, courage and fortitude, will, in a little time supply the place of every inferior passion and kindle the whole heart into heroism.

There is a mystery in the countenance of some causes, which we have not always present judgment enough to explain. It is distressing to see an enemy advancing into a country, but it is the only place in which we can beat them, and in which we have always beaten them, whenever they made the attempt. The nearer any disease approaches to a crisis, the nearer it is to a cure. Danger and deliverance make their advances together, and it is only the last push, that one or the other takes the lead.

There are many men who will do their duty when it is not wanted; but a genuine public spirit always appears most when there is most occasion for it. Thank God! our army though fatigued, is yet entire. The attack made by us yesterday, was under many disadvantages, naturally arising from the uncertainty of knowing which route the enemy would take; and from that circumstance, the whole of our force could not be brought up together time enough to engage all at once. Our strength is yet reserved; and it is evident that Howe does not think himself a gainer by the affair, otherwise he would this morning have moved down and attacked General Washington.

Gentlemen of the city and country, it is in your power, by a spirited improvement of the present circumstance, to turn it to a real advantage. Howe is now weaker than before, and every shot will contribute to reduce him. You are more immediately interested than any other part of the continent; your all is at stake; it is not so with the general cause; you are devoted by the enemy to plunder and destruction: It is the encouragement which Howe, the chief of plunderers, has promised his army. Thus circumstanced, you may save yourselves by a manly resistance, but you can have no hope in any other conduct. I never yet knew our brave general, or any part of the army, officers or men, out of heart, and I have seen them in circumstances a thousand times more trying than the present. It is only those that are not in action, that feel languor and heaviness, and the best way to rub it off is to turn out, and make sure work of it.

Our army must undoubtedly feel fatigue, and want a reinforcement of rest, though not of valor. Our own interest and happiness call upon us to give them every support in our power, and make the burden of the day, on which the safety of this city depends, light as possible. Remember, gentlemen, that we have forces both to the northward and southward of Philadelphia, and if the enemy be but stopt till those can arrive, this city will be saved, and the enemy finally routed. You have too much at stake to hesitate. You ought not to think an hour upon the matter, but to spring to action at once. Other states have been invaded, have likewise driven off the invaders. Now our time and turn is come, and perhaps the finishing stroke is reserved for us. When we look back on the dangers we have been saved from, and reflect on the success we have been blessed with, it would be sinful either to be idle or despair.

I close this paper with a short address to Gen. Howe. You, sir, are only lingering out the period that shall bring with it your defeat, You have yet scarce began upon the war, and the farther you enter, the faster will your troubles thicken. What you now enjoy is only a respite from ruin; an invitation to destruction: something that will lead on to our deliverance at your expence. We know the cause we are engaged in, and though a passionate fondness for it may make us grieve at every injury that threatens it, yet, when the moment of concern is over, the determination to duty returns. We are not moved by the gloomy smile of a worthless king, but by the ardent glow of generous patriotism. We fight not to enslave, but to set a country free, and to make room upon the earth for honest men to live in. In such a cause we are sure we are right; and we leave to you the despairing reflection of being the tool of a miserable tyrant.

NUMBER V

To General Sir William Howe

Lancaster, March 21, 1778

To argue with a man who has renounced the use and authority of reason, and whose philosophy consists in holding humanity in contempt, is like administering medicine to the dead, or endeavoring to convert an atheist by scripture. Enjoy, sir, your insensibility of feeling and reflecting. It is the prerogative of animals. And no man will envy you those honors, in which a savage only can be your rival and a bear your master.

As the generosity of this country rewarded your brother's services last war with an elegant monument in Westminster-Abbey, it is consistent that she should bestow some mark of distinction upon you. You certainly deserve her notice, and a conspicuous place in the catalogue of extraordinary persons. Yet it would be a pity to pass you from the world in state, and consign you to magnificent oblivion among the tombs, without telling the future beholder why. Judas is as much known as John, yet history ascribes their fame to very different actions.

Sir William hath undoubtedly merited a monument: But of what kind, or with what inscription, where placed or how embellished, is a question that would puzzle all the heralds of St. James' in the profoundest mood of historical deliberation. We are at no loss, sir, to ascertain your real character, but somewhat perplexed how to perpetuate its identity, and preserve it uninjured from the transformations of time or mistake. A statuary may give a false expression to your bust, or decorate it with some equivocal emblems, by which you may happen to steal into reputation and impose upon the hereafter traditionary world. Ill nature or ridicule may conspire, or a variety of accidents combine, to lessen, enlarge, or change Sir William's fame; and no doubt but he who has taken so much pains to be singular in his conduct, would choose to be just as singular in his exit, his monument and his epitaph.

The usual honors of the dead, to be sure, are not sufficiently sublime to escort a character like you to the republic of dust and ashes; for however men may differ in their ideas of grandeur or government here, the grave is nevertheless a perfect republic. Death is not the monarch of the dead, but of the dying. The moment he obtains a conquest he loses a subject, and, like the foolish king you serve, will, in the end, war himself out of all dominion.

As a proper preliminary towards the arrangement of your funeral honors, we readily admit your new rank of *knighthood.* The title is perfectly in character, and is your own, more by merit than creation. There are knights of various orders from the knight of the windmill to the knight of the post. The former is your patron for exploits, and the latter will assist you in settling your accounts. No honorary title could be more happily applied! The ingenuity is sublime! And your royal master hath discovered more genius in fitting you therewith, than in generating the most finished figure for a button, or discanting on the properties of a button-mould.

But how, sir, shall we dispose of you? The invention of a statuary is exhausted, and Sir William is yet unprovided with a monument. America is anxious to bestow her funeral favors upon you, and wishes to do it in a manner that shall distinguish you from the deceased heroes of the last war. The *Egyptian method of embalming* is not known to the present age, and hieroglyphical pageantry hath out-lived the science of decyphering it. Some other method, therefore, must be thought of to immortalize the new knight of the windmill and post. Sir William, thanks to his stars, is not oppressed with very delicate ideas. He has no ambition of being wrapt up and handed about in myrrh, aloes and cassia. Less chargeable odors will suffice; and it fortunately happens, that the simple genius of America hath discovered the art of prescrving bodies and embellishing them too, with much greater frugality than the ancients. In a balmage, sir, of humble tar, you will be as secure as Pharaoh, and in a hieroglyphic of feathers rival in finery all the mummies of Egypt.

As you have already made your exit from the moral world, and by numberless acts both of passionate and deliberate injustice engraved an *"Here Lyeth"* on your deceased honor, it must be mere affectation in you to pretend concern at the humors or opinions of mankind respecting you. What remains of you may expire at any time. The sooner the better. For he who survives his reputation, lives out of spite to himself, like a man listening to his own reproach.

Thus entombed and ornamented I leave you to the inspection of the curious, and return to the history of your yet surviving actions.———The character of Sir William hath undergone some extraordinary revolutions since his arrival in America. It is now fixed and known; and we have nothing to hope from your candor or to fear from your capacity. Indolence and inability have too large a share in your composition ever to suffer you to be any thing more than the hero of little villainies and unfinished adventures. That, which to some persons appeared moderation in you at first, was not produced by any real virtue of your own, but by a contrast of passions dividing and holding you in perpetual irresolution. One vice will frequently expel another without the least merit in the man, as powers in contrary directions reduce each other to rest.

It became you to have supported a dignified solemnity of character; to have shewn a superior liberality of soul; to have won respect by an obstinate perseverance in maintaining order, and to have exhibited on all occasions, such an unchangeable graciousness of conduct, that while we beheld in you the resolution of an enemy, we might admire in you the sincerity of a man. You came to America under the high-sounding titles of commander and commissioner; not only to suppress what you called rebellion by arms, but to shame it out of countenance by the excellence of your example. Instead of which, you have been the patron of low and vulgar frauds, the encourager of Indian cruelties; and have imported a cargo of vices blacker than those you pretended to suppress.

Mankind are not universally agreed in their determination of right and wrong; but there are certain actions which the consent of all nations and individuals hath branded with the unchangeable name of MEANNESS. In the list of human vices we find some of such a refined constitution, that they cannot be carried into practice without seducing some virtue to their assistance; but *meanness* hath neither alliance nor apology. It is generated in the dust and sweepings of other vices, and is of such a hateful figure that all the rest conspire to disown it. Sir William, the commissioner of George the Third, hath at last vouchsafed to give it rank and pedigree. He has placed the fugitive at the council board, and dubbed it companion of the order of knighthood.

The particular act of meanness which I allude to in this description, is forgery. You, sir, have abetted and patronized the forging and uttering counterfeit continental bills. In the same New-York newspapers in which your own proclamation under your master's authority was published, offering, or pretending to offer, pardon and protection to the inhabitants of these states, there were repeated advertisements of counterfeit money for sale, and persons who have come officially from you and under sanction of your flag, have been taken up in attempting to put them off.

A conduct so basely mean in a public character is without precedent or pretence. Every nation on earth, whether friends or enemies, will unite in despising you. 'Tis an incendiary war upon society which nothing can excuse or palliate—An improvement upon beggarly villainy—and shews an inbred wretchedness of heart made up between the venomous malignity of a serpent and the spiteful imbecility of an inferior reptile.

The laws of any civilized country would condemn you to the gibbet without regard to your rank or titles, because it is an action foreign to the usage and custom of war; and should you fall into our hands, which pray God you may, it will be a doubtful matter whether we are to consider you as a military prisoner or a prisoner for felony.

Besides, it is exceedingly unwise and impolitic in you, or any persons in the English service, to promote, or even encourage, or wink, at the crime of forgery in any case whatever. Because, as the riches of England, as a nation, are chiefly in paper, and the far greater part of trade among individuals is carried on by the same medium, that is, by notes and drafts on one another, they, therefore, of all people in the world ought to endeavor to keep forgery out of sight, and, if possible, not to revive the idea of it. It is dangerous to make men familiar with a crime which they may afterwards practise to much greater advantage against those who first taught them. Several officers in the English army have made their exit at the gallows for forgery on their agents; for we all know, who know any thing of England, that there is not a more necessitous body of men, taking them generally, than what the English officers are. They contrive to make a shew at the expence of the taylor, and appear clean at the charge of the washer-woman.

England hath at this time nearly two hundred million pounds sterling of public money in paper, for which she hath no real property, besides a large circulation of bank notes, bank post bills, and promissory notes and drafts of private bankers, merchants and tradesmen. She hath the greatest quantity of paper currency and the least quantity of gold and silver of any nation in Europe; the real specie, which is about sixteen millions sterling, serve only as change in large sums, which are always made in paper, or for payment in small ones. Thus circumstanced, the nation is put to its wit's end, and obliged to be severe almost to criminality, to prevent the practice and growth of forgery. Scarcely a session passes at the Old Bailey, or an execution at Tyburn, but witnesseth this truth. Yet you, sir, regardless of the policy which her necessity obliges her to adopt, have made your whole army intimate with the crime. And as all armies, at the conclusion of a war, are too apt to carry into practice the vices of the campaign, it will probably happen, that England will hereafter abound in forgeries, to which art, the practitioners were first initiated under your authority in America. You, sir, have the honor of adding a new vice to the military catalogue; and the reason, perhaps, why the invention was reserved for you is, because no General before was mean enough even to think of it.

That a man whose soul is absorbed in the low traffic of vulgar vice, is incapable of moving in any superior region, is clearly shewn in you by the event of every campaign. Your military exploits have been without plan, object or decision. Can it be possible that you or your employers can suppose the possession of Philadelphia to be any ways equal to the expence or expectation of the nation which supports you? What advantages does England derive from any achievements of yours? To *her* it is perfectly indifferent what place you are in, so long as the business of conquest is unperformed and the charge of maintaining you remains the same.

If the principal events of the three campaigns be attended to, the balance will appear strongly against you at the close of each; but the last, in point of importance to us, hath exceeded the former two. It is pleasant to look back on dangers past, and equally as pleasant to meditate on present ones when the way out begins to appear. *That* period is now arrived, and the long doubtful winter of war is changing to the sweeter prospects of victory and joy. At the close of the campaign in seventy-five, you were obliged to retreat from Boston. In the summer of seventy-six, you appeared with a numerous fleet and army in the harbor of New-York. By what miracle the Continent was preserved in that season of danger is a subject of admiration! If instead of wasting your time against Long-Island, you had run up the North-River and landed any where above New-York, the consequence must have been, that either you would have compelled General Washington to fight you with very unequal numbers, or he must have suddenly evacuated the city with the loss of nearly all the stores of the army, or have surrendered for want of provisions, the situation of the place naturally producing one or other of these events.

The preparations made to defend New-York were, nevertheless, wise and military; because your forces were then at sea, their numbers uncertain; storms, sickness, or a variety of accidents might have disabled their coming, or so diminished them on their passage, that those which survived would have been incapable of opening the campaign with any prospect of success;

in which case, the defence would have been sufficient and the place preserved; for cities that have been raised from nothing with an infinitude of labor and expence, are not to be thrown away on the bare probability of their being taken. On these grounds, the preparations made to maintain New-York were as judicious as the retreat afterwards. While you, in the interim, let slip the *very* opportunity which seemed to put conquest in your power.

Through the whole of that campaign you had nearly double the forces which General Washington immediately commanded. The principal plan, at that time, on our part, was to wear away the season with as little loss as possible, and to raise the army for the next year. Long-Island, New-York, Forts Washington and Lee were not defended, after your superior force was known, under any expectation of their being finally maintained, but as a range of out-works, in the attacking of which, your time might be wasted, your numbers reduced, and your vanity amused by possessing them on our retreat. It was intended to have withdrawn the garrison from Fort Washington after it had answered the former of those purposes, but the fate of that day put a prize into your hands without much honor to yourselves.

Your progress through the Jerseys was accidental; you had it not even in contemplation, or you would not have sent so principal a part of your force to Rhode-Island before-hand. The utmost hope of America in the year seventy-six reached no higher than that she might not *then* be conquered. She had no expectation of defeating you in that campaign. Even the most cowardly tory allowed, that, could she withstand the shock of *that* summer her independence would be past a doubt. You had *then* greatly the advantage of her. You were formidable. Your military knowledge was supposed to be complete. Your fleets and forces arrived without an accident. You had neither experience nor reinforcements to wait for. You had nothing to do but to begin, and your chance lay in the first vigorous onset.

America was young and unskilled. She was obliged to trust her defence to time and practice; and hath, by mere dint of perseverance, maintained her cause, and brought her enemy to a condition, in which, she is now capable of meeting him on any grounds.

It is remarkable that in the campaign of seventy-six, you gained no more, notwithstanding your great force than what was given you by consent of evacuation, except Fort Washington: While every advantage obtained by us was by fair and hard fighting. The defeat of Sir Peter Parker was complete. The conquest of the Hessians at Trenton by the remains of a retreating army, which but a few days before, you affected to despise, is an instance of heroic perseverance very seldom to be met with. And the victory over the British troops at Princeton, by a harassed and wearied party, who had been engaged the day before and marched all night without refreshment, is attended with such a scene of circumstances and superiority of generalship, as will ever give it a place on the first line in the history of great actions.

When I look back on the gloomy days of last winter and see America suspended by a thread, I feel a triumph of joy at the recollection of her delivery, and a reverence for the characters which snatched her from destruction. To doubt *now* would be a species of infidelity, and to forget the instruments which saved us *then* would be ingratitude.

The close of that campaign left us with the spirits of conquerors. The northern districts were relieved by the retreat of General Carleton over the lakes. The army under your command were hunted back and had their bounds prescribed. The Continent began to feel its military importance, and the winter passed pleasantly away in preparations for the next campaign.

However confident you might be on your first arrival, the course of the year seventy-six gave you some idea of the difficulty, if not impossibility, of conquest. To this reason I ascribe your delay in opening the campaign in seventy-seven. The face of matters, on the close of the former year, gave you no encouragement to pursue a discretionary war as soon as the spring admitted the taking the field: for though conquest, in that case, would have given you a double portion of fame, yet the experiment was too hazardous. The ministry, had you failed, would have shifted the whole blame upon you, charged you with having acted without orders, and condemned at once both your plan and your execution.

To avoid those misfortunes, which might have involved you and your money accounts in perplexity and suspicion, you prudently waited the arrival of a plan of operations from England, which was, that you should proceed for Philadelphia by the way of Chesapeake, and that Burgoyne, after reducing Ticonderoga, should take his route by Albany, and, if necessary, join you.

The splendid laurels of the last campaign have flourished in the north. In that quarter America hath surprized the world, and laid the foundation of her this year's glory. The conquest of Ticonderoga (if it may be called a conquest) has, like all your other victories, led on to ruin. Even the provisions taken in that fortress, (which by General Burgoyne's return was sufficient in bread and flour for nearly 5000 men for ten weeks, and in beef and pork for the same number of men for one month) served only to hasten his overthrow, by enabling him to proceed for Saratoga the place of his destruction. A short review of the operations of the last campaign will shew the condition of affairs on both sides.

You have taken Ticonderoga and marched into Philadelphia. These are all the events which the year hath produced on your part. A trifling campaign indeed, compared with the expences of England and the conquest of the continent. On the other side, a considerable part of your northern force has been routed by the New-York militia under General Herkemer. Fort Stanwix hath bravely survived a compounded attack of soldiers and savages, and the besiegers have fled. The battle of Bennington has put a thousand prisoners into our hands, with all their arms, stores, artillery and baggage. General Burgoyne in two engagements has been defeated; himself, his army, and all that were his and theirs are now ours. Ticonderoga and Independence are retaken, and not the shadow of an enemy remains in all the northern districts. At this instant we have upwards, of eleven thousand prisoners, between sixty and seventy pieces of brass ordnance, besides small arms, tents, stores, &c. &c.

In order to know the real value of those advantages we must reverse the scene, and suppose General Gates and the force he commanded, to be at your mercy as prisoners, and General Burgoyne with his army of soldiers and savages to be already joined to you in Pennsylvania. So dismal a picture can scarcely be looked at. It hath all the traces and colourings of horror and despair; and excites the most swelling emotions of gratitude by exhibiting the miseries we are so graciously preserved from.

I admire this distribution of laurels around the continent. It is the earnest of future union. South-Carolina has had her day of suffering and of fame; and the other southern states have exerted themselves in proportion to the force that invaded or insulted them. Towards the close of the campaign in seventy-six, these middle states were called upon and did their duty nobly. They were witnesses to the almost expiring flame of human freedom. It was the close struggle of life and death. The line of invisible division; and on which, the unabated fortitude of a Washington prevailed, and saved the spark, that has since blazed in the north with unrivalled lustre.

Let me ask, sir, what great exploits have you performed? Through all the variety of changes and opportunities which this war hath produced, I know no one action of yours that can be stiled masterly. You have moved in and out, backward and forward, round and round, as if valor consisted in a military jig. The history and figure of your movements would be truly ridiculous could they be justly delineated. They resemble the labors of a puppy pursuing his tail; the end is still at the same distance, and all the turnings round must be done over again.

The first appearance of affairs at Ticonderoga wore such an unpromising aspect, that it was necessary, in July, to detach a part of the forces to the support of that quarter, which were otherwise destined or intended to act against you, and this, perhaps, has been the means of postponing your downfall to another campaign. The destruction of one army at a time is work enough. We know, sir, what we are about, what we have to do, and how to do it.

Your progress from Chesapeake was marked by no capital stroke of policy or heroism. Your principal aim was to get General Washington between the Delaware and Schuylkill and between Philadelphia and your army. In that situation, with a river on each of his flanks, which united about five miles below the city, and your army above him, you could have intercepted his reinforcements and supplies, cut off all his communication with the country, and, if necessary, have dispatched assistance to open a passage for General Burgoyne. This scheme was too visible to succeed, for had General Washington suffered you to command the open country above him, I think it a very reasonable conjecture that the conquest of Burgoyne would not have taken place, because you could, in that case, have relieved him. It was therefore necessary, while that important victory was in suspence, to trepan *you* into a situation, in which you could only be on the defensive without the power of affording him assistance. The manoeuvre had its effect and Burgoyne was conquered.

There has been something unmilitarily passive in you from the time of your passing the Schuylkill and getting possession of Philadelphia to the close of the campaign. You mistook a trap for a conquest, the probability of which had been made known to Europe, and the edge of your triumph taken off by our own information long before.

Having got you into this situation, a scheme for a general attack upon you at Germantown was carried into execution on the fourth of October, and though the success was not equal to the excellence of the plan, yet the attempting it proved the genius of America to be on the rise and her power approaching to superiority. The obscurity of the morning was your best friend, for a fog is always favorable to a hunted enemy. Some weeks after this, you, likewise, planned an attack on General Washington while at Whitemarsh. Marched out with infinite parade, but on finding him preparing to attack you the next morning, you prudently cut about and retreated to Philadelphia with all the precipitation of a man conquered in imagination.

Immediately after the battle of Germantown, the probability of Burgoyne's defeat gave a new policy to affairs in Pennsylvania, and it was judged most consistent with the general safety of America to wait the issue of the Northern campaign. Slow and sure is sound work. The news of that victory arrived in our camp on the 18th of October, and no sooner did the shout of joy and the report of the thirteen cannon reach your ears, than you resolved upon a retreat, and the next day, that is, on the 19th, withdrew your drooping army into Philadelphia. This movement was evidently dictated by fear; and carried with it a positive confession that you dreaded a second attack. It was hiding yourself among women and children, and sleeping away the choicest part of a campaign in expensive inactivity. An army in a city can never be a conquering army. The situation admits only of defence. It is mere shelter; and every military power in Europe will conclude you to be eventually defeated.

The time when you made this retreat was the very time you ought to have fought a battle, in order to put yourself in a condition of recovering in Pennsylvania what you had lost at Saratoga. And the reason why you did not, must be either prudence or cowardice; the former supposes your inability, and the latter needs no explanation. I draw no conclusions, sir, but such as are naturally deduced from known and visible facts, and such as will always have a being while the facts which produced them remain unaltered.

After this retreat a new difficulty arose which exhibited the power of Britain in a very contemptible light, which was the attack and defence of Mud-Island. For several weeks did that little unfinished fortress stand out against all the attempts of Admiral and General Howe. It was the fable of Bendar realized on the Delaware. Scheme after scheme, and force upon force were tried and defeated. The garrison, with scarce any thing to cover them but their bravery, survived in the midst of mud, shot and shells, and were at last obliged to give it up more to the powers of time and gunpowder than to the military superiority of the besiegers.

It is my sincere opinion that matters are in a much worse condition with you than what is generally known. Your master's speech at the opening of parliament is like a soliloquy on ill luck. It shews him to be coming a little to his reason, for sense of pain is the first symptom of recovery in profound stupefactions. His condition is deplorable. He is obliged to submit to all the insults of France and Spain without daring to know or resent them, and thankful for the most trivial evasions to the most humble remonstrances. The time *was* when he could not *deign* an answer to a petition from America, and the time now *is* when he dare not *give* an answer to an affront from France. The capture of Burgoyne's army will sink his consequence as much in Europe as in America. In his speech he expresses his suspicions at the warlike preparations of France and Spain, and as he has only the one army which you command to support his character in the world with, it remains very uncertain when, or in what quarter, it will be most wanted or can be best employed; and this will partly account for the great care you take to keep it from action and attacks, for should Burgoyne's fate be yours, which it probably will, England may take her endless farewell not only of all America but of all the West-Indies.

Never did a nation invite destruction upon itself with the eagerness and ignorance with which Britain has done. Bent upon the ruin of a young and unoffending country, she hath drawn the sword that hath wounded herself to the heart, and in the agony of her resentment hath applied a poison for a cure. Her conduct towards America is a compound of rage and lunacy; she aims at the government of it, yet preserves neither dignity nor character in her methods to obtain it. Were government a mere manufacture or article of commerce immaterial by whom it should be made or sold, we might as well employ her as another, but when we consider it as the fountain from whence the general manners and morality of a country take their rise, that the persons entrusted with the execution thereof are by their serious example and authority to support these principles, how abominably absurd is the idea of being hereafter governed by a set of men who have been guilty of forgery, perjury, treachery, theft, and every species of villainy which the lowest wretches on earth could practise or invent. What

greater public curse can befall any country than to be
under such authority, and what greater blessing than
to be delivered therefrom. The soul of any man of
sentiment would rise in brave rebellion against them
and spurn them from the earth.

The malignant and venomous tempered General
Vaughan has amused his savage fancy in burning the
whole town of Kingston, in York government, and the
late Governor of that State, Mr. Tryon, in his letter
to General Parsons, has endeavored to justify it, and
declared his wish to burn the houses of every
committee-man in the country. Such a confession from
one who was once entrusted with the powers of civil
government, is a reproach to the character. But it is
the wish and the declaration of a man whom anguish
and disappointment have driven to despair, and who
is daily decaying into the grave with constitutional
rottenness.

There is not in the compass of language a sufficiency
of words to express the baseness of your king, his
ministry and his army. They have refined upon villainy
till it wants a name. To the fiercer vices of former
ages they have added the dregs and scummings of the
most finished rascality, and are so completely sunk in
serpentine deceit, that there is not left among them
one generous enemy.

From such men and such masters may the gracious
hand of Heaven preserve America! And though the
sufferings she now endures are heavy and severe, they
are like straws in the wind compared to the weight of
evils she would feel under the government of your
king, and his pensioned parliament.

There is something in meanness which excites a species of resentment that never subsides, and something
in cruelty which stirs up the heart to the highest agony
of human hatred; Britain hath filled up both these
characters till no addition can be made, and hath not
reputation left with us to obtain credit for the slightest

promise. The will of God hath parted us, and the deed is registered for eternity. When she shall be a spot scarcely visible among the nations, America shall flourish the favorite of Heaven and the friend of mankind.

For the domestic happiness of Britain and the peace of the world I wish she had not a foot of land but what is circumscribed within her own island. Extent of dominion hath been her ruin, and instead of civilizing others hath brutalized herself. Her late reduction of India, under Clive and his successors, was not so properly a conquest as an extermination of mankind. She is the only power who could practise the prodigal barbarity of tying men to the mouths of loaded cannon and blowing them away. It happens that General Burgoyne, who made the report of that horrid transaction in the house of commons, is now a prisoner with us, and though an enemy, I can appeal to him for the truth of it, being confident that he neither can nor will deny it. Yet Clive received the approbation of the last parliament.

When we take a survey of mankind we cannot help cursing the wretch, who, to the unavoidable misfortunes of nature shall willfully add the calamities of war. One would think there were evils enough in the world without studying to increase them, and that life is sufficiently short without shaking the sand that measures it. The histories of Alexander, and Charles of Sweden, are the histories of human devils; a good man cannot think of their actions without abhorrence nor of their deaths without rejoicings. To see the bounties of Heaven destroyed, the beautiful face of nature laid waste, and the choicest works of creation and art tumbled into ruin, would fetch a curse from the soul of piety itself. But in this country the aggravation is heightened by a new combination of affecting circumstances. America was young, and, compared with other countries, was virtuous. None but a Herod of uncommon malice would have made war upon infancy and innocence, and none but a people of the most finished fortitude dared, under those circumstances, have resisted the tyranny. The natives, or their ancestors, had fled from the former oppressions of England, and with the industry of bees had changed a wilderness into a habitable world. To Britain they were indebted for nothing. The country was the gift of Heaven, and God alone is their Lord and Sovereign.

The time, sir, will come when you, in a melancholy hour, shall reckon up your miseries by your murders in America. Life, with you, begins to wear a clouded aspect. The vision of pleasurable delusion is wearing away, and changing to the barren wild of age and sorrow. The poor reflection of having served your king will yield you no consolation in your parting moments. He will crumble to the same undistinguished ashes with yourself, and have sins enough of his own to answer for. It is not the farcical benedictions of a bishop, nor the cringing hypocrisy of a court of chaplains, nor the formality of an act of parliament, that can change guilt into innocence, or make the punishment *one* pang the less. You may, perhaps, be unwilling to be serious, but this destruction of the goods of Providence, this havoc of the human race, and this sowing the world with mischief, must be accounted for to him who made and governs it. To us they are only present sufferings, but to him they are deep rebellions.

If there is a sin superior to every other it is that of willful and offensive war. Most other sins are circumscribed within narrow limits, that is, the power of *one* man cannot give them a very general extension, and many kind of sins have only a mental existence from which no infection arises; but he who is the author of a war, lets loose the whole contagion of hell, and opens a vein that bleeds a nation to death. We leave it to England and Indians to boast of these honors; we feel no thirst for such savage glory; a nobler flame, a purer spirit animates America. She hath taken up the sword of virtuous defence; she hath bravely put herself between Tyranny and Freedom, between a curse and a blessing, determined to expel the one, and protect the other.

It is the object only of war that makes it honorable. And if there were ever a *just* war since the world began, it is this which America is now engaged in. She invaded no land of yours. She hired no mercenaries to burn your towns, nor Indians to massacre their inhabitants. She wanted nothing from you and was indebted for nothing to you; and thus circumstanced, her defence is honorable and her prosperity certain.

Yet it is not on the *justice* only, but likewise on the *importance* of this cause that I ground my seeming enthusiastical confidence of our success. The vast extension of America makes her of too much value in the scale of Providence, to be cast, like a pearl before swine, at the feet of an European island; and of much less consequence would it be that Britain were sunk in the sea than that America should miscarry. There has been such a chain of extraordinary events in the discovery of this country at first, in the peopling and planting it afterwards, in the rearing and nursing it to its present state, and in the protection of it through the present war, that no man can doubt, but Providence hath some nobler end to accomplish than the gratification of the petty elector of Hanover or the ignorant and insignificant king of Britain.

As the blood of the martyrs hath been the seed of the Christian church, so the political persecutions of England will and hath already enriched America with industry, experience, union and importance. Before the present aera she was a mere chaos of uncemented Colonies, individually exposed to the ravages of the Indians and the invasion of any power that Britain should be at war with. She had nothing she could call her own. Her felicity depended upon accident. The convulsions of Europe might have thrown her from one conqueror to another, till she had been the slave of all and ruined by every one; for until she had spirit enough to become her own master, there was no knowing to which master she should belong. *That* period, thank God, is past, and she is no longer the dependant, disunited Colonies of Britain, but the independent and United States of America, knowing no master but Heaven and herself. You or your king may call this "Delusion," "Rebellion," or what name you please. To us it is perfectly indifferent. The issue will determine the character and time will give it a name as lasting as his own.

You have now, sir, tried the fate of three campaigns, and can fully declare to England, that nothing is to be got on your part but blows and broken bones, and nothing on hers but waste of trade and credit and an increase of poverty and taxes. You are now only where you might have been two years ago without the loss of a single ship, and yet not a step the forwarder towards the conquest of the Continent; because, as I have already hinted, "An army in a city can never be a conquering army." The full amount of your losses since the beginning of the war exceeds twenty thousand men, besides millions of treasure for which you have nothing in exchange. Our expences, though great, are circulated within ourselves. Yours is a direct sinking of money, and that from both ends at once, first in hiring troops out of the nation, and in paying them afterwards, because the money in neither case can return again to Britain. We are already in possession of the prize, you only in suit for it. To us it is a real treasure, to you it would be only an empty triumph. Our expences will repay themselves with ten-fold interest, while yours entail upon you everlasting poverty.

Take a review, sir, of the ground you have gone over, and let it teach you policy, if it cannot honesty.

You stand but on a very tottering foundation. A change of the ministry in England may probably bring your measures into question and your head to the block. Clive, with all his successes, had some difficulty in escaping, and yours being all a war of losses, will afford you less pretensions and your enemies more grounds for impeachment.

Go home, sir, and endeavor to save the remains of your ruined country by a just representation of the madness of her measures. A few moments well applied may yet preserve her from political destruction. I am not one of those who wish to see Europe in a flame, because I am persuaded such an event will not shorten the war. The rupture, at present, is confined between the two powers of America and England. England finds she cannot conquer America, and America has no wish to conquer England. You are fighting for what you can never obtain, and we defending what we mean never to part with. A few words, therefore, settle the bargain. Let England mind her own business and we will mind ours. Govern yourselves and we will govern ourselves. You may then trade where you please unmolested by us, and we will trade where we please unmolested by you; and such articles as we can purchase of each other better than elsewhere may be mutually done. If it were possible that you could carry on the war for twenty years you must still come to this point at last, or worse, and the sooner you think of it the better it will be for you.

My official situation enables me to know the repeated insults which Britain is obliged to put up with from foreign powers, and the wretched shifts she is driven to, to gloss them over. Her reduced strength and exhausted coffers in a three years' war with America have given a powerful superiority to France and Spain. She is not now a match for them——But if neither counsels can prevail on her to think, nor sufferings awaken her to reason, she must e'en go on, till the honor of England becomes a proverb of contempt, and Europe dub her the Land of Fools.

I am, Sir,
With every wish for an honorable peace,
Your friend, enemy, and countryman,
COMMON SENSE

To the Inhabitants of America

With all the pleasure with which a man exchanges bad company for good, I take my leave of Sir William and return to you. It is now nearly three years since the tyranny of Britain received its first repulse by the arms of America. A period, which has given birth to a new world and erected a monument to the folly of the old.

I cannot help being sometimes surprised at the complimentary references which I have seen and heard made to ancient histories and transactions. The wisdom, civil governments, and sense of honor of the states of Greece and Rome, are frequently held up as objects of excellence and imitation. Mankind have lived for very little purpose, if, at this period of the world, they must go two or three thousand years back for lessons and examples. We do dishonorary injustice to ourselves by placing them in such a superior line. We have no just authority for it, neither can we tell why it is that we should suppose ourselves inferior.

Could the mist of antiquity be taken away, and men and things viewed as they then really were, it is more than probable that they would admire us, rather than we them. America has surmounted a greater variety and combination of difficulties than, I believe, ever fell to the share of any one people in the same space of time, and has replenished the world with more useful knowledge and sounder maxims of civil government than were ever produced in any age before. Had it not been for America there had been no such thing as freedom left throughout the whole universe. England hath lost hers in a long chain of right reasoning from wrong principles, and it is from this country now she must learn the resolution to redress herself, and the wisdom how.

The Grecians and Romans were strongly possessed of the *Spirit* of liberty but *not* the *principle,* for at the time they were determined not to be slaves themselves, they employed their power to enslave the rest of mankind. But this distinguished aera is blotted by no one misanthropical vice. In short, if the principle on which the cause is founded, the universal blessings that are to arise from it, the difficulties that accompanied it, the wisdom with which it has been debated, the fortitude by which it has been supported, the strength of the power we had to oppose, and the condition in which we undertook it, be all taken in one view, we may justly stile it the most virtuous and illustrious revolution that ever graced the history of mankind.

A good opinion of ourselves is exceedingly necessary in private life, but absolutely necessary in public life, and of the utmost importance in supporting national character. I have no notion of yielding the palm of the United States to any Grecians or Romans that were ever born. We have equalled the bravest in times of danger, and excelled the wisest in the construction of civil governments, *no one in America excepted.*

From this agreeable eminence let us take a review of present affairs. The spirit of corruption is so inseparably interwoven with British politics, that their ministry suppose all mankind are governed by the same motive. They have no idea of a people submitting even to temporary inconvenience from an attachment to rights and privileges. Their plans of business are calculated *by* the hour and *for* the hour, and are uniform in nothing but the corruption which gives them birth. They never had, neither have they at this time, any regular plan for the conquest of America by arms. They know not how to go about it, neither have they power to effect it if they could know. The thing is not within the compass of human practicability, for America is too extensive either to be fully conquered or *passively* defended. But she may be *actively* defended by defeating or making prisoners of the army that invades her. And this is the only system of defence that can be effectual in a large country.

There is something in a war carried on by invasion which makes it differ in circumstances from any other mode of war, because he who conducts it cannot tell whether the ground he gains, be for him, or against him, when he first makes it. In the winter of seventy-six General Howe marched with an air of victory through the Jerseys, the consequence of which was his defeat, and General Burgoyne at Saratoga experienced the same fate from the same cause. The Spaniards about two years ago were defeated by the Algerines in the same manner, that is, their first triumphs became a trap in which they were totally routed. And whoever will attend to the circumstances and events of a war carried on by invasion, will find, that any invader, in order to be finally conquered must first begin to conquer.

I confess myself one of those who believe the loss of Philadelphia to be attended with more advantages than injuries. The case stood thus. The enemy imagined Philadelphia to be of more importance to us than it really was; for we all know that it had long ceased to be a port, not a cargo of goods had been brought into it for near a twelve-month, nor any fixed manufactories, nor even ship-building carried on in it; yet as the enemy believed the conquest of it to be practicable, and to that belief added the absurd idea that the soul of all America was centered there, and would be conquered there, it naturally follows, that their possession of it, by not answering the end proposed, must break up the plans they had so foolishly gone upon, and either oblige them to form a new one, for which their present strength is not sufficient, or to give over the attempt.

We never had so small an army to fight against, nor so fair an opportunity of final success as *now*. The death wound is already given. The day is our own if we follow it up. The enemy by his situation is within our reach, and by his reduced strength is within our power. The ministers of Britain may rage as they please, but our part is to conquer their armies. Let them wrangle and welcome, but let it not draw our attention from the *one* thing needful. *Here, in this* spot is our business to be accomplished, our felicity secured. What we have now to do is as clear as light, and the way to do it is as strait as a line. It needs not to be commented upon, yet, in order to be perfectly understood I will put a case that cannot admit of a mistake.

Had the armies under the Generals Howe and Burgoyne been united and taken post at Germantown, and had the Northern army, under General Gates been joined to that under General Washington at Whitemarsh, the consequence would have been a general action; and if in the action we had killed and taken the same number of officers and men, that is, between nine and ten thousand, with the same quantity of artillery, arms, stores, &c. as have been taken at the Northward, and obliged General Howe with the remains of his army, that is, with the same number he now commands, to take shelter in Philadelphia, we should certainly have thought ourselves the greatest heroes in the world; and should, as soon as the season permitted, have collected together all the force of the Continent and laid siege to the city, for it requires a much greater force to besiege an enemy in a town than to defeat them in the field. The case *now* is just the same as if it had been produced by the means I have here supposed. Between nine and ten thousand have been killed and taken, all their stores are in our possession, and General Howe, in consequence of that victory, has thrown himself for shelter into Philadelphia. He, or his trifling friend Galloway, may form what pretences they please, yet no just reason can be given for their going into winter quarters so early as the 19th of October, but their apprehension of a defeat if they continued out, or their conscious inability of keeping the field with safety. I see no advantage which can arise to America by hunting the enemy from state to state. It is a triumph without a prize, and wholly unworthy the attention of a people determined to conquer. Neither can any state promise itself security while the enemy remains in a condition to transport themselves from one part of the Continent to another. Howe, likewise, cannot conquer where we have no army to oppose, therefore any such removals in him are mean and cowardly, and reduces Britain to a common pilferer. If he retreats from Philadelphia, he will be despised; if he stays, he may be shut up and starved out, and the country, if he advances into it, may become his Saratoga. He has his choice of evils and we of opportunities. If he moves early, it is not only a sign but a proof that he expects no reinforcement, and his delays will prove that he either waits for the arrival of a plan to go upon, or force to execute it, or both; in *which* case, our strength will increase more than his, therefore in *any* case we cannot be wrong if we do but proceed.

The particular condition of Pennsylvania deserves the attention of all the other states. Her military strength must not be estimated by the number of inhabitants. Here are men of all nations, characters, professions and interests. Here are the firmest whigs, surviving, like sparks in the ocean, unquenched and uncooled in the midst of discouragement and disaffection. Here are men losing their all with cheerfulness, and collecting fire and fortitude from the flames of their own estates. Here are others skulking in secret, many making a market of the times, and numbers who are changing whig and tory with the circumstances of every day.

It is by mere dint of fortitude and perseverance that the whigs of this state have been able to maintain so good a countenance, and do even what they have done. We want help, and the sooner it can arrive the more effectual it will be. The invaded state, be it which it may, will always feel an additional burthen upon its back, and be hard set to support its civil power with sufficient authority: and this difficulty will always rise or fall, in proportion as the other states throw in their assistance to the common cause.

The enemy will most probably make many manoeuvres at the opening of this campaign, to amuse and draw off the attention of the several states from the *one thing needful.* We may expect to hear of alarms and pretended expeditions to *this* place and *that* place, to the Southward, the Eastward and the Northward, all intended to prevent our forming into one formidable body. The less the enemy's strength is, the more subtleties of this kind will they make use of. Their existence depends upon it, because the force of America, when collected, is sufficient to swallow their present army up. It is therefore our business to make short work of it, by bending our whole attention to *this one principal point,* for the instant that the main body under General Howe is defeated, all the inferior alarms thro'out the Continent, like so many shadows, will follow his downfall.

The only way to finish a war with the least possible bloodshed, or perhaps without any, is to collect an army, against the power of which, the enemy shall have no chance. By not doing this, we prolong the war, and double both the calamities and the expences of it. What a rich and happy country would America be, were she, by a vigorous exertion, to reduce Howe as she has reduced Burgoyne. Her currency would rise to millions beyond its present value. Every man would be rich, and every man would have it in his power to be happy. And why not do these things? What is there to hinder? America is her own mistress and can do what she pleases.

If we had not at this time a man in the field, we could, nevertheless, raise an army in a few weeks sufficient to overwhelm all the force which General Howe at present commands. Vigor and determination will do any thing and every thing. We began the war with this kind of spirit, why not end it with the same? Here, gentlemen, is the enemy. Here is the army. The interest, the happiness, of all America is centered in this half ruined spot. Come on and help us. Here are laurels, come and share them. Here are tories, come and help us to expel them. Here are whigs that will make you welcome, and enemies that dread your coming.

The worst of all policy is that of doing things by halves. Penny wise and pound foolish, has been the ruin of thousands. The present spring, if rightly improved, will free us from all our troubles, and save us the expence of millions. We have now only one army to cope with. No opportunity can be fairer; no prospect more promising. I shall conclude this paper with a few outlines of a plan, either for filling up the battalions with expedition, or for raising an additional force, for any limited time, on any sudden emergency.

That in which every man is interested, is every man's duty to support. And any burthen which falls equally on all men, and, from which every man is to receive an equal benefit, is consistent with the most perfect ideas of liberty. I would wish to revive something of that virtuous ambition which first called

America into the field. Then every man was eager to do his part, and perhaps the principal reason why we have in any degree fallen therefrom, is, because we did not set a sufficient value by it at first, but left it to blaze out of itself, instead of regulating and preserving it by just proportions of rest and service.

Suppose any state whose number of effective inhabitants was 80,000, should be required to furnish 3,200 men towards the defence of the Continent, on any sudden emergency.

First, Let the whole number of effective inhabitants be divided into hundreds; then if each of those hundreds turn out four men, the whole number of 3,200 will be had.

Secondly, Let the names of each hundred men be entered in a book, and let four dollars be collected from each man, with as much more as any of the gentlemen, whose abilities can afford it, shall please to throw in, which gifts shall likewise be entered against the donors' names.

Thirdly, Let the sums so collected be offered as a present, over and above the bounty of twenty dollars, to any four who may be inclined to propose themselves as volunteers; if more than four offer, the majority of the subscribers present shall determine which; if none offer, then four out of the hundred shall be taken by lot, who shall be entitled to the said sums, and shall either go, or provide others that will, in the space of six days.

Fourthly, As it will always happen, that in the space of ground on which an hundred men shall live, there will be always a number of persons who, by age and infirmity, are incapable of doing personal service, and as such persons are generally possessed of the greatest part of the property in any county, their portion of service, therefore, will be to furnish each man with a blanket, which will make a regimental coat, jacket and breeches, or cloaths in lieu thereof, and another for a watch cloak, and two pair of shoes—for however choice people may be of these things matters not in cases of this kind—Those who live always in houses can find many ways to keep themselves warm, but it is a shame and a sin to suffer a soldier in the field to want a blanket while there is one in the country.

Should the cloathing not be wanted, the superannuated or infirm persons possessing property, may, in lieu thereof, throw in their money subscriptions towards increasing the bounty, for though age will naturally exempt a person from personal service, it cannot exempt him from his share of the charge, because the men are raised for the defence of property and liberty, jointly.

There never was a scheme against which objections might not be raised. But this alone is not a sufficient reason for rejection. The only line to judge truly upon, is, to draw out and admit all the objections which can fairly be made, and place against them all the contrary qualities, conveniences and advantages, then by striking a balance you come at the true character of any scheme, principle or position.

The most material advantages of the plan here proposed are ease, expedition, and cheapness; yet the men so raised get a much larger bounty than is any where at present given; because all the expences, extravagance, and consequent idleness of recruiting are saved or prevented. The country incurs no new debt, nor interest thereon; the whole matter being all settled at once and entirely done with. It is a subscription answering all the purposes of a tax, without either the charge or trouble of collecting. The men are ready for the field with the greatest possible expedition, because it becomes the duty of the inhabitants themselves, in every part of the country, to find up their proportion of men, instead of leaving it to a recruiting sergeant, who, be he ever so industrious, cannot know always where to apply.

I do not propose this as a regular digested plan, neither will the limits of this paper admit of any further remarks upon it. I believe it to be a hint capable of much improvement, and as such submit it to the public.

NUMBER VII (Selections)

To the People *of* England

Philadelphia, Nov. 21, 1778

. . . a set of very interesting and rational questions.

First, What is the original fountain of power and honor in any country?

Secondly, Whether the prerogative does not belong to the people?

Thirdly, Whether there is any such thing as the English constitution?

Fourthly, Of what use is the crown to the people?

Fifthly, Whether he who invented a crown was not an enemy to mankind?

Sixthly, Whether it is not a shame for a man to spend a million a year and do no good for it, and whether the money might not be better applied?

Seventhly, Whether such a man is not better dead than alive?

Eighthly, Whether a congress constituted like that of America, is not the most happy and consistent form of government in the world? . . .

NUMBER VIII (Selections)

Addressed to the People of England

. . . Make but the case of others your own, and your own theirs, and you will then have a clear idea of the whole. Had France acted towards her colonies as you have done, you would have branded her with every epithet of abhorrence; and had you like her, stept in to succour a struggling people, all Europe must have echoed with your own applauses. But entangled in the passion of dispute, you see it not as you ought, and form opinions thereon which suit with no interest but your own. You wonder America does not rise in union with you to impose on herself a portion of your taxes and reduce herself to unconditional submission. You are amazed that the southern powers of Europe do not assist you in conquering a country which is afterwards to be turned against themselves; and that the northern ones do not contribute to reinstate you in America, who already enjoy the market for naval stores by the separation. You seem surprised that Holland does not pour in her succours, to maintain you mistress of the seas, when her own commerce is suffering by your act of navigation, or that any country should study her own interests while yours is on the carpet.

Such excesses of passionate folly, and unjust as well

as unwise resentment, have driven you on, like Pharaoh, to unpitied miseries, and while the importance of the quarrel shall perpetuate your disgrace, the flag of America will carry it round the world. The natural feelings of every rational being will take against you, and wherever the story shall be told, you will have neither excuse nor consolation left. With an unsparing hand and an unsatiable mind, you have havocked the world, both to gain dominion and to lose it, and while in a phrenzy of avarice and ambition, the east and the west are doomed to tributary bondage, you rapidly earned destruction as the wages of a nation. . . .

NUMBER XIII

Philadelphia, April 19, 1783

"The times that tried mens souls," are over—and the greatest and completest revolution the world ever knew, gloriously and happily accomplished.

But to pass from the extremes of danger to safety—from the tumult of war, to the tranquility of peace, though sweet in contemplation, requires a gradual composure of the senses to receive it. Even calmness has the power of stunning, when it opens too instantly upon us. The long and raging hurricane that should cease in a moment, would leave us in a state rather of wonder than enjoyment; and some moments of recollection must pass, before we could be capable of tasting the full felicity of repose. There are but few instances, in which the mind is fitted for sudden transitions: It takes in its pleasures by reflection and comparison, and those must have time to act, before the relish for new scenes is complete.

In the present case—the mighty magnitude of the object—the various uncertainties of fate it has undergone—the numerous and complicated dangers we have suffered or escaped—the eminence we now stand on, and the vast prospect before us, must all conspire to impress us with contemplation.

To see it in our power to make a world happy—to

teach mankind the art of being so—to exhibit on the theatre of the universe, a character hitherto unknown—and to have, as it were, a new creation entrusted to our hands, are honors that command reflection, and can neither be too highly estimated, nor too gratefully received.

In this pause then of recollection—while the storm is ceasing, and the long agitated mind vibrating to a rest, let us look back on the scenes we have passed, and learn from experience what is yet to be done.

Never, I say, had a country so many openings to happiness as this. Her setting out into life, like the rising of a fair morning, was unclouded and promising. Her cause was good. Her principles just and liberal. Her temper serene and firm. Her conduct regulated by the nicest steps, and every thing about her wore the mark of honor.

It is not every country (perhaps there is not another in the world) that can boast so fair an origin. Even the first settlement of America corresponds with the character of the revolution. Rome, once the proud mistress of the universe, was originally a band of ruffians. Plunder and rapine made her rich, and her oppression of millions made her great. But America needs never be ashamed to tell her birth, nor relate the stages by which she rose to empire.

The remembrance then of what is past, if it operates rightly, must inspire her with the most laudable of all ambition, that of adding to the fair fame she began with. The world has seen her great in adversity. Struggling without a thought of yielding beneath accumulated difficulties. Bravely, nay proudly, encountering distress, and rising in resolution as the storm increased. All this is justly due to her, for her fortitude has merited the character. Let then the world see that she can bear prosperity: and that her honest virtue in time of peace, is equal to the bravest virtue in time of war.

She is now descending to the scenes of quiet and domestic life. Not beneath the cypress shade of disappointment, but to enjoy in her own land, and under her own vine, the sweet of her labors, and the reward of her toil—In this situation, may she never forget that a fair national reputation, is of as much importance as independence. That it possesses a charm which wins upon the world, and makes even enemies civil. That it gives a dignity which is often superior to power, and commands a reverence where pomp and splendor fail.

It would be a circumstance ever to be lamented and never to be forgotten, were a single blot, from any cause whatever, suffered to fall on a revolution, which to the end of time must be an honor to the age that accomplished it: and which has contributed more to enlighten the world, and diffuse a spirit of freedom and liberality among mankind, than any human event (if this may be called one) that ever preceded it.

It is not among the least of the calamities of a long continued war, that it unhinges the mind from those nice sensations which at other times appear so amiable. The continual spectacle of woe, blunts the finer feelings, and the necessity of bearing with the sight, renders it familiar. In like manner, are many of the moral obligations of society weakened, till the custom of acting by necessity, becomes an apology where it is truly a crime. Yet let but a nation conceive rightly of its character, and it will be chastely just in protecting it. None ever began with a fairer than America, and none can be under a greater obligation to preserve it.

The debt which America has contracted, compared with the cause she has gained, and the advantages to flow from it, ought scarcely to be mentioned. She has it in her choice to do, and to live, as happily, as she pleases. The world is in her hands. She has no foreign power to monopolize her commerce, perplex her legislation, or controul her prosperity. The struggle is over, which must one day have happened, and, perhaps,

never could have happened at a better time.* And
instead of a domineering master, she has gained an
ally, whose exemplary greatness, and universal liberality, have extorted a confession even from her enemies.

With the blessings of peace, independence, and an
universal commerce, the states individually and collectively, will have leisure and opportunity to regulate
and establish their domestic concerns, and to put it
beyond the power of calumny to throw the least reflection on their honor. Character is much easier kept
than recovered, and that man, if any such there be,
who, from any sinister views, or littleness of soul, lends
unseen his hand to injure it, contrives a wound it will
never be in his power to heal.

As we have established an inheritance for posterity,
let that inheritance descend, with every mark of an
honorable conveyance. The little it will cost, compared

---

* That the revolution began at the exact period of time best fitted
to the purpose, is sufficiently proved by the event—But the great
hinge on which the whole machine turned is the UNION OF THE
STATES: and this union was naturally produced by the inability of
any one state to support itself against any foreign enemy without
the assistance of the rest.

Had the states severally been less able than they were when the
war began, their united strength would not have been equal to the
undertaking, and they must, in all human probability, have failed—
And on the other hand, had they severally been more able, they
might not have seen, or, what is more, might not have felt the
necessity of uniting; and either by attempting to stand alone, or in
small confederacies, would have been separately conquered.

Now, as we cannot see a time (and many years must pass away
before it can arrive) when the strength of any one state, or several
united, can be equal to the whole of the present United States, and
as we have seen the extreme difficulty of collectively prosecuting
the war to a successful issue, and preserving our national importance
in the world, therefore, from the experience we have had, and the
knowledge we have gained, we must, unless we make a waste of
wisdom, be strongly impressed with the advantage, as well as the
necessity of strengthening that happy union which has been our
salvation, and without which we should have been a ruined people.

with the worth of the states, the greatness of the object, and the value of national character, will be a profitable exchange.

But that which must more forcibly strike a thoughtful penetrating mind, and which includes and renders easy all inferior concerns, is the UNION OF THE STATES. On this, our great national character depends. It is this which must give us importance abroad and security at home. It is through this only that we are, or can be nationally known in the world. It is the flag of the United States which renders our ships and commerce safe on the seas, or in a foreign port. Our Mediterranean passes must be obtained under the same stile. All our treaties whether of alliance, peace or commerce, are formed under the sovereignty of the United States, and Europe knows us by no other name or title.

The division of the empire into states is for our own convenience, but abroad this distinction ceases. The affairs of each state are local. They can go no farther than to itself. And were the whole worth of even the richest of them expended in revenue, it would not be sufficient to support sovereignty against a foreign attack. In short, we have no other national sovereignty than as United States. It would even be fatal for us if we had—too expensive to be maintained, and impossible to be supported. Individuals or individual states may call themselves what they please: but the world, and especially the world of enemies, is not to be held in awe by the whistling of a name. Sovereignty must have power to protect all the parts that compose and constitute it: and as UNITED STATES we are equal to the importance of the title, but otherwise we are not. Our union well and wisely regulated and cemented, is the cheapest way of being great—the easiest way of being powerful, and the happiest invention in government which the circumstances of America can admit of—Because it collects from each state, that which, by being inadequate, can be of no use to it, and forms an aggregate that serves for all.

The states of Holland are an unfortunate instance of the effects of individual sovereignty. Their disjointed condition exposes them to numerous intrigues, losses, calamities and enemies; and the almost impossibility of bringing their measures to a decision, and that decision into execution, is to them, and would be to us, a source of endless misfortune.

It is with confederated states as with individuals in society; something must be yielded up to make the whole secure. In this view of things we gain by what we give, and draw an annual interest greater than the capital.—I ever feel myself hurt when I hear the union, that great palladium of our liberty and safety, the least irreverently spoken of. It is the most sacred thing in the constitution of America, and that which every man should be most proud and tender of. Our citizenship in the United States is our national character. Our citizenship in any particular state is only our local distinction. By the latter we are known at home, by the former to the world. Our great title is, AMERICANS—our inferior one varies with the place.

So far as my endeavors could go, they have all been directed to conciliate the affections, unite the interests and draw and keep the mind of the country together; and the better to assist in this foundation-work of the revolution, I have avoided all places of profit or office, either in the state I live in, or in the United States; kept myself at a distance from all parties and party connections, and even disregarded all private and inferior concerns: and when we take into view the great work we have gone through, and feel, as we ought to feel, the just importance of it, we shall then see, that the little wranglings and indecent contentions of personal parley, are as dishonorable to our characters, as they are injurious to our repose.

It was the cause of America that made me an author. The force with which it struck my mind, and the dangerous condition the country appeared to me in, by courting an impossible and an unnatural reconciliation with those who were determined to reduce her, instead of striking out into the only line that could cement and save her, A DECLARATION OF INDEPENDENCE, made it impossible for me, feeling as I did, to be silent: and if, in the course of more than seven years, I have rendered her any service, I have likewise added something to the reputation of literature, by freely and disinterestedly employing it in the great cause of mankind, and shewing there may be genius without prostitution.

Independence always appeared to me practicable and probable; provided the sentiment of the country could be formed and held to the object; and there is no instance in the world, where a people so extended, and wedded to former habits of thinking, and under such a variety of circumstances, were so instantly and effectually pervaded, by a turn in politics, as in the case of independence, and who supported their opinion, undiminished, through such a succession of good and ill fortune, till they crowned it with success.

But as the scenes of war are closed, and every man preparing for home and happier times, I therefore take my leave of the subject. I have most sincerely followed it from beginning to end, and through all its turns and windings: and whatever country I may hereafter be in, I shall always feel an honest pride at the part I have taken and acted, and a gratitude to Nature and Providence for putting it in my power to be of some use to mankind.

COMMON SENSE

RIGHTS OF MAN

BEING AN ANSWER TO MR. BURKE'S ATTACK ON THE FRENCH REVOLUTION

1791

PART THE FIRST

To George Washington
PRESIDENT OF THE UNITED STATES OF AMERICA

SIR,

I present you a small treatise in defense of those principles of freedom which your exemplary virtue hath so eminently contributed to establish. That the rights of man may become as universal as your benevolence can wish, and that you may enjoy the happiness of seeing the New World regenerate the Old, is the prayer of

Sir
Your much obliged, and
Obedient humble servant,
THOMAS PAINE

Prefaces

1. Preface to the French Edition

The astonishment which the French Revolution has caused throughout Europe should be considered from two different points of view; first as it affects foreign people, secondly as it affects their governments.

The cause of the French people is that of all Europe, or rather of the whole world; but the governments of all those countries are by no means favorable to it. It is important that we should never lose sight of this distinction. We must not confuse the peoples with their governments; especially not the English people with its government.

The government of England is no friend to the revolution of France. Of this we have sufficient proofs in the thanks given by that weak and witless person, the Elector of Hanover, sometimes called the King of England, to Mr. Burke for the insults heaped on it in his book, and in the malevolent comments of the English Minister, Mr. Pitt, in his speeches in Parliament.

In spite of the professions of sincerest friendship found in the official correspondence of the English government with that of France, its conduct gives the lie to all its declarations and shows us clearly that it is not a court to be trusted, but an insane court, plunging in all the quarrels and intrigues of Europe in quest of a war to satisfy its folly and countenance its extravagance.

The English nation, on the contrary, is very favorably disposed towards the French Revolution and to the progress of liberty in the whole world; and this feeling will become more general in England as the intrigues and artifices of its government are better known, and the principles of the revolution better understood. The French should know that most English newspapers are directly in the pay of government or, if indirectly connected with it, always under its orders; and that these papers constantly distort and attack the revolution in France in order to deceive the nation. But, as it is impossible long to prevent the prevalence of truth, the daily falsehoods of those papers no longer have the desired effect.

To be convinced that the voice of truth has been stifled in England, the world needs only to be told that the government regards and prosecutes as a libel that which it should protect.* This outrage on morality is called *law,* and judges are found wicked enough to inflict penalties on truth.

The English government presents just now a curious phenomenon. Seeing that the French and English nations are getting rid of the prejudices and false notions formerly entertained against each other, and which have cost them so much money, that government seems to be placarding its need of a foe; for unless it finds one somewhere, no pretext exists for the enormous revenue and taxation now deemed necessary.

Therefore it seeks in Russia the enemy it has lost in France, and appears to say to the universe, or to say to itself: "If nobody will be so kind as to become my foe, I shall need no more fleets or armies, and shall be forced to reduce my taxes. The American war enabled me to double the taxes; the Dutch business to add more; the Nootka humbug gave me a pretext for raising three millions sterling more; but unless I can make an enemy of Russia the harvest from wars will end. I was the first to incite Turk against Russian, and now I hope to reap a fresh crop of taxes."

If the miseries of war and the flood of evils it spreads over a country did not check all inclination to mirth and turn laughter into grief, the frantic conduct

---

* The main and uniform maxim of the judges is, the greater the truth the greater the libel.

of the government of England would only excite ridicule. But it is impossible to banish from one's mind the images of suffering which the contemplation of such vicious policy presents. To reason with governments, as they have existed for ages, is to argue with brutes. It is only from the nations themselves that reforms can be expected. There ought not now to exist any doubt that the peoples of France, England, and America, enlightened and enlightening each other, shall henceforth be able, not merely to give the world an example of good government, but by their united influence enforce its practice.

2. Preface to the English Edition

From the part Mr. Burke took in the American Revolution it was natural that I should consider him a friend to mankind; and as our acquaintance commenced on that ground, it would have been more agreeable to me to have had cause to continue in that opinion than to change it.

At the time Mr. Burke made his violent speech last winter in the English Parliament against the French Revolution and the National Assembly, I was in Paris, and had written to him but a short time before to inform him how prosperously matters were going on. Soon after this I saw his advertisement of the pamphlet he intended to publish: As the attack was to be made in a language but little studied and less understood in France, and as everything suffers by translation, I promised some of the friends of the Revolution in that country that whenever Mr. Burke's pamphlet came forth, I would answer it. This appeared to me the more necessary to be done when I saw the flagrant misrepresentations which Mr. Burke's pamphlet contains; and that while it is an outrageous abuse on the

French Revolution and the principles of Liberty, it is an imposition on the rest of the world.

I am the more astonished and disappointed at this conduct in Mr. Burke, as (from the circumstances I am going to mention) I had formed other expectations.

I had seen enough of the miseries of war to wish it might never more have existence in the world, and that some other mode might be found out to settle the differences that should occasionally arise in the neighborhood of nations. This certainly might be done if courts were disposed to set honestly about it, or if countries were enlightened enough not to be made the dupes of courts. The people of America had been bred up in the same prejudices against France which at that time characterized the people of England; but experience and an acquaintance with the French nation have most effectually shown to the Americans the falsehood of those prejudices; and I do not believe that a more cordial and confidential intercourse exists between any two countries than between America and France.

When I came to France in the spring of 1787, the Archbishop of Toulouse was then Minister, and at that time highly esteemed. I became much acquainted with the private secretary of that minister, a man of an enlarged benevolent heart; and found that his sentiments and my own perfectly agreed with respect to the madness of war and the wretched impolicy of two nations, like England and France, continually worrying each other to no other end than that of a mutual increase of burdens and taxes. That I might be assured I had not misunderstood him, nor he me, I put the substance of our opinions into writing and sent it to him; subjoining a request, that if I should see among the people of England any disposition to cultivate a better understanding between the two nations than had hitherto prevailed, how far I might be authorized to say that the same disposition prevailed on the part of France? He answered me by letter in the most unreserved manner, and that not for himself only, but for the minister with whose knowledge the letter was declared to be written.

I put this letter into the hands of Mr. Burke almost three years ago, and left it with him, where it still remains; hoping, and at the same time naturally expecting, from the opinion I had conceived of him, that he would find some opportunity of making good use of it for the purpose of removing those errors and prejudices which two neighboring nations, from the want of knowing each other, had entertained to the injury of both.

When the French Revolution broke out it certainly afforded to Mr. Burke an opportunity of doing some good had he been disposed to it; instead of which, no sooner did he see the old prejudices wearing away, than he immediately began sowing the seeds of a new inveteracy, as if he were afraid that England and France would cease to be enemies. That there are men in all countries who get their living by war, and by keeping up the quarrels of nations, is as shocking as it is true; but when those who are concerned in the government of a country make it their study to sow discord and cultivate prejudices between nations, it becomes more unpardonable.

With respect to a paragraph in this work alluding to Mr. Burke's having a pension, the report has been some time in circulation, at least two months; and as a person is often the last to hear what concerns him the most to know, I have mentioned it, that Mr. Burke may have an opportunity of contradicting the rumor, if he thinks proper.

RIGHTS OF MAN

Among the incivilities by which nations or individuals provoke and irritate each other, Mr. Burke's pamphlet on the French Revolution is an extraordinary instance. Neither the people of France, nor the National Assembly, were troubling themselves about the affairs of England, or the English Parliament; and why Mr. Burke should commence an unprovoked attack upon them, both in Parliament and in public, is a conduct that cannot be pardoned on the score of manners, nor justified on that of policy.

There is scarcely an epithet of abuse to be found in the English language, with which Mr. Burke has not loaded the French Nation and the National Assembly. Everything which rancour, prejudice, ignorance or knowledge could suggest, is poured forth in the copious fury of near four hundred pages. In the strain and on the plan Mr. Burke was writing, he might have written on to as many thousands. When the tongue or the pen is let loose in a phrenzy of passion, it is the man, and not the subject, that becomes exhausted.

Hitherto Mr. Burke has been mistaken and disappointed in the opinions he had formed of the affairs of France; but such is the ingenuity of his hope, or the malignancy of his despair, that it furnishes him with new pretences to go on. There was a time when it was impossible to make Mr. Burke believe there would be any Revolution in France. His opinion then was, that the French had neither spirit to undertake it nor fortitude to support it; and now that there is one, he seeks an escape by condemning it.

Not sufficiently content with abusing the National Assembly, a great part of his work is taken up with abusing Dr. Price (one of the best-hearted men that lives) and the two societies in England known by the name of the Revolution Society and the Society for Constitutional Information.

Dr. Price had preached a sermon on the 4th of November, 1789, being the anniversary of what is called in England the Revolution, which took place 1688. Mr. Burke, speaking of this sermon, says, "The political Divine proceeds dogmatically to assert, that by the principles of the Revolution, the people of England have acquired three fundamental rights:

1. To choose their own governors.
2. To cashier them for misconduct.
3. To frame a government for ourselves."

Dr. Price does not say that the right to do these things exists in this or in that person, or in this or in that description of persons, but that it exists in the *whole;* that it is a right resident in the Nation. Mr. Burke, on the contrary, denies that such a right exists in the Nation, either in whole or in part, or that it exists anywhere; and, what is still more strange and marvellous, he says, "that the people of England utterly disclaim such a right, and that they will resist the practical assertion of it with their lives and fortunes." That men should take up arms and spend their lives and fortunes, *not* to maintain their rights, but to maintain they have *not* rights, is an entirely new species of discovery, and suited to the paradoxical genius of Mr. Burke.

The method which Mr. Burke takes to prove that the people of England have no such rights, and that such rights do not now exist in the Nation, either in

whole or in part, or anywhere at all, is of the same
marvellous and monstrous kind with what he has already said; for his arguments are that the persons, or
the generation of persons, in whom they did exist, are
dead, and with them the right is dead also. To prove
this, he quotes a declaration made by parliament
about a hundred years ago, to William and Mary, in
these words: "The Lords Spiritual and Temporal, and
Commons, do, in the name of the people aforesaid
[meaning the people of England then living], most
humbly and faithfully *submit* themselves, their *heirs*
and *posterities,* for EVER." He also quotes a clause of
another act of Parliament made in the same reign, the
terms of which, he says, "bind us [meaning the people
of that day], our *heirs* and our *posterity,* to *them,* their
heirs and *posterity,* to the end of time."

Mr. Burke conceives his point sufficiently established by producing those clauses, which he enforces
by saying that they exclude the right of the Nation for
ever. And not yet content with making such declarations, repeated over and over again, he farther says,
"that if the people of England possessed such a right
before the Revolution [which he acknowledges to
have been the case, not only in England, but throughout Europe, at an early period], yet that the *English
Nation* did, at the time of the Revolution, most solemnly renounce and abdicate it, for themselves, and
for *all their posterity, for ever.*"

As Mr. Burke occasionally applies the poison drawn
from his horrid principles (if it is not prophanation to
call them by the name of principles) not only to the
English Nation, but to the French Revolution and the
National Assembly, and charges that august, illumi-
nated and illuminating body of men with the epithet
of *usurpers,* I shall, *sans cérémonie,* place another system of principles in opposition to his.

The English Parliament of 1688 did a certain thing,
which, for themselves and their constituents, they had

a right to do, and which it appeared right should be done: but, in addition to this right, which they possessed by delegation, *they set up another right by assumption,* that of binding and controuling posterity to the end of time. The case, therefore, divides itself into two parts; the right which they possessed by delegation, and the right which they set up by assumption. The first is admitted; but with respect to the second, I reply—

There never did, there never will, and there never can, exist a Parliament, or any description of men, or any generation of men, in any country, possessed of the right or the power of binding and controuling posterity to the *"end of time,"* or of commanding for ever how the world shall be governed, or who shall govern it; and therefore all such clauses, acts or declarations by which the makers of them attempt to do what they have neither the right nor the power to do, nor the power to execute, are in themselves null and void. Every age and generation must be as free to act for itself *in all cases* as the ages and generations which preceded it. The vanity and presumption of governing beyond the grave is the most ridiculous and insolent of all tyrannies. Man has no property in man; neither has any generation a property in the generations which are to follow. The Parliament or the people of 1688, or of any other period, had no more right to dispose of the people of the present day, or to bind or to controul them *in any shape whatever,* than the Parliament or the people of the present day have to dispose of, bind or controul those who are to live a hundred or a thousand years hence. Every generation is, and must be, competent to all the purposes which its occasions require. It is the living, and not the dead, that are to be accommodated. When man ceases to be, his power and his wants cease with him; and having no longer any participation in the concerns of this world, he has no longer any authority in directing who shall be its governors, or how its Government shall be organised, or how administered.

I am not contending for nor against any form of Government, nor for nor against any party, here or elsewhere. That which a whole Nation chooses to do, it has a right to do. Mr. Burke says, No. Where, then, does the right exist? I am contending for the rights of the *living,* and against their being willed away, and controuled and contracted for, by the manuscript assumed authority of the dead; and Mr. Burke is contending for the authority of the dead over the rights and freedom of the living. There was a time when Kings disposed of their Crowns by will upon their deathbeds, and consigned the people, like beasts of the field, to whatever successor they appointed. This is now so exploded as scarcely to be remembered, and so monstrous as hardly to be believed; but the Parliamentary clauses upon which Mr. Burke builds his political church are of the same nature.

The laws of every country must be analogous to some common principle. In England no parent or master, nor all the authority of Parliament, omnipotent as it has called itself, can bind or controul the personal freedom even of an individual beyond the age of twenty-one years. On what ground of right, then, could the Parliament of 1688, or any other Parliament, bind all posterity for ever?

Those who have quitted the world, and those who are not yet arrived at it, are as remote from each other as the utmost stretch of mortal imagination can conceive. What possible obligation, then, can exist between them; what rule or principle can be laid down that of two non-entities, the one out of existence and the other not in, and who never can meet in this world, the one should controul the other to the end of time?

In England it is said that money cannot be taken out of the pockets of the people without their consent.

But who authorised, or who could authorise, the Parliament of 1688 to controul and take away the freedom of posterity (who were not in existence to give or to withhold their consent), and limit and confine their right of acting in certain cases for ever?

A greater absurdity cannot present itself to the understanding of man than what Mr. Burke offers to his readers. He tells them, and he tells the world to come, that a certain body of men who existed a hundred years ago, made a law, and that there does not now exist in the Nation, nor ever will, nor ever can, a power to alter it. Under how many subtilties or absurdities has the divine right to govern been imposed on the credulity of mankind! Mr. Burke has discovered a new one, and he has shortened his journey to Rome by appealing to the power of this infallible Parliament of former days; and he produces what it has done as of divine authority, for that power must certainly be more than human which no human power to the end of time can alter.

But Mr. Burke has done some service, not to his cause, but to his country, by bringing those clauses into public view. They serve to demonstrate how necessary it is at all times to watch against the attempted encroachment of power, and to prevent its running to excess. It is somewhat extraordinary that the offence for which James II. was expelled, that of setting up power by *assumption,* should be re-acted, under another shape and form, by the Parliament that expelled him. It shows that the rights of man were but imperfectly understood at the Revolution; for certain it is that the right which that Parliament set up by *assumption* (for by delegation it had it not, and could not have it, because none could give it) over the persons and freedom of posterity for ever, was of the same tyrannical unfounded kind which James attempted to set up over the Parliament and the Nation, and for which he was expelled. The only difference is (for in principle they differ not) that the one was an usurper over the living, and the other over the unborn; and as the one has no better authority to stand upon than the other, both of them must be equally null and void, and of no effect.

From what, or from whence, does Mr. Burke prove the right of any human power to bind posterity for ever? He has produced his clauses, but he must produce also his proofs that such a right existed, and show how it existed. If it ever existed it must now exist, for whatever appertains to the nature of man cannot be annihilated by man. It is the nature of man to die, and he will continue to die as long as he continues to be born. But Mr. Burke has set up a sort of political Adam, in whom all posterity are bound for ever; he must, therefore, prove that his Adam possessed such a power, or such a right.

The weaker any cord is the less will it bear to be stretched, and the worse is the policy to stretch it, unless it is intended to break it. Had any one proposed the overthrow of Mr. Burke's positions, he would have proceeded as Mr. Burke has done. He would have magnified the authorities, on purpose to have called the *right* of them into question; and the instant the question of right was started, the authorities must have been given up.

It requires but a very small glance of thought to perceive that altho' laws made in one generation often continue in force through succeeding generations, yet that they continue to derive their force from the consent of the living. A law not repealed continues in force, not because it *cannot* be repealed, but because it *is not* repealed; and the non-repealing passes for consent.

But Mr. Burke's clauses have not even this qualification in their favour. They become null, by attempting to become immortal. The nature of them precludes consent. They destroy the right which they *might* have, by grounding it on a right which they *cannot* have. Immortal power is not a human right, and therefore cannot be a right of Parliament. The Parliament of 1688 might as well have passed an act to have authorized themselves to live for ever, as to make their authority live for ever. All, therefore, that can be said of those clauses is that they are a formality of words, of as much import as if those who used them had addressed a congratulation to themselves, and in the oriental stile of antiquity had said: O Parliament, live for ever!

The circumstances of the world are continually changing, and the opinions of men change also; and as Government is for the living, and not for the dead, it is the living only that has any right in it. That which may be thought right and found convenient in one age may be thought wrong and found inconvenient in another. In such cases, Who is to decide, the living, or the dead?

As almost one hundred pages of Mr. Burke's book are employed upon these clauses, it will consequently follow that if the clauses themselves, so far as they set up an *assumed usurped* dominion over posterity for ever, are unauthoritative, and in their nature null and void; that all his voluminous inferences, and declamation drawn therefrom, or founded thereon, are null and void also; and on this ground I rest the matter.

We now come more particularly to the affairs of France. Mr. Burke's book has the appearance of being written as instruction to the French Nation; but if I may permit myself the use of an extravagant metaphor, suited to the extravagance of the case, It is darkness attempting to illuminate light.

While I am writing this there are accidentally before me some proposals for a declaration of rights by the Marquis de la Fayette (I ask his pardon for using his former address, and do it only for distinction's sake) to the National Assembly, on the 11th of July, 1789, three days before the taking of the Bastille; and I cannot but remark with astonishment how opposite the sources are from which that gentleman and Mr. Burke draw their principles. Instead of referring to musty records and mouldy parchments to prove that the rights of the living are lost, "renounced and abdicated for ever," by those who are now no more, as Mr. Burke has done, M. de la Fayette applies to the living world, and emphatically says, "Call to mind the sentiments which Nature has engraved in the heart of every citizen, and which take a new force when they are solemnly recognised by all: For a Nation to love Liberty, it is sufficient that she knows it; and to be free, it is sufficient that she wills it." How dry, barren, and obscure is the source from which Mr. Burke labours; and how ineffectual, though gay with flowers, are all his declamation and his arguments compared with these clear, concise, and soul-animating sentiments! Few and short as they are, they lead to a vast field of generous and manly thinking, and do not finish, like Mr. Burke's periods, with music in the ear, and nothing in the heart.

As I have introduced M. de la Fayette, I will take the liberty of adding an anecdote respecting his farewell address to the Congress of America in 1783, which occurred fresh to my mind, when I saw Mr. Burke's thundering attack on the French Revolution. M. de la Fayette went to America at an early period of the war, and continued a volunteer in her service to the end. His conduct through the whole of that enterprise is one of the most extraordinary that is to be found in the history of a young man, scarcely then twenty years of age. Situated in a country that was like the lap of sensual pleasure, and with the means of enjoying it, how few are there to be found who would exchange such a scene for the woods and wildernesses of America, and pass the flowery years of youth in unprofitable danger and hardship! But such is the fact. When the war ended, and he was on the point of taking his final departure, he presented himself to Congress, and contemplating, in his affectionate farewell, the Revolution he had seen, expressed himself in these words: "May this great monument raised to Liberty, serve as a lesson to the oppressor, and an example to the oppressed!" When this address came to the hands of Dr. Franklin, who was then in France, he applied to Count Vergennes to have it inserted in the French Gazette, but never could obtain his consent. The fact was that Count Vergennes was an aristocratical despot at home, and dreaded the example of the American Revolution in France, as certain other persons now dread the example of the French Revolution in England; and Mr. Burke's tribute of fear (for in this light his book must be considered) runs parallel with Count Vergennes' refusal. But to return more particularly to his work—

"We have seen," says Mr. Burke, "the French rebel against a mild and lawful Monarch, with more fury, outrage, and insult, than any people has been known to rise against the most illegal usurper, or the most sanguinary tyrant." This is one among a thousand other instances, in which Mr. Burke shows that he is ignorant of the springs and principles of the French Revolution.

It was not against Louis XVI., but against the despotic principles of the government, that the Nation revolted. These principles had not their origin in him, but in the original establishment, many centuries back; and they were become too deeply rooted to be removed, and the Augean stable of parasites and plunderers too abominably filthy to be cleansed, by anything short of a complete and universal Revolution. When it becomes necessary to do a thing, the whole heart and soul should go into the measure, or not attempt it. That crisis was then arrived, and there remained no choice but to act with determined vigour, or not to act at all. The King was known to be the friend of the Nation, and this circumstance was favourable to the enterprise. Perhaps no man bred up in the style of an absolute King, ever possessed a heart so little disposed to the exercise of that species of power as the present King of France. But the principles of the Government itself still remained the same. The Monarch and the Monarchy were distinct and separate things; and it was against the established despotism of the latter, and not against the person or principles of the former, that the revolt commenced, and the Revolution has been carried.

Mr. Burke does not attend to the distinction between *men* and *principles;* and, therefore, he does not see that a revolt may take place against the despotism of the latter, while there lies no charge of despotism against the former.

The natural moderation of Louis XVI. contributed nothing to alter the hereditary despotism of the Monarchy. All the tyrannies of former reigns, acted under that hereditary despotism, were still liable to be revived in the hands of a successor. It was not the respite of a reign that would satisfy France, enlightened as she then was become. A casual discontinuance of the *practice* of despotism, is not a discontinuance of its *principles;* the former depends on the virtue of the individual who is in immediate possession of the power; the latter, on the virtue and fortitude of the nation. In the case of Charles I. and James II. of England, the revolt was against the personal despotism of the men; whereas in France, it was against the hereditary despotism of the established government. But men who can consign over the rights of posterity for ever on the authority of a mouldy parchment, like Mr. Burke, are not qualified to judge of this Revolution. It takes in a field too vast for their views to explore, and proceeds with a mightiness of reason they cannot keep pace with.

But there are many points of view in which this Revolution may be considered. When despotism has established itself for ages in a country, as in France, it is not in the person of the King only that it resides. It has the appearance of being so in show, and in nominal authority; but it is not so in practice and in fact. It has its standard everywhere. Every office and department has its despotism, founded upon custom and usage. Every place has its Bastille, and every Bastille its despot. The original hereditary despotism resident in the person of the King, divides and subdivides itself into a thousand shapes and forms, till at last the whole of it is acted by deputation. This was the case in France; and against this species of despotism, proceeding on through an endless labyrinth of office till the source of it is scarcely perceptible, there is no mode of redress. It strengthens itself by assuming the appearance of duty, and tyrannises under the pretence of obeying.

When a man reflects on the condition which France was in from the nature of her Government, he will see other causes for revolt than those which immediately connect themselves with the person or character of Louis XVI. There were, if I may so express it, a thousand despotisms to be reformed in France, which had grown up under the hereditary despotism of the monarchy, and became so rooted as to be in great measure independent of it. Between the Monarchy, the Parliament, and the Church, there was a *rivalship* of despotism; besides the feudal despotism operating locally, and the ministerial despotism operating everywhere. But Mr. Burke, by considering the King as the only possible object of a revolt, speaks as if France was a village, in which everything that passed must be known to its commanding officer, and no oppression could be acted but what he could immediately controul. Mr. Burke might have been in the Bastille his whole life, as well under Louis XVI. as Louis XIV., and neither the one nor the other have known that such a man as Mr. Burke existed. The despotic principles of the Government were the same in both reigns, though the dispositions of the men were as remote as tyranny and benevolence.

What Mr. Burke considers as a reproach to the French Revolution (that of bringing it forward under a reign more mild than the preceding ones) is one of its highest honours. The Revolutions that have taken place in other European countries, have been excited by personal hatred. The rage was against the man, and he became the victim. But, in the instance of France we see a revolution generated in the rational contemplation of the rights of man, and distinguishing from the beginning between persons and principles.

But Mr. Burke appears to have no idea of principles when he is contemplating Governments. "Ten years ago," says he, "I could have felicitated France on her having a Government, without inquiring what the nature of that Government was, or how it was administered." Is this the language of a rational man? Is it the language of a heart feeling as it ought to feel for the rights and happiness of the human race? On this ground, Mr. Burke must compliment all the Governments in the world, while the victims who suffer under them, whether sold into slavery, or tortured out of existence, are wholly forgotten. It is power, and not principles, that Mr. Burke venerates; and under this abominable depravity he is disqualified to judge between them. Thus much for his opinion as to the occasions of the French Revolution. I now proceed to other considerations.

I know a place in America called Point-no-Point, because as you proceed along the shore, gay and flowery as Mr. Burke's language, it continually recedes and presents itself at a distance before you; but when you have got as far as you can go, there is no point at all. Just thus it is with Mr. Burke's three hundred

and fifty-six pages. It is therefore difficult to reply to
him. But as the points he wishes to establish may be
inferred from what he abuses, it is in his paradoxes
that we must look for his arguments.

As to the tragic paintings by which Mr. Burke has
outraged his own imagination, and seeks to work upon
that of his readers, they are very well calculated for
theatrical representation, where facts are manufac-
tured for the sake of show, and accommodated to produce, through the weakness of sympathy, a weeping
effect. But Mr. Burke should recollect that he is writing history, and not *plays,* and that his readers will
expect truth, and not the spouting rant of high-toned
exclamation.

When we see a man dramatically lamenting in a
publication intended to be believed that *"The age of
chivalry is gone!* that *The glory of Europe is extinguished for ever!* that *the unbought grace of life* (if any
one knows what it is), *the cheap defence of nations,
the nurse of manly sentiment and heroic enterprise is
gone!"* and all this because the Quixote age of chivalry
nonsense is gone, what opinion can we form of his
judgment, or what regard can we pay to his facts? In
the rhapsody of his imagination he has discovered a
world of windmills, and his sorrows are that there are
no Quixotes to attack them. But if the age of Aristocracy, like that of Chivalry, should fall (and they had
originally some connection), Mr. Burke, the trumpeter
of the order, may continue his parody to the end, and
finish with exclaiming: *"Othello's occupation's gone!"*

Notwithstanding Mr. Burke's horrid paintings, when
the French Revolution is compared with the Revolutions of other countries, the astonishment will be that
it is marked with so few sacrifices; but this astonishment will cease when we reflect that *principles,* and
not *persons,* were the meditated objects of destruction.
The mind of the nation was acted upon by a higher
stimulus than what the consideration of persons could

inspire, and sought a higher conquest than could be produced by the downfall of an enemy. Among the few who fell there do not appear to be any that were intentionally singled out. They all of them had their fate in the circumstances of the moment, and were not pursued with that long, cold-blooded, unabated revenge which pursued the unfortunate Scotch in the affair of 1745.

Through the whole of Mr. Burke's book I do not observe that the Bastille is mentioned more than once, and that with a kind of implication as if he were sorry it was pulled down, and wished it were built up again. "We have rebuilt Newgate," says he, "and tenanted the mansion; and we have prisons almost as strong as the Bastille for those who dare to libel the Queens of France." As to what a madman like the person called Lord G——— G——— might say, to whom Newgate is rather a bedlam than a prison, it is unworthy a rational consideration. It was a madman that libelled, and that is sufficient apology; and it afforded an opportunity for confining him, which was the thing that was wished for. But certain it is that Mr. Burke, who does not call himself a madman (whatever other people may do), has libelled in the most unprovoked manner, and in the grossest stile of the most vulgar abuse, the whole representative authority of France, and yet Mr. Burke takes his seat in the British House of Commons! From his violence and his grief, his silence on some points and his excess on others, it is difficult not to believe that Mr. Burke is sorry, extremely sorry, that arbitrary power, the power of the Pope and the Bastille, are pulled down.

Not one glance of compassion, not one commiserating reflection that I can find throughout his book, has he bestowed on those who lingered out the most wretched of lives, a life without hope in the most miserable of prisons. It is painful to behold a man employing his talents to corrupt himself. Nature has been kinder to Mr. Burke than he is to her. He is not affected by the reality of distress touching his heart, but by the showy resemblance of it striking his imagination. He pities the plumage, but forgets the dying bird. Accustomed to kiss the aristocratical hand that hath purloined him from himself, he degenerates into a composition of art, and the genuine soul of nature forsakes him. His hero or his heroine must be a tragedy-victim expiring in show, and not the real prisoner of misery, sliding into death in the silence of a dungeon.

As Mr. Burke has passed over the whole transaction of the Bastille (and his silence is nothing in his favour), and has entertained his readers with reflections on supposed facts distorted into real falsehoods, I will give, since he has not, some account of the circumstances which preceded that transaction. They will serve to show that less mischief could scarcely have accompanied such an event when considered with the treacherous and hostile aggravations of the enemies of the Revolution.

The mind can hardly picture to itself a more tremendous scene than what the city of Paris exhibited at the time of taking the Bastille, and for two days before and after, nor conceive the possibility of its quieting so soon. At a distance this transaction has appeared only as an act of heroism standing on itself, and the close political connection it had with the Revolution is lost in the brilliancy of the achievement. But we are to consider it as the strength of the parties brought man to man, and contending for the issue. The Bastille was to be either the prize or the prison of the assailants. The downfall of it included the idea of the downfall of despotism, and this compounded image was become as figuratively united as Bunyan's Doubting Castle and Giant Despair.

The National Assembly, before and at the time of taking the Bastille, was sitting at Versailles, twelve miles distance from Paris. About a week before the rising of the Parisians, and their taking the Bastille, it was discovered that a plot was forming, at the head of which was the Count d'Artois, the king's youngest brother, for demolishing the National Assembly, seizing its members, and thereby crushing, by a *coup de main,* all hopes and prospects of forming a free government. For the sake of humanity, as well as of freedom, it is well this plan did not succeed. Examples are not wanting to show how dreadfully vindictive and cruel are all old Governments, when they are successful against what they call a revolt.

This plan must have been some time in contemplation; because, in order to carry it into execution, it was necessary to collect a large military force round Paris, and cut off the communication between that city and the National Assembly at Versailles. The troops destined for this service were chiefly the foreign troops in the pay of France, and who, for this particular purpose, were drawn from the distant provinces where they were then stationed. When they were collected to the amount of about twenty-five and thirty thousand, it was judged time to put the plan in execution. The ministry who were then in office, and who were friendly to the Revolution, were instantly dismissed and a new ministry formed of those who had concerted the project, among whom was Count de Broglio, and to his share was given the command of those troops. The character of this man as described to me in a letter which I communicated to Mr. Burke before he began to write his book, and from an authority which Mr. Burke well knows was good, was that of "a high-flying aristocrat, cool, and capable of every mischief."

While these matters were agitating, the National Assembly stood in the most perilous and critical situation that a body of men can be supposed to act in. They were the devoted victims, and they knew it. They had the hearts and wishes of their country on their side, but military authority they had none. The guards of Broglio surrounded the hall where the assembly sat, ready, at the word of command, to seize their persons, as had been done the year before to the Parliament of Paris. Had the National Assembly deserted their trust, or had they exhibited signs of weakness or fear, their enemies had been encouraged and the country depressed. When the situation they stood in, the cause they were engaged in and the crisis then ready to burst, which was to determine their personal and political fate and that of their country, and probably of Europe, are taken into one view, none but a heart callous with prejudice or corrupted by dependence can avoid interesting itself in their success.

The Archbishop of Vienne was at this time president of the National Assembly—a person too old to undergo the scene that a few days or a few hours might bring forth. A man of more activity and greater fortitude was necessary, and the National Assembly chose (under the form of a vice-president, for the presidency still resided in the Archbishop) M. de la Fayette; and this is the only instance of a vice-president being chosen. It was at the moment that this storm was pending (July 11th) that a declaration of rights was brought forward by M. de la Fayette; and is the same which is alluded to in page 144. It was hastily drawn up, and makes only a part of the more extensive declaration of rights agreed upon and adopted afterwards by the National Assembly. The particular reason for bringing it forward at this moment (M. de la Fayette has since informed me) was that if the National Assembly should fall in the threatened destruction that then surrounded it, some traces of its principles might have the chance of surviving the wreck.

Everything now was drawing to a crisis. The event

was to be freedom or slavery. On one side, an army of nearly thirty thousand men; on the other, an unarmed body of citizens; for the citizens of Paris, on whom the National Assembly must then immediately depend, were as unarmed and as undisciplined as the citizens of London are now. The French guards had given strong symptoms of their being attached to the national cause; but their numbers were small, not a tenth part of the force that Broglio commanded, and their officers were in the interest of Broglio.

Matters being now ripe for execution, the new ministry made their appearance in office. The reader will carry in his mind that the Bastille was taken the 14th of July; the point of time I am now speaking to is the 12th. Immediately on the news of the change of ministry reaching Paris, in the afternoon, all the playhouses and places of entertainment, shops and houses, were shut up. The change of ministry was considered as the prelude of hostilities, and the opinion was rightly founded.

The foreign troops began to advance towards the city. The Prince de Lambesc, who commanded a body of German cavalry, approached by the Palace of Louis XV., which connects itself with some of the streets. In his march, he insulted and struck an old man with his sword. The French are remarkable for their respect to old age; and the insolence with which it appeared to be done, uniting with the general fermentation they were in, produced a powerful effect, and a cry of *"To arms! To arms!"* spread itself in a moment over the city.

Arms they had none, nor scarcely any who knew the use of them; but desperate resolution, when every hope is at stake, supplies, for a while, the want of arms. Near where the Prince de Lambesc was drawn up, were large piles of stones collected for building the new bridge, and with these the people attacked the cavalry. A party of the French guards, upon hearing the firing, rushed from their quarters and joined the people; and night coming on, the cavalry retreated.

The streets of Paris, being narrow, are favourable for defence, and the loftiness of the houses, consisting of many stories, from which great annoyance might be given, secured them against nocturnal enterprises; and the night was spent in providing themselves with every sort of weapon they could make or procure: guns, swords, blacksmiths' hammers, carpenters' axes, iron crows, pikes, halberts, pitchforks, spits, clubs, etc., etc. The incredible numbers in which they assembled the next morning, and the still more incredible resolution they exhibited, embarrassed and astonished their enemies. Little did the new ministry expect such a salute. Accustomed to slavery themselves, they had no idea that Liberty was capable of such inspiration, or that a body of unarmed citizens would dare to face the military force of thirty thousand men. Every moment of this day was employed in collecting arms, concerting plans, and arranging themselves into the best order which such an instantaneous movement could afford. Broglio continued lying round the city, but made no farther advances this day, and the succeeding night passed with as much tranquillity as such a scene could possibly admit.

But defence only was not the object of the citizens. They had a cause at stake, on which depended their freedom or their slavery. They every moment expected an attack, or to hear of one made on the National Assembly; and in such a situation, the most prompt measures are sometimes the best. The object that now presented itself was the Bastille; and the *éclat* of carrying such a fortress in the face of such an army, could not fail to strike a terror into the new ministry, who had scarcely yet had time to meet. By some intercepted correspondence, it was discovered that the Mayor of Paris, M. Defflesselles, who appeared to be in the interest of the citizens, was betraying them; from this discovery, there remained no doubt that Broglio would reinforce the Bastille the ensuing evening. It was therefore necessary to attack it that day; but before this could be done, it was first necessary to procure a better supply of arms than they were then possessed of.

There was, adjoining to the city, a large magazine of arms deposited at the Hospital of the Invalids, which the citizens summoned to surrender; and as the place was not defensible, nor attempted much defence, they soon succeeded. Thus supplied, they marched to attack the Bastille; a vast mixed multitude of all ages, and of all degrees, armed with all sorts of weapons. Imagination would fail in describing to itself the appearance of such a procession, and of the anxiety for the events which a few hours or few minutes might produce. What plans the ministry was forming, were as unknown to the people within the city, as what the citizens were doing was unknown to the ministry; and what movements Broglio might make for the support or relief of the place, were to the citizens equally as unknown. All was mystery and hazard.

That the Bastille was attacked with an enthusiasm of heroism, such only as the highest animation of Liberty could inspire, and carried in the space of a few hours, is an event which the world is fully possessed of. I am not undertaking a detail of the attack, but bringing into view the conspiracy against the nation which provoked it, and which fell with the Bastille. The prison to which the new ministry were dooming the National Assembly, in addition to its being the high altar and castle of despotism, became the proper object to begin with. This enterprise broke up the new ministry, who began now to fly from the ruin they had prepared for others. The troops of Broglio dispersed, and himself fled also.

Mr. Burke has spoken a great deal about plots, but

he has never once spoken of this plot against the National Assembly, and the liberties of the Nation; and that he might not, he has passed over all the circumstances that might throw it in his way. The exiles who have fled from France, whose case he so much interests himself in, and from whom he has had his lesson, fled in consequence of the miscarriage of this plot. No plot was formed against them; they were plotting against others; and those who fell, met, not unjustly, the punishment they were preparing to execute. But will Mr. Burke say, that if this plot, contrived with the subtilty of an ambuscade, had succeeded, the successful party would have restrained their wrath so soon? Let the history of all old Governments answer the question.

Whom has the National Assembly brought to the scaffold? None. They were themselves the devoted victims of this plot, and they have not retaliated; why, then, are they charged with revenge they have not acted? In the tremendous breaking forth of a whole people, in which all degrees, tempers, and characters are confounded, delivering themselves by a miracle of exertion from the destruction meditated against them, is it to be expected that nothing will happen? When men are sore with the sense of oppressions, and menaced with the prospect of new ones, is the calmness of philosophy or the palsy of insensibility to be looked for? Mr. Burke exclaims against outrage; yet the greatest is that which himself has committed. His book is a volume of outrage, not apologised for by the impulse of a moment, but cherished through a space of ten months; yet Mr. Burke had no provocation, no life, no interest at stake.

More of the citizens fell in this struggle than of their opponents; but four or five persons were seized by the populace and instantly put to death; the Governor of the Bastille, and the Mayor of Paris, who was detected in the act of betraying them; and afterwards Foulon, one of the new ministry, and Berthier, his son-in-law, who had accepted the office of intendant of Paris. Their heads were stuck upon spikes, and carried about the city; and it is upon this mode of punishment that Mr. Burke builds a great part of his tragic scenes. Let us therefore examine how men came by the idea of punishing in this manner.

They learn it from the Governments they live under, and retaliate the punishments they have been accustomed to behold. The heads stuck upon spikes, which remained for years upon Temple Bar, differed nothing in the horror of the scene from those carried about upon spikes at Paris; yet this was done by the English Government. It may perhaps be said that it signifies nothing to a man what is done to him after he is dead; but it signifies much to the living; it either tortures their feelings or hardens their hearts, and in either case it instructs them how to punish when power falls into their hands.

Lay then the axe to the root, and teach Governments humanity. It is their sanguinary punishments which corrupt mankind. In England the punishment in certain cases is by *hanging, drawing* and *quartering;* the heart of the sufferer is cut out and held up to the view of the populace. In France, under the former Government, the punishments were not less barbarous. Who does not remember the execution of Damien, torn to pieces by horses? The effect of those cruel spectacles exhibited to the populace is to destroy tenderness or excite revenge; and by the base and false idea of governing men by terror, instead of reason, they become precedents. It is over the lowest class of mankind that Government by terror is intended to operate, and it is on them that it operates to the worst effect. They have sense enough to feel they are the objects aimed at; and they inflict in their turn the examples of terror they have been instructed to practise.

There is in all European countries a large class of

people of that description, which in England is called the *Mob*. Of this class were those who committed the burnings and devastations in London in 1780, and of this class were those who carried the heads upon spikes in Paris. Foulon and Berthier were taken up in the country, and sent to Paris, to undergo their examination at the Hotel de Ville; for the National Assembly, immediately on the new ministry coming into office, passed a decree, which they communicated to the King and Cabinet, that they (the National Assembly) would hold the ministry, of which Foulon was one, responsible for the measures they were advising and pursuing; but the mob, incensed at the appearance of Foulon and Berthier, tore them from their conductors before they were carried to the Hotel de Ville, and executed them on the spot. Why then does Mr. Burke charge outrages of this kind on a whole people? As well may he charge the riots and outrages of 1780 on all the people of London, or those in Ireland on all his countrymen.

But everything we see or hear offensive to our feelings and derogatory to the human character should lead to other reflections than those of reproach. Even the beings who commit them have some claim to our consideration. How then is it that such vast classes of mankind as are distinguished by the appellation of the vulgar, or the ignorant mob, are so numerous in all old countries? The instant we ask ourselves this question, reflection feels an answer. They arise, as an unavoidable consequence, out of the ill construction of all old Governments in Europe, England included with the rest. It is by distortedly exalting some men, that others are distortedly debased, till the whole is out of nature. A vast mass of mankind are degradedly thrown into the background of the human picture, to bring forward, with greater glare, the puppet-show of State and Aristocracy. In the commencement of a Revolution, those men are rather the followers of the *camp* than of the *standard* of Liberty, and have yet to be instructed how to reverence it.

I give to Mr. Burke all his theatrical exaggerations for facts, and I then ask him if they do not establish the certainty of what I here lay down? Admitting them to be true, they show the necessity of the French Revolution, as much as any one thing he could have asserted. These outrages were not the effect of the principles of the Revolution, but of the degraded mind that existed before the Revolution, and which the Revolution is calculated to reform. Place them then to their proper cause, and take the reproach of them to your own side.

It is to the honour of the National Assembly and the city of Paris that, during such a tremendous scene of arms and confusion, beyond the controul of all authority, they have been able, by the influence of example and exhortation, to restrain so much. Never were more pains taken to instruct and enlighten mankind, and to make them see that their interest consisted in their virtue, and not in their revenge, than have been displayed in the Revolution of France. I now proceed to make some remarks on Mr. Burke's account of the expedition to Versailles, October the 5th and 6th.

I cannot consider Mr. Burke's book in any other light than a dramatic performance; and he must, I think, have considered it in the same light himself, by the poetical liberties he has taken of omitting some facts, distorting others, and making the whole machinery bend to produce a stage effect. Of this kind is his account of the expedition to Versailles. He begins this account by omitting the only facts which as causes are known to be true; everything beyond these is conjecture even in Paris; and he then works up a tale accommodated to his own passions and prejudices.

It is to be observed throughout Mr. Burke's book that he never speaks of plots *against* the Revolution; and it is from those plots that all the mischiefs have

arisen. It suits his purpose to exhibit the consequences
without their causes. It is one of the arts of the drama
to do so. If the crimes of men were exhibited with
their sufferings, the stage effect would sometimes be
lost, and the audience would be inclined to approve
where it was intended they should commiserate.

After all the investigations that have been made
into this intricate affair (the expedition to Versailles),
it still remains enveloped in all that kind of mystery
which ever accompanies events produced more from
a concurrence of awkward circumstances than from
fixed design. While the characters of men are forming,
as is always the case in Revolutions, there is a reciprocal suspicion, and a disposition to misinterpret each
other; and even parties directly opposite in principle
will sometimes concur in pushing forward the same
movement with very different views, and with the
hopes of its producing very different consequences. A
great deal of this may be discovered in this embarrassed affair, and yet the issue of the whole was what
nobody had in view.

The only things certainly known are that considerable uneasiness was at this time excited at Paris by
the delay of the King in not sanctioning and forward-
ing the decrees of the National Assembly, particularly
that of the *Declaration of the Rights of Man,* and the
decrees of the *fourth of August,* which contained the
foundation principles on which the constitution was
to be erected. The kindest, and perhaps the fairest
conjecture upon this matter is, that some of the ministers intended to make remarks and observations upon
certain parts of them before they were finally sanc-
tioned and sent to the provinces; but be this as it may,
the enemies of the Revolution derived hope from the
delay, and the friends of the Revolution uneasiness.

During this state of suspense, the *Garde du Corps,*
which was composed, as such regiments generally are,
of persons much connected with the Court, gave an

entertainment at Versailles (October 1) to some foreign regiments then arrived; and when the entertainment was at the height, on a signal given the *Garde du Corps* tore the national cockade from their hats, trampled it under foot, and replaced it with a counter-cockade prepared for the purpose. An indignity of this kind amounted to defiance. It was like declaring war; and if men will give challenges they must expect consequences. But all this Mr. Burke has carefully kept out of sight. He begins his account by saying: "History will record that on the morning of the 6th of October, 1789, the King and Queen of France, after a day of confusion, alarm, dismay, and slaughter, lay down under the pledged security of public faith to indulge nature in a few hours of respite, and troubled melancholy repose." This is neither the sober stile of history, nor the intention of it. It leaves everything to be guessed at and mistaken. One would at least think there had been a battle; and a battle there probably would have been had it not been for the moderating prudence of those whom Mr. Burke involves in his censures. By his keeping the *Garde du Corps* out of sight Mr. Burke has afforded himself the dramatic licence of putting the King and Queen in their places, as if the object of the expedition was against them. But to return to my account—

This conduct of the *Garde du Corps,* as might well be expected, alarmed and enraged the Parisians. The colours of the cause, and the cause itself, were become too united to mistake the intention of the insult, and the Parisians were determined to call the *Garde du Corps* to an account. There was certainly nothing of the cowardice of assassination in marching in the face of day to demand satisfaction, if such a phrase may be used, of a body of armed men who had voluntarily given defiance. But the circumstance which serves to throw this affair into embarrassment is, that the enemies of the Revolution appear to have encouraged it as well as its friends. The one hoped to prevent a civil war by checking it in time, and the other to make one. The hopes of those opposed to the Revolution rested in making the King of their party, and getting him from Versailles to Metz, where they expected to collect a force and set up a standard. We have, therefore, two different objects presenting themselves at the same time, and to be accomplished by the same means; the one to chastise the *Garde du Corps,* which was the object of the Parisians; the other to render the confusion of such a scene an inducement to the King to set off for Metz.

On the 5th of October a very numerous body of women, and men in the disguise of women, collected round the Hotel de Ville or town-hall at Paris, and set off for Versailles. Their professed object was the *Garde du Corps;* but prudent men readily recollect that mischief is more easily begun than ended; and this impressed itself with the more force from the suspicions already stated, and the irregularity of such a cavalcade. As soon, therefore, as a sufficient force could be collected, M. de la Fayette, by orders from the civil authority of Paris, set off after them at the head of twenty thousand of the Paris militia. The Revolution could derive no benefit from confusion, and its opposers might. By an amiable and spirited manner of address he had hitherto been fortunate in calming disquietudes, and in this he was extraordinarily successful; to frustrate, therefore, the hopes of those who might seek to improve this scene into a sort of justifiable necessity for the King's quitting Versailles and withdrawing to Metz, and to prevent at the same time the consequences that might ensue between the *Garde du Corps* and this phalanx of men and women, he forwarded expresses to the King, that he was on his march to Versailles, by the orders of the civil authority of Paris, for the purpose of peace and protection, expressing at the same time the necessity of restraining the *Garde du Corps* from firing upon the people.

He arrived at Versailles between ten and eleven at night. The *Garde du Corps* was drawn up, and the people had arrived some time before, but everything had remained suspended. Wisdom and policy now consisted in changing a scene of danger into a happy event. M. de la Fayette became the mediator between the enraged parties; and the King, to remove the uneasiness which had arisen from the delay already stated, sent for the President of the National Assembly, and signed the Declaration of the Rights of Man, and such other parts of the Constitution as were in readiness.

It was now about one in the morning. Everything appeared to be composed, and a general congratulation took place. By the beat of drum a proclamation was made that the citizens of Versailles would give the hospitality of their houses to their fellow-citizens of Paris. Those who could not be accommodated in this manner remained in the streets, or took up their quarters in the churches; and at two o'clock the King and Queen retired.

In this state matters passed till the break of day, when a fresh disturbance arose from the censurable conduct of some of both parties, for such characters there will be in all such scenes. One of the *Garde du Corps* appeared at one of the windows of the palace, and the people who had remained during the night in the streets accosted him with reviling and provocative language. Instead of retiring, as in such a case prudence would have dictated, he presented his musket, fired, and killed one of the Paris militia. The peace being thus broken, the people rushed into the palace in quest of the offender. They attacked the quarters of the *Garde du Corps* within the palace, and pursued them throughout the avenues of it, and to the apartments of the King. On this tumult, not the Queen only, as Mr. Burke has represented it, but every person in the palace was awakened and alarmed; and M. de la Fayette had a second time to interpose between the parties, the event of which was that the *Garde du Corps* put on the national cockade, and the matter ended as by oblivion, after the loss of two or three lives.

During the latter part of the time in which this confusion was acting, the King and Queen were in public at the balcony, and neither of them concealed for safety's sake, as Mr. Burke insinuates. Matters being thus appeased, and tranquillity restored, a general acclamation broke forth of *Le Roi à Paris—Le Roi à Paris—* The King of Paris. It was the shout of peace, and immediately accepted on the part of the King. By this measure all future projects of trepanning the King to Metz, and setting up the standard of opposition to the Constitution, were prevented, and the suspicions extinguished. The King and his family reached Paris in the evening, and were congratulated on their arrival by M. Bailley, the Mayor of Paris, in the name of the citizens. Mr. Burke, who throughout his book confounds things, persons, and principles, as in his remarks on M. Bailley's address, confounded time also. He censures M. Bailley for calling it *"un bon jour,"* a good day. Mr. Burke should have informed himself that this scene took up the space of two days, the day on which it began with every appearance of danger and mischief, and the day on which it terminated without the mischiefs that threatened; and that it is to this peaceful termination that M. Bailley alludes, and to the arrival of the King at Paris. Not less than three hundred thousand persons arranged themselves in the procession from Versailles to Paris, and not an act of molestation was committed during the whole march.

Mr. Burke, on the authority of M. Lally Tollendal,

a deserter from the National Assembly, says, that on entering Paris, the people shouted *"Tous les évêques à la lanterne."* All Bishops to be hanged at the lanthorn or lamp-posts. It is surprising that nobody could hear this but Lally Tollendal, and that nobody should believe it but Mr. Burke. It has not the least connection with any part of the transaction, and is totally foreign to every circumstance of it. The Bishops had never been introduced before into any scene of Mr. Burke's drama: why then are they, all at once, and altogether, *tout à coup, et tous ensemble,* introduced now? Mr. Burke brings forward his bishops and his lanthorn-like figures in a magic lanthorn, and raises his scenes by contrast instead of connection. But it serves to show, with the rest of his book, what little credit ought to be given where even probability is set at defiance, for the purpose of defaming; and with this reflection, instead of a soliloquy in praise of chivalry, as Mr. Burke has done, I close the account of the expedition to Versailles.

I have now to follow Mr. Burke through a pathless wilderness of rhapsodies, and a sort of descant upon Governments, in which he asserts whatever he pleases, on the presumption of its being believed, without offering either evidence or reasons for so doing.

Before anything can be reasoned upon to a conclusion, certain facts, principles, or data, to reason from, must be established, admitted, or denied. Mr. Burke, with his usual outrage, abuses the *Declaration of the Rights of Man,* published by the National Assembly of France as the basis on which the constitution of France is built. This he calls "paltry and blurred sheets of paper about the rights of man." Does Mr. Burke mean to deny that *man* has any rights? If he does, then he must mean that there are no such things as rights anywhere, and that he has none himself; for who is there in the world but man? But if Mr. Burke means to admit that man has rights, the question then will be: What are those rights, and how came man by them originally?

The error of those who reason by precedents drawn from antiquity, respecting the rights of man, is that they do not go far enough into antiquity. They do not go the whole way. They stop in some of the intermediate stages of an hundred or a thousand years, and produce what was then done, as a rule for the present day. This is not authority at all. If we travel still farther into antiquity, we shall find a direct contrary opinion and practice prevailing; and if antiquity is to be authority, a thousand such authorities may be produced, successively contradicting each other; but if we proceed on, we shall at last come out right; we shall come to the time when man came from the hand of his Maker. What was he then? Man. Man was his high and only title, and a higher cannot be given him. But of titles I shall speak hereafter.

We are now got at the origin of man, and at the origin of his rights. As to the manner in which the world has been governed from that day to this, it is no farther any concern of ours than to make a proper use of the errors or the improvements which the history of it presents. Those who lived a hundred or a thousand years ago, were then moderns, as we are now. They had *their* ancients, and those ancients had others, and we also shall be ancients in our turn. If the mere name of antiquity is to govern in the affairs of life, the people who are to live an hundred or a thousand years hence, may as well take us for a precedent, as we make a precedent of those who lived an hundred or a thousand years ago. The fact is, that portions of antiquity, by proving everything, establish nothing. It is authority against authority all the way, till we come to the divine origin of the rights of man at the creation. Here our inquiries find a resting-place, and our reason finds a home. If a dispute about the rights of man had arisen at the distance of an hundred years from the creation, it is to this source of authority they must have referred, and it is to this same source of authority that we must now refer.

Though I mean not to touch upon any sectarian principle of religion, yet it may be worth observing, that the genealogy of Christ is traced to Adam. Why then not trace the rights of man to the creation of man? I will answer the question. Because there have been upstart Governments, thrusting themselves between and presumptuously working to *un-make* man.

If any generation of men ever possessed the right of dictating the mode by which the world should be governed for ever, it was the first generation that existed; and if that generation did it not, no succeeding generation can show any authority for doing it, nor can set any up. The illuminating and divine principle of the equal rights of man (for it has its origin from the Maker of man) relates, not only to the living individuals, but to generations of men succeeding each other. Every generation is equal in rights to the generations which preceded it, by the same rule that every individual is born equal in rights with his contemporary.

Every history of the creation, and every traditionary account, whether from the lettered or unlettered world, however they may vary in their opinion or belief of certain particulars, all agree in establishing one point, *the unity of man;* by which I mean that men are all of *one degree,* and consequently that all men are born equal, and with equal natural rights, in the same manner as if posterity had been continued by *creation* instead of *generation,* the latter being only the mode by which the former is carried forward; and consequently every child born into the world must be considered as deriving its existence from God. The world is as new to him as it was to the first man that existed, and his natural right in it is of the same kind.

The Mosaic account of the creation, whether taken as divine authority or merely historical, is fully up to this point, *the unity or equality of man.* The expressions admit of no controversy. "And God said, Let us make man in our own image. In the image of God created he him; male and female created he them." The distinction of sexes is pointed out, but no other distinction is even implied. If this be not divine authority, it is at least historical authority, and shows that the equality of man, so far from being a modern doctrine, is the oldest upon record.

It is also to be observed that all the religions known in the world are founded, so far as they relate to man, on the *unity of man,* as being all of one degree. Whether in heaven or in hell, or in whatever state man may be supposed to exist hereafter, the good and the bad are the only distinctions. Nay, even the laws of Governments are obliged to slide into this principle, by making degrees to consist in crimes and not in persons.

It is one of the greatest of all truths, and of the highest advantage to cultivate. By considering man in this light, and by instructing him to consider himself in this light, it places him in a close connection with all his duties, whether to his Creator or to the creation, of which he is part; and it is only when he forgets his origin, or, to use a more fashionable phrase, his *birth and family,* that he becomes dissolute. It is not among the least of the evils of the present existing Governments in all parts of Europe that man, considered as man, is thrown back to a vast distance from his Maker, and the artificial chasm filled up by a succession of barriers, or sort of turnpike gates, through which he has to pass. I will quote Mr. Burke's catalogue of barriers that he has set up between Man and his Maker. Putting himself in the character of a herald, he says: *We fear God—we look with* AWE *to kings—with affection to Parliaments—with duty to magistrates—with*

reverence to priests, and with respect to nobility. Mr.
Burke has forgotten to put in *"chivalry."* He has also
forgotten to put in Peter.

The duty of man is not a wilderness of turnpike
gates, through which he is to pass by tickets from one
to the other. It is plain and simple, and consists but
of two points. His duty to God, which every man must
feel; and with respect to his neighbour, to do as he
would be done by. If those to whom power is delegated do well, they will be respected; if not, they will
be despised; and with regard to those to whom no
power is delegated, but who assume it, the rational
world can know nothing of them.

Hitherto we have spoken only (and that but in part)
of the natural rights of man. We have now to consider
the civil rights of man, and to show how the one origi-
nates from the other. Man did not enter into society
to become *worse* than he was before, not to have
fewer rights than he had before, but to have those
rights better secured. His natural rights are the foundation of all his civil rights. But in order to pursue this
distinction with more precision, it will be necessary to
mark the different qualities of natural and civil rights.

A few words will explain this. Natural rights are
those which appertain to man in right of his existence.
Of this kind are all the intellectual rights, or rights of
the mind, and also all those rights of acting as an
individual for his own comfort and happiness, which
are not injurious to the natural rights of others. Civil
rights are those which appertain to man in right of his
being a member of society. Every civil right has for
its foundation some natural right pre-existing in the
individual, but to the enjoyment of which his individual power is not, in all cases, sufficiently competent.
Of this kind are all those which relate to security
and protection.

From this short view it will be easy to distinguish
between that class of natural rights which man retains

after entering into society and those which he throws into the common stock as a member of society.

The natural rights which he retains are all those in which the *power* to execute it is as perfect in the individual as the right itself. Among this class, as is before mentioned, are all the intellectual rights, or rights of the mind; consequently religion is one of those rights. The natural rights which are not retained, are all those in which, though the right is perfect in the individual, the power to execute them is defective. They answer not his purpose. A man, by natural right, has a right to judge in his own cause; and so far as the right of the mind is concerned, he never surrenders it. But what availeth it him to judge, if he has not power to redress? He therefore deposits this right in the common stock of society, and takes the arm of society, of which he is a part, in preference and in addition to his own. Society *grants* him nothing. Every man is a proprietor in society, and draws on the capital as a matter of right.

From these premises two or three certain conclusions will follow:

First, *That every civil right grows out of a natural right; or, in other words, is a natural right exchanged.*

Secondly, *That civil power properly considered as such is made up of the aggregate of that class of the natural rights of man, which becomes defective in the individual in point of power, and answers not his purpose, but when collected to a focus becomes competent to the purpose of every one.*

Thirdly, *That the power produced from the aggregate of natural rights, imperfect in power in the individual, cannot be applied to invade the natural rights which are retained in the individual, and in which the power to execute is as perfect as the right itself.*

We have now, in a few words, traced man from a natural individual to a member of society, and shown, or endeavoured to show, the quality of the natural rights retained, and of those which are exchanged for civil rights. Let us now apply these principles to Governments.

In casting our eyes over the world, it is extremely easy to distinguish the Governments which have arisen out of society, or out of the social compact, from those which have not; but to place this in a clearer light than what a single glance may afford, it will be proper to take a review of the several sources from which Governments have arisen and on which they have been founded.

They may be all comprehended under three heads.

First, *Superstition.*

Secondly, *Power.*

Thirdly, *The common interest of society and the common rights of man.*

The first was a Government of Priestcraft, the second of Conquerors, and the third of Reason.

When a set of artful men pretended, through the medium of oracles, to hold intercourse with the Deity, as familiarly as they now march up the back-stairs in European Courts, the world was completely under the government of superstition. The oracles were consulted, and whatever they were made to say became the law; and this sort of Government lasted as long as this sort of superstition lasted.

After these a race of conquerors arose, whose Government, like that of William the Conqueror, was founded in power, and the sword assumed the name of a sceptre. Governments thus established last as long as the power to support them lasts; but that they might avail themselves of every engine in their favour, they united fraud to force, and set up an idol which they called *Divine Right,* and which, in imitation of the Pope, who affects to be spiritual and temporal, and in contradiction to the Founder of the Christian religion, twisted itself afterwards into an idol of another shape, called *Church and State.* The key of St. Peter and the key of the Treasury became quartered on one another, and the wondering cheated multitude worshipped the invention.

When I contemplate the natural dignity of man, when I feel (for Nature has not been kind enough to me to blunt my feelings) for the honour and happiness of its character, I become irritated at the attempt to govern mankind by force and fraud, as if they were all knaves and fools and can scarcely avoid disgust at those who are thus imposed upon.

We have now to review the governments which arise out of the society, in contradistinction to those which arose out of superstition and conquest.

It has been thought a considerable advance towards establishing the principles of Freedom to say that Government is a compact between those who govern and those who are governed; but this cannot be true, because it is putting the effect before the cause; for as man must have existed before Governments existed, there necessarily was a time when Governments did not exist, and consequently there could originally exist no governors to form such a compact with. The fact therefore must be that the *individuals themselves*, each in his own personal and sovereign right, *entered into a compact with each other* to produce a Government: and this is the only mode in which Governments have a right to arise, and the only principle on which they have a right to exist.

To possess ourselves of a clear idea of what Government is, or ought to be, we must trace it to its origin. In doing this we shall easily discover that Governments must have arisen either *out* of the people or *over* the people. Mr. Burke has made no distinction. He investigates nothing to its source, and therefore he confounds everything; but he has signified his intention of undertaking, at some future opportunity, a comparison between the Constitutions of England and France. As he thus renders it a subject of controversy by throwing the gauntlet, I take him up on his own ground. It is in high challenges that high truths have the right of appearing; and I accept it with the more readiness because it affords me, at the same time, an opportunity of pursuing the subject with respect to Governments arising out of society.

But it will be first necessary to define what is meant by a *Constitution*. It is not sufficient that we adopt the word; we must fix also a standard signification to it.

A Constitution is not a thing in name only, but in fact. It has not an ideal, but a real existence; and wherever it cannot be produced in a visible form, there is none. A Constitution is a thing *antecedent* to a Government, and a Government is only the creature of a Constitution. The Constitution of a country is not the act of its Government, but of the people constituting a Government. It is the body of elements, to which you can refer, and quote article by article; and which contains the principles on which the Government shall be established, the manner in which it shall be organised, the powers it shall have, the mode of elections, the duration of Parliaments, or by what other name such bodies may be called; the powers which the executive part of the Government shall have; and in fine, everything that relates to the complete organisation of a civil Government, and the principles on which it shall act, and by which it shall be bound. A Constitution, therefore, is to a Government what the laws made afterwards by that Government are to a Court of Judicature. The Court of Judicature does not make the laws, neither can it alter them; it only acts in conformity to the laws made: and the Government is in like manner governed by the Constitution.

Can, then, Mr. Burke produce the English Constitution? If he cannot, we may fairly conclude that though it has been so much talked about, no such thing as a Constitution exists, or ever did exist, and consequently that the people have yet a Constitution to form.

Mr. Burke will not, I presume, deny the position I have already advanced—namely, that Governments arise either *out* of the people or *over* the people. The English Government is one of those which arose out of a conquest, and not out of society, and consequently it arose over the people; and though it has been much modified from the opportunity of circumstances since the time of William the Conqueror, the country has never yet regenerated itself, and is therefore without a Constitution.

I readily perceive the reason why Mr. Burke declined going into the comparison between the English and French Constitutions, because he could not but perceive, when he sat down to the task, that no such thing as a Constitution existed on his side the question. His book is certainly bulky enough to have contained all he could say on this subject, and it would have been the best manner in which people could have judged of their separate merits. Why then has he declined the only thing that was worth while to write upon? It was the strongest ground he could take, if the advantages were on his side, but the weakest if they were not; and his declining to take it is either a sign that he could not possess it or could not maintain it.

Mr. Burke said, in a speech last winter in Parliament, that *when the National Assembly first met in three Orders,* the Tiers Etats, the Clergy, and the Noblesse), *France had then a good constitution.* This shows among numerous other instances, that Mr. Burke does not understand what a constitution is. The persons so met were not a *Constitution,* but a *Convention,* to make a Constitution.

The present National Assembly of France is, strictly speaking, the *personal social compact.* The members of it are the delegates of the Nation in its *original* character; future assemblies will be the delegates of the Nation in its *organised* character. The authority of the present assembly is different to what the authority of future assemblies will be. The authority of the present one is to form a Constitution; the authority of future assemblies will be to legislate according to the principles and forms prescribed in that Constitution; and if experience should hereafter show that alterations, amendments, or additions are necessary, the Constitution will point out the mode by which such things shall be done, and not leave it to the discretionary power of the future Government.

A Government on the principles on which constitutional Governments arising out of society are established, cannot have the right of altering itself. If it had, it would be arbitrary. It might make itself what it pleased; and wherever such a right is set up, it shows there is no Constitution. The act by which the English Parliament empowered itself to sit seven years, shows there is no Constitution in England. It might, by the same self-authority, have sat any greater number of years, or for life. The bill which the present Mr. Pitt brought into Parliament some years ago, to reform Parliament, was on the same erroneous principle. The right of reform is in the nation in its original character, and the constitutional method would be by a general convention elected for the purpose. There is, moreover, a paradox in the idea of vitiated bodies reforming themselves.

From these preliminaries I proceed to draw some comparisons. I have already spoken of the declaration of rights; and as I mean to be as concise as possible, I shall proceed to other parts of the French Constitution.

The Constitution of France says, *That every man who pays a tax of sixty sous per annum* (2s. 6d. English) *is an elector.* What article will Mr. Burke place against this? Can anything be more limited, and at the same time more capricious, than the qualifications of electors are in England? Limited—because not one man in an hundred (I speak much within compass) is admitted to vote. Capricious—because the lowest character that can be supposed to exist, and who has not so much as the visible means of an honest livelihood, is an elector in some places: while in other places, the man who pays very large taxes, and has a known fair character, and the farmer who rents to the amount of three or four hundred pounds a year, with a property on that farm to three or four times that amount, is not admitted to be an elector.

Everything is out of nature, as Mr. Burke says on another occasion, in this strange chaos, and all sorts of follies are blended with all sorts of crimes.

William the Conqueror and his descendants parcelled out the country in this manner, and bribed some parts of it by what they called charters to hold the other parts of it the better subjected to their will. This is the reason why so many of those charters abound in Cornwall; the people were averse to the Government established at the conquest, and the towns were garrisoned and bribed to enslave the country. All the old charters are the badges of this conquest, and it is from this source that the capriciousness of elections arises.

The French Constitution says, *that the number of representatives for any place shall be in a ratio to the number of taxable inhabitants or electors.*

What article will Mr. Burke place against this? The county of Yorkshire, which contains nearly a million of souls, sends two county members; and so does the county of Rutland, which contains not an hundredth part of that number. The town of Old Sarum, which contains not three houses, sends two members; and the town of Manchester, which contains upwards of sixty thousand souls, is not admitted to send any. Is there any principle in these things? Is there anything by which you can trace the marks of freedom, or discover those of wisdom? No wonder then Mr. Burke has declined the comparison, and endeavoured to lead his readers from the point by a wild, unsystematical display of paradoxical rhapsodies.

The French Constitution says, *that the National Assembly shall be elected every two years.*

What article will Mr. Burke place against this? Why, that the Nation has no right at all in the case; that the Government is perfectly arbitrary with respect to this point; and he can quote for his authority the precedent of a former Parliament.

The French Constitution says, *there shall be no game laws, that the farmer on whose lands wild game shall be found (for it is by the produce of his lands they are fed) shall have a right to what he can take; that there shall be no monopolies of any kind—that all trade shall be free and every man free to follow any occupation by which he can procure an honest livelihood, and in any place, town, or city throughout the Nation.*

What will Mr. Burke say to this? In England, game is made the property of those at whose expense it is not fed; and with respect to monopolies, the country is cut up into monopolies. Every chartered town is an aristocratical monopoly in itself, and the qualification of electors proceeds out of those chartered monopolies. Is this freedom? Is this what Mr. Burke means by a Constitution?

In these chartered monopolies, a man coming from another part of the country is hunted from them as if he were a foreign enemy. An Englishman is not free of his own country; every one of those places presents a barrier in his way, and tells him he is not a freeman—that he has no rights. Within these monopolies are other monopolies. In a city, such for instance as Bath, which contains between twenty and thirty thousand inhabitants, the right of electing representatives to Parliament is monopolized by about thirty-one persons. And within these monopolies are still others. A man even of the same town, whose parents were not in circumstances to give him an occupation, is debarred, in many cases, from the natural right of acquiring one, be his genius or industry what it may.

Are these things examples to hold out to a country regenerating itself from slavery, like France? Certainly they are not, and certain am I, that when the people of England come to reflect upon them they will, like France, annihilate those badges of ancient oppression, those traces of a conquered nation. Had Mr. Burke possessed talents similar to the author of "On the Wealth of Nations," he would have comprehended all the parts which enter into, and, by assemblage, form a constitution. He would have reasoned from minutiae to magnitude. It is not from his prejudices only, but from the disorderly cast of his genius, that he is unfitted for the subject he writes upon. Even his genius is without a Constitution. It is a genius at random, and not a genius constituted. But he must say something. He has therefore mounted in the air like a balloon, to draw the eyes of the multitude from the ground they stand upon.

Much is to be learned from the French Constitution. Conquest and tyranny transplanted themselves with William the Conqueror from Normandy into England, and the country is yet disfigured with the marks. May, then, the example of all France contribute to regenerate the freedom which a province of it destroyed!

The French Constitution says *that to preserve the national representation from being corrupt no member of the National Assembly shall be an officer of the Government, a placeman or a pensioner.*

What will Mr. Burke place against this? I will whisper his answer—Loaves and Fishes. Ah! this Government of loaves and fishes has more mischief in it than people have yet reflected on. The National Assembly has made the discovery, and it holds out the example to the world. Had Governments agreed to quarrel on purpose to fleece their countries by taxes, they could not have succeeded better than they have done.

Many things in the English Government appear to me the reverse of what they ought to be and what they are said to be. The Parliament, imperfectly and capriciously elected as it is, is nevertheless *supposed* to hold the national purse in *trust* for the nation; but in the manner in which an English Parliament is constructed it is like a man being both mortgager and mortgagee, and in the case of misapplication of trust it is the criminal sitting in judgment upon himself. If those who vote the supplies are the same persons who receive the supplies when voted, and arc to account for the expenditure of those supplies to those who voted them, it is *themselves accountable to themselves,* and the Comedy of Errors concludes with the Pantomime of Hush. Neither the ministerial party nor the Opposition will touch upon this case. The national purse is the common hack which each mounts upon. It is like what the country people call "Ride and tie— You ride a little way, and then I." They order these things better in France.

The French Constitution says *that the right of war and peace is in the nation.*

Where else should it reside but in those who are to pay the expence?

In England this right is said to reside in a *metaphor* shown at the Tower for sixpence or a shilling a piece: so are the lions; and it would be a step nearer to reason to say it resided in them, for any inanimate metaphor is no more than a hat or a cap. We can all see the absurdity of worshipping Aaron's molten calf, or Nebuchadnezzar's golden image; but why do men continue to practise themselves the absurdities they despise in others?

It may with reason be said that in the manner the English Nation is represented it signifies not where this right resides, whether in the Crown or in the Parliament. War is the common harvest of all those who participate in the division and expenditure of public money, in all countries. It is the art of *conquering at home;* the object of it is an increase of revenue; and as revenue cannot be increased without taxes, a pretence must be made for expenditures. In reviewing the history of the English Government, its wars and its taxes, a bystander, not blinded by prejudice nor warped by interest, would declare that taxes were not raised to carry on wars, but that wars were raised to carry on taxes.

Mr. Burke, as a member of the House of Commons, is a part of the English Government; and though he professes himself an enemy of war, he abuses the French Constitution, which seeks to explode it. He holds up the English Government as a model, in all its parts, to France; but he should first know the remarks which the French make upon it. They contend in favour of their own, that the portion of liberty enjoyed in England is just enough to enslave a country more productively than by despotism, and that as the real object of all despotism is revenue, a Government so formed obtains more than it could do either by direct despotism, or in a full state of freedom, and is, therefore, on the ground of interest, opposed to both. They account also for the readiness which always appears in such Governments for engaging in wars by remarking on the different motives which produce them. In despotic Governments wars are the effect of pride; but in those Governments in which they become the means of taxation, they acquire thereby a more permanent promptitude.

The French Constitution, therefore, to provide against both these evils, has taken away the power of declaring war from kings and ministers, and placed the right where the expence must fall.

When the question of the right of war and peace

was agitating in the National Assembly, the people of England appeared to be much interested in the event, and highly to applaud the decision. As a principle it applies as much to one country as another. William the Conqueror, *as a conqueror,* held this power of war and peace in himself, and his descendants have ever since claimed it under him as a right.

Although Mr. Burke has asserted the right of the Parliament at the Revolution to bind and control the Nation and posterity *for ever,* he denies at the same time that the Parliament or the nation had any right to alter what he calls the succession of the Crown in anything but in part, or by a sort of modification. By his taking this ground he throws the case back to the *Norman Conquest,* and by thus running a line of succession springing from William the Conqueror to the present day, he makes it necessary to inquire who and what William the Conqueror was, and where he came from, and into the origin, history and nature of what are called prerogatives. Everything must have had a beginning, and the fog of time and antiquity should be penetrated to discover it. Let, then, Mr. Burke bring forward his William of Normandy, for it is to this origin that his argument goes. It also unfortunately happens, in running this line of succession, that another line parallel thereto presents itself, which is, that if the succession runs in the line of the conquest, the Nation runs in the line of being conquered, and it ought to rescue itself from this reproach.

But it will perhaps be said that tho' the power of declaring war descends in the heritage of the conquest, it is held in check by the right of the Parliament to withhold the supplies. It will always happen when a thing is originally wrong that amendments do not make it right, and it often happens that they do as much mischief one way as good the other, and such is the case here, for if the one rashly declares war as a matter of right, and the other peremptorily withholds the supplies as a matter of right, the remedy becomes as bad, or worse, than the disease. The one forces the Nation to a combat, and the other ties its hands; but the more probable issue is that the contest will end in a collusion between the parties, and be made a screen to both.

On this question of war, three things are to be considered. First, the right of declaring it; secondly, the expence of supporting it; thirdly, the mode of conducting it after it is declared. The French Constitution places the *right* where the *expence* must fall, and this union can be only in the Nation. The mode of conducting it after it is declared, it consigns to the executive department. Were this the case in all countries, we should hear but little more of wars.

Before I proceed to consider other parts of the French Constitution, and by way of relieving the fatigue of argument, I will introduce an anecdote which I had from Dr. Franklin.

While the Doctor resided in France as Minister from America during the war, he had numerous proposals made to him by projectors of every country and of every kind, who wished to go to the land that floweth with milk and honey, America; and among the rest, there was one who offered himself to be King. He introduced his proposal to the Doctor by letter, which is now in the hands of M. Beaumarchais, of Paris—stating first, that as the Americans had dismissed or sent away their King, that they would want another. Secondly, that himself was a Norman. Thirdly, that he was of a more ancient family than the Dukes of Normandy, and of a more honourable descent, his line having never been bastardised. Fourthly, that there was already a precedent in England of Kings coming out of Normandy, and on these grounds he rested his offer, *enjoining* that the Doctor would forward it to America. But as the Doctor neither did this, nor yet sent him an answer, the projector wrote a second letter in which he did not, it is true, threaten to go over and conquer America, but only with great dignity proposed that if his offer was not accepted, an acknowledgment of about £30,000 might be made to him for his generosity! Now, as all arguments respecting succession must necessarily connect that succession with some beginning, Mr. Burke's arguments on this subject go to show that there is no English origin of Kings, and that they are descendants of the Norman line in right of the Conquest. It may, therefore, be of service to his doctrine to make this story known and to inform him, that in case of that natural extinction to which all mortality is subject, Kings may again be had from Normandy, on more reasonable terms than William the Conqueror; and consequently that the good people of England at the Revolution of 1688, *might have done much better,* had such a generous Norman as *this* known *their* wants, and they had known *his!* The chivalric character which Mr. Burke so much admires, is certainly much easier to make a bargain with than a *hard dealing Dutchman.* But to return to the matters of the Constitution.

The French Constitution says, *There shall be no titles;* and, of consequence, all that class of equivocal generation which in some countries is called *"aristocracy"* and in others *"nobility,"* is done away, and the *peer* is exalted into MAN.

Titles are but nicknames, and every nickname is a title. The thing is perfectly harmless in itself, but it marks a sort of foppery in the human character, which degrades it. It reduces man into the diminutive of man in things which are great, and the counterfeit of woman in things which are little. It talks about its fine *blue ribbon* like a girl, and shows its new *garter* like a child. A certain writer, of some antiquity, says: *"When I was a child, I thought as a child; but when I became a man, I put away childish things."*

It is, properly, from the elevated mind of France

that the folly of titles has fallen. It has outgrown the baby cloaths of *Count* and *Duke,* and breeched itself in manhood. France has not levelled, it has exalted. It has put down the dwarf, to set up the man. The puny-ism of a senseless word like *Duke* or *Count* or *Earl* has ceased to please. Even those who possessed them have disowned the gibberish, and as they outgrew the rickets, have despised the rattle. The genuine mind of man, thirsting for its native home, society, contemns the gewgaws that separate him from it. Titles are like circles drawn by the magician's wand, to contract the sphere of man's felicity. He lived immured within the Bastille of a word, and surveys at a distance the envied life of man.

Is it, then, any wonder that titles should fall in France? Is it not a greater wonder they should be kept up anywhere? What are they? What is their worth, and "what is their amount"?

When we think or speak of a *Judge* or a *General,* we associate with it the ideas of office and character; we think of gravity in the one and bravery in the other; but when we use a word *merely as a title,* no ideas associate with it. Through all the vocabulary of Adam there is not such an animal as a Duke or a Count; neither can we connect any certain idea with the words. Whether they mean strength or weakness, wisdom or folly, a child or a man, or the rider or the horse, is all equivocal. What respect then can be paid to that which describes nothing, and which means nothing? Imagination has given figure and character to centaurs, satyrs, and down to all the fairy tribe; but titles baffle even the powers of fancy, and are a chimerical nondescript.

But this is not all. If a whole country is disposed to hold them in contempt, all their value is gone, and none will own them. It is common opinion only that makes them anything or nothing, or worse than noth-ing. There is no occasion to take titles away, for they take themselves away when society concurs to ridicule them. This species of imaginary consequence has visibly declined in every part of Europe, and it hastens to its exit as the world of reason continues to rise. There was a time when the lowest class of what are called *nobility* was more thought of than the highest is now, and when a man in armour riding through Christendom in quest of adventures was more stared at than a modern Duke. The world has seen this folly fall, and it has fallen by being laughed at, and the farce of titles will follow its fate. The patriots of France have discovered in good time that rank and dignity in society must take a new ground. The old one has fallen through. It must now take the substantial ground of character, instead of chimerical ground of titles; and they have brought their titles to the altar, and made of them a burnt-offering to Reason.

If no mischief had annexed itself to the folly of titles they would not have been worth a serious and formal destruction, such as the National Assembly have decreed them; and this makes it necessary to inquire farther into the nature and character of Aristocracy.

That, then, which is called Aristocracy in some countries and Nobility in others arose out of the Governments founded upon conquest. It was originally a military order for the purpose of supporting military Government (for such were all Governments founded in conquest); and to keep up a succession of this order for the purpose for which it was established, all the younger branches of those families were disinherited and the law of *primogenitureship* set up.

The nature and character of Aristocracy shows itself to us in this law. It is a law against every law of nature, and Nature herself calls for its destruction. Establish family justice and Aristocracy falls. By the aristocractical law of primogenitureship, in a family of six children five are exposed. Aristocracy has never more than one child. The rest are begotten to be devoured.

They are thrown to the cannibal for prey, and the natural parent prepares the unnatural repast.

As everything which is out of nature in man affects, more or less, the interest of society, so does this. All the children which the Aristocracy disowns (which are all except the eldest) are, in general, cast like orphans on a parish, to be provided for by the public, but at a greater charge. Unnecessary offices and places in Governments and Courts are created at the expence of the public to maintain them.

With what kind of parental reflections can the father or mother contemplate their younger offspring? By Nature they are children, and by Marriage they are heirs; but by Aristocracy they are bastards and orphans. They are the flesh and blood of their parents in one line, and nothing akin to them in the other. To restore, therefore, parents to their children, and children to their parents—relations to each other, and man to society—and to exterminate the monster Aristocracy, root and branch—the French Constitution has destroyed the law of PRIMOGENITURESHIP. Here then lies the monster; and Mr. Burke, if he pleases, may write its epitaph.

Hitherto we have considered Aristocracy chiefly in one point of view. We have now to consider it in another. But whether we view it before or behind, or sideways, or any way else, domestically or publicly, it is still a monster.

In France Aristocracy had one feature less in its countenance than what it has in some other countries. It did not compose a body of hereditary legislators. It was not a *"Corporation of Aristocracy,"* for such I have heard M. de la Fayette describe an English House of Peers. Let us then examine the grounds upon which the French Constitution has resolved against having such a House in France.

Because, in the first place, as is already mentioned, Aristocracy is kept up by family tyranny and injustice.

Secondly, because there is an unnatural unfitness in an Aristocracy to be legislators for a Nation. Their ideas of *distributive justice* are corrupted at the very source. They begin life by trampling on all their younger brothers and sisters, and relations of every kind, and are taught and educated so to do. With what ideas of justice or honour can that man enter a house of legislation, who absorbs in his own person the inheritance of a whole family of children or doles out to them some pitiful portion with the insolence of a gift?

Thirdly, because the idea of hereditary legislators is as inconsistent as that of hereditary judges, or hereditary juries; and as absurd as an hereditary mathematician, or an hereditary wise man; and as ridiculous as an hereditary poet-laureate.

Fourthly, because a body of men, holding themselves accountable to nobody, ought not to be trusted by any body.

Fifthly, because it is continuing the uncivilised principle of Governments founded in conquest, and the base idea of man having property in man, and governing him by personal right.

Sixthly, because Aristocracy has a tendency to degenerate the human species. By the universal economy of nature it is known, and by the instance of the Jews it is proved, that the human species has a tendency to degenerate, in any small number of persons, when separated from the general stock of society, and inter-marrying constantly with each other. It defeats even its pretended end, and becomes in time the opposite of what is noble in man. Mr. Burke talks of nobility; let him show what it is. The greatest characters the world have known have risen on the democratic floor. Aristocracy has not been able to keep a proportionate pace with Democracy. The artificial NOBLE shrinks into a dwarf before the noble of Nature; and in the few instances of those (for there are some in all countries) in whom nature, as by a miracle, has survived in Aristocracy, THOSE MEN DESPISE IT. But it is time to proceed to a new subject.

The French Constitution has reformed the condition of the clergy. It has raised the income of the lower and middle classes, and taken from the higher. None is now less than twelve hundred livres (fifty pounds sterling) nor any higher than about two or three thousand pounds. What will Mr. Burke place against this? Hear what he says. He says—

"That the people of England can see without pain or grudging, an archbishop precede a duke; they can see a Bishop of Durham, or a Bishop of Winchester in possession of £10,000 a-year; and cannot see why it is in worse hands than estates to a like amount, in the hands of this earl or that 'squire."

And Mr. Burke offers this as an example to France.

As to the first part, whether the Archbishop precedes the Duke, or the Duke the Bishop, it is, I believe, to the people in general, somewhat like *Sternhold* and *Hopkins,* or *Hopkins* and *Sternhold*; you may put which you please first; and as I confess that I do not understand the merits of this case, I will not contend it with Mr. Burke.

But with respect to the latter, I have something to say:—Mr. Burke has not put the case right. The comparison is out of order, by being put between the bishop and the earl or the squire. It ought to be put between the bishop and the curate, and then it will stand thus:—

"The people of England can see without pain or grudging, a Bishop of Durham, or a Bishop of Winchester, in possession of ten thousand pounds a-year, and a curate on thirty or forty pounds a-year, or less."

No, sir, they certainly do not see those things without great pain or grudging. It is a case that applies itself to every man's sense of justice, and is one among many that calls aloud for a Constitution.

In France the cry of *"the Church! the Church!"* was repeated as often as in Mr. Burke's book, and as loudly as when the Dissenters' Bill was before the English Parliament; but the generality of the French clergy were not to be deceived by this cry any longer. They knew that whatever the pretence might be it was themselves who were one of the principal objects of it. It was the cry of the high beneficed clergy, to prevent any regulation of income taking place between those of ten thousand pounds a-year and the parish priest. They therefore joined their case to those of every other oppressed class of men, and by this union obtained redress.

The French Constitution *has abolished Tythes,* that source of perpetual discontent between the tythe-holder and the parishioner. When land is held on tythe, it is in the condition of an estate held between two parties; the one receiving one-tenth, and the other nine-tenths of the produce: and consequently, on principles of equity, if the estate can be improved, and made to produce by that improvement double or treble what it did before, or in any other ratio, the expense of such improvement ought to be borne in like proportion between the parties who are to share the produce. But this is not the case in tythes; the farmer bears the whole expence, and the tythe-holder takes a tenth of the improvement, in addition to the original tenth, and by this means gets the value of two-tenths instead of one. This is another case that calls for a Constitution.

The French Constitution hath abolished or renounced *Toleration* and *Intoleration* also, and hath established UNIVERSAL RIGHT OF CONSCIENCE.

Toleration is not the *opposite* of Intolerance, but is the *counterfeit* of it. Both are despotisms. The one assumes to itself the right of withholding Liberty of Conscience, and the other of granting it. The one is the Pope armed with fire and faggot, and the other is the Pope selling or granting indulgences. The former is Church and State, and the latter is Church and traffic.

But Toleration may be viewed in a much stronger light. Man worships not himself, but his Maker; and the liberty of conscience which he claims is not for the service of himself, but of his God. In this case, therefore, we must necessarily have the associated idea of two beings; the *mortal* who renders the worship, and the IMMORTAL BEING who is worshipped. Toleration, therefore, places itself, not between man and man, nor between Church and Church, nor between one denomination of religion and another, but between God and man; between the being who worships, and the BEING who is worshipped; and by the same act of assumed authority by which it tolerates man to pay his worship, it presumptuously and blasphemously sets itself up to tolerate the Almighty to receive it.

Were a Bill brought into any Parliament, entitled, *"An Act to tolerate or grant liberty to the Almighty to receive the worship of a Jew or a Turk,"* or "to prohibit the Almighty from receiving it," all men would startle and call it blasphemy. There would be an uproar. The presumption of toleration in religious matters would then present itself unmasked; but the presumption is not the less because the name of "Man" only appears to those laws, for the associated idea of the *worshipped* and the *worshipper* cannot be separated. Who then art thou, vain dust and ashes! by whatever name thou art called, whether a King, a Bishop, a Church, or a State, a Parliament, or anything else, that obtrudest thine insignificance between the soul of man and its maker? Mind thine own concerns. If he believes not as thou believest, it is a proof that thou believest not as he believeth, and there is no earthly power can determine between you.

With respect to what are called denominations of religion, if every one is left to judge of his own religion, there is no such thing as a religion that is wrong; but if they are to judge of each other's religion, there is no such thing as a religion that is right; and therefore all the world is right, or all the world is wrong. But with respect to religion itself, without regard to names, and as directing itself from the universal family of mankind to the Divine object of all adoration, *it is man bringing to his Maker the fruits of his heart;* and though those fruits may differ from each other like the fruits of the earth, the grateful tribute of every one is accepted.

A Bishop of Durham, or a Bishop of Winchester, or the Archbishop who heads the Dukes, will not refuse a tythe-sheaf of wheat because it is not a cock of hay, nor a cock of hay because it is not a sheaf of wheat; nor a pig, because it is neither one nor the other; but these same persons, under the figure of an established church, will not permit their Maker to receive the varied tythes of man's devotion.

One of the continual choruses of Mr. Burke's book is "Church and State." He does not mean some one particular Church, or some one particular State, but any Church and State; and he uses the term as a general figure to hold forth the political doctrine of always uniting the Church with the State in every country, and he censures the National Assembly for not having done this in France. Let us bestow a few thoughts on this subject.

All religions are in their nature kind and benign, and united with principles of morality. They could not have made proselytes at first by professing anything that was vicious, cruel, persecuting, or immoral. Like everything else, they had their beginning; and they proceeded by persuasion, exhortation, and example. How then is it that they lose their native mildness, and become morose and intolerant?

It proceeds from the connection which Mr. Burke recommends. By engendering the Church with the State, a sort of mule-animal, capable only of destroying, and not of breeding up, is produced, called *The Church established by Law*. It is a stranger, even from its birth, to any parent mother, on whom it is begotten, and whom in time it kicks out and destroys.

The Inquisition in Spain does not proceed from the religion originally professed but from this mule-animal engendered between the Church and the State. The burnings in Smithfield proceeded from the same heterogeneous production; and it was the regeneration of this strange animal in England afterwards that renewed rancour and irreligion among the inhabitants, and that drove the people called Quakers and Dissenters to America. Persecution is not an original feature in *any* religion; but it is always the strongly-marked feature of all law-religions, or religions established by law. Take away the law-establishment and every religion reassumes its original benignity. In America a Catholic priest is a good citizen, a good character, and a good neighbour; an Episcopalian minister is of the same description; and this proceeds, independently of the men, from there being no law establishment in America.

If also we view this matter in a temporal sense we shall see the ill effects it has had on the prosperity of nations. The union of Church and State has impoverished Spain. The revoking the Edict of Nantes drove the silk manufacture from France into England; and Church and State are driving the cotton manufacture from England to America and France. Let then Mr. Burke continue to preach his antipolitical doctrine of Church and State. It will do some good. The National Assembly will not follow his advice, but will benefit by his folly. It was by observing the ill effects of it in England, that America has been warned against it; and it is by experiencing them in France, that the National Assembly have abolished it, and, like America, have established UNIVERSAL RIGHT OF CONSCIENCE AND UNIVERSAL RIGHT OF CITIZENSHIP.

I will here cease the comparison with respect to the principles of the French Constitution, and conclude this part of the subject with a few observations on the organisation of the formal parts of the French and English Governments.

The executive power in each country is in the hands of a person stiled the King; but the French Constitution distinguishes between the King and the Sovereign. It considers the station of King as official, and places Sovereignty in the Nation.

The representatives of the Nation who compose the National Assembly, and who are the legislative power, originate in and from the people by election, as an inherent right in the people. In England it is otherwise; and this arises from the original establishment of what is called its monarchy; for as by the Conquest all the rights of the people or the Nation were absorbed into the hands of the Conqueror, and who added the title of King to that of Conqueror, those same matters which in France are now held as rights in the people, or in the Nation, are held in England as grants from what is called the Crown. The Parliament in England, in both its branches, was erected by patents from the descendants of the Conqueror. The House of Commons did not originate as a matter of right in the people to delegate or elect, but as a grant or boon.

By the French Constitution the Nation is always named before the King. The third article of the Declaration of Rights says: *"The Nation is essentially the source (or fountain) of all sovereignty."* Mr. Burke argues that in England a King is the fountain—that he is the fountain of all honour. But as this idea is evidently descended from the Conquest I shall make no other remark upon it, than that it is the nature of conquest to turn everything upside down; and as Mr. Burke will not be refused the privilege of speaking twice, and as there are but two parts in the figure, the *fountain* and the *spout,* he will be right the second time.

The French Constitution puts the legislative before the executive, the Law before the King; *la Loi, le Roi.* This also is in the natural order of things, because laws must have existence before they can have execution.

A King in France does not, in addressing himself to the National Assembly, say "My Assembly," similar to the phrase used in England of "*my* Parliament"; neither can he use it consistently with the Constitution, nor could it be admitted. There may be propriety in the use of it in England, because as is before mentioned, both Houses of Parliament originated from what is called the Crown by patent or boon—and not from the inherent rights of the people, as the National Assembly does in France, and whose name designates its origin.

The President of the National Assembly does not ask the King *to grant to the Assembly liberty of speech,* as is the case with the English House of Commons. The constitutional dignity of the National Assembly cannot debase itself. Speech is, in the first place, one of the natural rights of man always retained; and with respect to the National Assembly the use of it is their *duty,* and the nation is their *authority.* They were elected by the greatest body of men exercising the right of election the European world ever saw. They sprung not from the filth of rotten boroughs, nor are they the vassal representatives of aristocratical ones. Feeling the proper dignity of their character, they support it. Their parliamentary language, whether for or against the question, is free, bold and manly, and extends to all the parts and circumstances of the case.

If any matter or subject respecting the executive department or the person who presides in it (the King) comes before them it is debated on with the spirit of men, and the language of gentlemen; and their answer or their address is returned in the same stile. They stand not aloof with the gaping vacuity of vulgar ignorance, nor bend with the cringe of sycophantic insignificance. The graceful pride of truth knows no extremes, and preserves, in every latitude of life, the right-angled character of man.

Let us now look to the other side of the question. In the addresses of the English Parliaments to their Kings we see neither the intrepid spirit of the old Parliaments of France, nor the serene dignity of the present National Assembly; neither do we see in them anything of the style of English manners, which borders somewhat on bluntness. Since then they are neither of foreign extraction, nor naturally of English production, their origin must be sought for elsewhere, and that origin is the Norman Conquest. They are evidently of the vassalage class of manners, and emphatically mark the prostrate distance that exists in no other condition of men than between the conqueror and the conquered. That this vassalage idea and stile of speaking was not got rid of even at the Revolution of 1688, is evident from the declaration of Parliament to William and Mary in these words: "We do most humbly and faithfully *submit* ourselves, our heirs and posterities, for ever." Submission is wholly a vassalage term, repugnant to the dignity of freedom, and an echo of the language used at the Conquest.

As the estimation of all things is by comparison, the Revolution of 1688, however from circumstances it may have been exalted beyond its value, will find its level. It is already on the wane, eclipsed by the enlarging orb of reason, and the luminous Revolutions of America and France. In less than another century it will go, as well as Mr. Burke's labours, "to the family vault of all the Capulets." Mankind will then scarcely believe that a country calling itself free would send to Holland for a man, and cloath him with power on purpose to put themselves in fear of him, and give him almost a million sterling a year for leave to *submit* themselves and their posterity, like bondmen and bondwomen, for ever.

But there is a truth that ought to be made known: I have had the opportunity of seeing it; which is, *that notwithstanding appearances, there is not any description of men that despise monarchy so much as courtiers.* But they well know, that if it were seen by others, as it is seen by them, the juggle could not be kept up. They are in the condition of men who get their living by a show, and to whom the folly of that show is so familiar that they ridicule it; but were the audience to be made as wise in this respect as themselves, there would be an end to the show and the profits with it. The difference between a republican and a courtier with respect to monarchy, is that the one opposes monarchy, believing it to be something; and the other laughs at it, knowing it to be nothing.

As I used sometimes to correspond with Mr. Burke believing him then to be a man of sounder principles than his book shows him to be, I wrote to him last winter from Paris, and gave him an account how prosperously matters were going on. Among other subjects in that letter, I referred to the happy situation the National Assembly were placed in; that they had taken a ground on which their moral duty and their political interest were united. They have not to hold out a language which they do not themselves believe, for the fraudulent purpose of making others believe it. Their station requires no artifice to support it, and can only be maintained by enlightening mankind. It is not their interest to cherish ignorance, but to dispel it. They are not in the case of a ministerial or an opposition party in England, who, though they are opposed, are still united to keep up the common mystery. The National Assembly must throw open a magazine of light. It must show man the proper character of man; and the nearer it can bring him to that standard, the stronger the National Assembly becomes.

In contemplating the French Constitution, we see in it a rational order of things. The principles harmonize with the forms, and both with their origin. It may perhaps be said as an excuse for bad forms, that they are nothing more than forms; but this is a mistake. Forms grow out of principles, and operate to continue the principles they grow from. It is impossible to practise a bad form on anything but a bad principle. It cannot be ingrafted on a good one; and wherever the forms in any government are bad, it is a certain indication that the principles are bad also.

I will here finally close this subject. I began it by remarking that Mr. Burke had *voluntarily* declined going into a comparison of the English and French Constitutions. He apologises for not doing it, by saying that he had not time. Mr. Burke's book was upwards of eight months in hand, and is extended to a volume of three hundred and sixty-six pages. As his omission does injury to his cause, his apology makes it worse; and men on the English side of the water will begin to consider, whether there is not some radical defect in what is called the English Constitution, that made it necessary for Mr. Burke to suppress the comparison, to avoid bringing it into view.

As Mr. Burke has not written on Constitutions so neither has he written on the French Revolution. He gives no account of its commencement or its progress. He only expresses his wonder. "It looks," says he, "to me, as if I were in a great crisis, not of the affairs of France alone, but of all Europe, perhaps of more than Europe. All circumstances taken together, the French Revolution is the most astonishing that has hitherto happened in the world."

As wise men are astonished at foolish things, and other people at wise ones, I know not on which ground to account for Mr. Burke's astonishment; but certain it is, that he does not understand the French Revolution. It has apparently burst forth like a creation from a chaos, but it is no more than the consequence of a mental Revolution priorily existing in France. The mind of the Nation had changed beforehand, and the new order of things has naturally followed the new order of thoughts. I will here, as concisely as I can, trace out the growth of the French Revolution, and mark the circumstances that have contributed to produce it.

The despotism of Louis XIV., united with the gaiety of his Court, and the gaudy ostentation of his character had so humbled, and at the same time so fascinated the mind of France, that the people appear to have lost all sense of their own dignity, in contemplating that of their Grand Monarch; and the whole reign of Louis XV., remarkable only for weakness and effeminacy, made no other alteration than that of spreading a sort of lethargy over the nation, from which it showed no disposition to rise.

The only signs which appeared of the spirit of Liberty during those periods, are to be found in the writings of the French philosophers. Montesquieu, President of the Parliament of Bordeaux, went as far as a writer under a despotic Government could well proceed; and being obliged to divide himself between principle and prudence, his mind often appears under a veil, and we ought to give him credit for more than he has expressed.

Voltaire, who was both the flatterer and the satirist of despotism, took another line. His forte lay in exposing and ridiculing the superstitions which priestcraft, united with statecraft, had interwoven with Governments. It was not from the purity of his principles, or his love of mankind (for satire and philanthropy are not naturally concordant), but from his strong capacity of seeing folly in its true shape, and his irresistible propensity to expose it, that he made those attacks. They were, however, as formidable as if the motives had been virtuous; and he merits the thanks rather than the esteem of mankind.

On the contrary, we find in the writings of Rousseau, and the Abbé Raynal, a loveliness of sentiment in favour of liberty, that excites respect, and elevates the human faculties; but having raised this animation, they do not direct its operations, and leave the mind in love with an object, without describing the means of possessing it.

The writings of Quesnay, Turgot, and the friends of those authors, are of the serious kind; but they laboured under the same disadvantage with Montesquieu; their writings abound with moral maxims of Government, but are rather directed to economise and reform the administration of the Government, than the Government itself.

But all those writings and many others had their weight; and by the different manner in which they treated the subject of Government, Montesquieu by his judgment and knowledge of laws, Voltaire by his wit, Rousseau and Raynal by their animation, and Quesnay and Turgot by their moral maxims and systems of economy, readers of every class met with something to their taste, and a spirit of political inquiry began to diffuse itself through the Nation at the time the dispute between England and the then colonies of America broke out.

In the war which France afterwards engaged in, it is very well known that the nation appeared to be beforehand with the French ministry. Each of them had its view: but those views were directed to different objects; the one sought liberty, and the other retaliation on England. The French officers and soldiers, who after this went to America, were eventually placed in the school of Freedom, and learned the practice as well as the principles of it by heart.

As it was impossible to separate the military events which took place in America from the principles of the American Revolution, the publication of those events in France necessarily connected themselves with the principles which produced them. Many of the facts were in themselves principles; such as the Declaration of American Independence, and the treaty of alliance between France and America, which recognised the natural right of man, and justified resistance to oppression. The then Minister of France, Count Vergennes, was not the friend of America; and it is both justice and gratitude to say, that it was the Queen of France who gave the cause of America a fashion at the French Court. Count Vergennes was the personal and social friend of Dr. Franklin; and the Doctor had obtained, by his sensible gracefulness, a sort of influence over him; but with respect to principles Count Vergennes was a despot.

The situation of Dr. Franklin, as Minister from America to France, should be taken into the chain of circumstances. The diplomatic character is of itself the narrowest sphere of society that man can act in. It forbids intercourse by the reciprocity of suspicion: and a diplomatic is a sort of unconnected atom, continually repelling and repelled. But this was not the case with Dr. Franklin. He was not the diplomatic of a Court, but of MAN. His character as a philosopher had been long established, and his circle of society in France was universal. Count Vergennes resisted for a considerable time the publication in France of the American Constitutions, translated into the French language: but even in this he was obliged to give way to public opinion, and a sort of propriety in admitting to appear what he had undertaken to defend. The American Constitutions were to Liberty what a grammar is to language: they define its parts of speech, and practically construct them into syntax. The peculiar situation of the then Marquis de la Fayette is another link in the great chain. He served in America as an American officer under a commission of Congress, and by the universality of his acquaintance was in close friendship with the civil government of America, as well as with the military line. He spoke the language of the country, entered into the discussions on the principles of Government, and was always a welcome friend at any election.

When the war closed, a vast reinforcement to the cause of Liberty spread itself over France, by the return of the French officers and soldiers. A knowledge of the practice was then joined to the theory; and all that was wanting to give it real existence was opportunity. Man cannot, properly speaking, make circumstances for his purpose, but he always has it in his power to improve them when they occur, and this was the case in France.

M. Neckar was displaced in May, 1781; and by the ill-management of the finances afterwards, and particularly during the extravagant administration of M. Calonne, the revenue of France, which was nearly twenty-four millions sterling per year, was become unequal to the expenditure, not because the revenue had decreased, but because the expences had increased; and this was a circumstance which the Nation laid hold of to bring forward a Revolution. The English Minister, Mr. Pitt, has frequently alluded to the state of the French finances in his budgets, without understanding the subject. Had the French Parliaments been as ready to register edicts for new taxes as an English Parliament is to grant them, there had been no derangement in the finances, nor yet any Revolution; but this will better explain itself as I proceed. It will be necessary here to show how taxes were formerly raised in France. The King, or rather the Court or Ministry acting under the use of that name, framed the edicts for taxes at their own discretion, and sent them to the Parliaments to be registered; for until they were registered by the Parliaments they were not operative. Disputes had long existed between the Court and the Parliaments with respect to the extent of the Parliaments' authority on this head. The Court insisted that the authority of Parliaments went no farther than to remonstrate or show reasons against the tax, reserving to itself the right of determining whether the reasons were well or ill-founded; and in consequence thereof, either to withdraw the edict as a matter of choice, or to *order* it to be enregistered as a matter of authority. The Parliaments on their part insisted that they had not only a right to remonstrate, but to reject; and on this ground they were always supported by the Nation. But to return to the order of my narrative M. Calonne wanted money: and as he knew the sturdy disposition of the Parliaments with respect to new taxes, he ingeniously sought either to approach them by a more gentle means than that of direct authority, or to get over their heads by a manoeuvre; and for this purpose he revived the project of assembling a body of men from the several provinces, under the style of an "Assembly of the Notables," or men of note, who met in 1787, and who were either to recommend taxes to the Parliaments, or to act as a Parliament themselves. An assembly under this name had been called in 1617.

As we are to view this as the first practical step towards the Revolution, it will be proper to enter into some particulars respecting it. The Assembly of the Notables has in some places been mistaken for the States-General, but was wholly a different body, the States-General being always by election. The persons who composed the Assembly of the Notables were all nominated by the King, and consisted of one hundred and forty members. But as M. Calonne could not depend upon a majority of this Assembly in his favour, he very ingeniously arranged them in such a manner as to make forty-four a majority of one hundred and forty; to effect this he disposed of them into seven separate committees, of twenty members each. Every general question was to be decided, not by a majority of persons, but by a majority of committees; and as eleven votes would make a majority in a committee and four committees a majority of seven, M. Calonne had good reason to conclude that as forty-four would determine any general question he could not be out-voted. The then Marquis de la Fayette was placed in the second committee, of which the Count D'Artois was president, and as money matters were the object, it naturally brought into view every circumstance connected with it. M. de la Fayette made a verbal charge against Calonne for selling crown lands to the amount of two millions of livres, in a manner that appeared to be unknown to the King. The Count D'Artois (as if to intimidate, for the Bastille was then in being) asked the Marquis if he would render the charge in writing? He replied that he would. The Count D'Artois did not demand it, but brought a message from the King to that purport. M. de la Fayette then delivered in his charge in writing, to be given to the King, undertaking to support it. No farther proceedings were had upon this affair, but M. Calonne was soon after dismissed by the King and sent off to England.

As M. de la Fayette, from the experience of what he had seen in America, was better acquainted with the science of civil Government than the generality of the members who composed the Assembly of the Notables could then be, the brunt of the business fell considerably to his share. The plan of those who had a Constitution in view was to contend with the Court on the ground of taxes, and some of them openly professed their object. Disputes frequently arose between Count D'Artois and M. de la Fayette upon various subjects. With respect to the arrears already incurred the latter proposed to remedy them by accommodating the expences to the revenue instead of the revenue to the expences; and as objects of reform he proposed to abolish the Bastille and all the State prisons throughout the Nation (the keeping of which was attended with great expense), and to suppress *lettres de cachet;* but those matters were not then much attended to, and with respect to *lettres de cachet, a majority of the nobles appeared to be in favour of them.*

On the subject of supplying the Treasury by new taxes the Assembly declined taking the matter on themselves, concurring in the opinion that they had not authority. In a debate on this subject M. de la Fayette said that raising money by taxes could only be done by a National Assembly, freely elected by the people, and acting as their representatives. Do you mean, said the Count D'Artois, the *States-General?* M. de la Fayette replied that he did. Will you, said the Count D'Artois, sign what you say to be given to the King? The other replied that he would not only do this but that he would go farther, and say that the effectual mode would be for the King to agree to the establishment of a Constitution.

As one of the plans had thus failed, that of getting the Assembly to act as a Parliament, the other came into view, that of recommending. On this subject the Assembly agreed to recommend two new taxes to be enregistered by the Parliament: the one a stamp-tax and the other a territorial or sort of land-tax. The two have been estimated at about five millions sterling per annum. We have now to turn our attention to the Parliaments, on whom the business was again devolving.

The Archbishop of Toulouse (since Archbishop of Sens, and now a Cardinal) was appointed to the administration of the finances soon after the dismission of Calonne. He was also made Prime Minister, an office that did not always exist in France. When this office did not exist, the chiefs of the principal departments transacted business immediately with the King, but when a Prime Minister was appointed they did business only with him. The Archbishop arrived to more state-authority than any Minister since the Duke de Choiseul, and the Nation was strongly disposed in his favour; but by a line of conduct scarcely to be accounted for he perverted every opportunity, turned out a despot, and sunk into disgrace, and a Cardinal.

The Assembly of the Notables having broken up, the new Minister sent the edicts for the two taxes recommended by the Assembly to the Parliaments to be enregistered. They of course came first before the Parliament of Paris, who returned for answer, *That with such a revenue as the nation then supported the name of taxes ought not to be mentioned but for the purpose of reducing them,* and threw both the edicts out.

On this refusal the Parliament was ordered to Versailles, where, in the usual form, the King held what under the old Government was called a Bed of Justice; and the two edicts were enregistered in presence of the Parliament by an order of State.

On this the Parliament immediately returned to Paris, renewed their session in form, and ordered the enregistering to be struck out, declaring that everything done at Versailles was illegal. All the members of the Parliament were then served with *Lettres de Cachet,* and exiled to Trois; but as they continued as inflexible in exile as before, and as vengeance did not supply the place of taxes, they were after a short time recalled to Paris.

The edicts were again tendered to them, and the Count D'Artois undertook to act as representative of the King. For this purpose he came from Versailles to Paris, in a train of procession; and the Parliament were assembled to receive him. But show and parade had lost their influence in France; and whatever ideas of importance he might set off with, he had to return with those of mortification and disappointment. On alighting from his carriage to ascend the steps of the Parliament House, the crowd (which was numerously collected) threw out trite expressions saying: "This is Monsieur D'Artois, who wants more of our money to spend." The marked disapprobation which he saw impressed him with apprehensions, and the word *Aux armes! (To arms!)* was given out by the officer of the guard who attended him. It was so loudly vociferated, that it echoed through the avenues of the House, and produced a temporary confusion. I was then standing in one of the apartments through which he had to pass, and could not avoid reflecting how wretched was the condition of a disrespected man.

He endeavoured to impress the Parliament by great words, and opened his authority by saying, "The King, our Lord and Master." The Parliament received him very coolly and with their usual determination not to register the taxes; and in this manner the interview ended.

After this a new subject took place: In the various debates and contests which arose between the Court and the Parliaments on the subject of taxes, the Parliament of Paris at last declared that although it had been customary for Parliaments to enregister edicts for taxes as a matter of convenience, the right belonged only to the *States-General;* and that, therefore, the Parliament could no longer with propriety continue to debate on what it had not authority to act. The King after this came to Paris and held a meeting with the Parliament, in which he continued from ten in the morning till about six in the evening, and, in a manner that appeared to proceed from him as if unconsulted upon with the Cabinet or Ministry, gave his word to the Parliament that the States-General should be convened.

But after this another scene arose, on a ground different from all the former. The Minister and the Cabinet were averse to calling the States-General. They well knew that if the States-General were assembled, themselves must fall; and as the King had not mentioned *any time,* they hit on a project calculated to elude, without appearing to oppose.

For this purpose, the Court set about making a sort of Constitution itself. It was principally the work of M. Lamoignon, Keeper of the Seals, who afterwards shot himself. This new arrangement consisted in establishing a body under the name of a *Cour Plénière,* or full Court, in which were invested all the powers that the Government might have occasion to make use of. The persons composing this Court were to be nominated by the King. The contended right of taxation was given up on the part of the King, and a new criminal code of laws and law proceedings was substituted in the room of the former. The thing, in many points, contained better principles than those upon which the Government had hitherto been administered; but with respect to the *Cour Plénière,* it was no other than a medium through which despotism was to pass, without appearing to act directly from itself.

The Cabinet had high expectations from their new contrivance. The persons who were to compose the *Cour Plénière* were already nominated; and as it was necessary to carry a fair appearance, many of the best characters in the Nation were appointed among the number. It was to commence on the 8th of May, 1788; but an opposition arose to it on two grounds—the one as to principle, the other as to form.

On the ground of principle it was contended that Government had not a right to alter itself, and that if the practice was once admitted it would grow into a principle and be made a precedent for any future alterations the Government might wish to establish; that the right of altering the Government was a national right, and not a right of Government. And on the ground of form it was contended that the *Cour Plénière* was nothing more than a larger Cabinet.

The then Duke de la Rouchefoucault, Luxembourg, De Noailles, and many others, refused to accept the nomination, and strenuously opposed the whole plan. When the edict for establishing this new Court was sent to the Parliaments to be enregistered and put into execution, they resisted also. The Parliament of Paris not only refused, but denied the authority; and the contest renewed itself between the Parliament and the Cabinet more strongly than ever. While the Parliament were sitting in debate on this subject, the Ministry ordered a regiment of soldiers to surround the House and form a blockade. The members sent out for beds and provisions, and lived as in a besieged citadel; and as this had no effect, the commanding officer was ordered to enter the Parliament House and seize them, which he did, and some of the principal members were shut up in different prisons. About the same time a deputation of persons arrived from the province of Brittany to remonstrate against the establishment of the *Cour Plénière,* and those the Archbishop sent to the Bastille. But the spirit of the Nation was not to be overcome, and it was so fully sensible of the strong ground it had taken, that of withholding taxes, that it contented itself with keeping up a sort of quiet resistance, which effectually overthrew all the plans at that time formed against it. The project of the *Cour Plénière* was at last obliged to be given up, and the Prime Minister not long afterwards followed its fate, and M. Neckar was recalled into office.

The attempt to establish the *Cour Plénière* had an effect upon the Nation which itself did not perceive. It was a sort of new form of Government that insensibly served to put the old one out of sight and to unhinge it from the superstitious authority of antiquity. It was Government dethroning Government; and the old one, by attempting to make a new one, made a chasm.

The failure of this scheme renewed the subject of convening the States-General; and this gave rise to a new series of politics.

There was no settled form for convening the States-General; all that it positively meant was a deputation from what was then called the Clergy, the Noblesse, and the Commons; but their numbers or their proportions had not been always the same. They had been convened only on extraordinary occasions, the last of which was in 1614; their numbers were then in equal proportions, and they voted by orders.

It could not well escape the sagacity of M. Neckar, that the mode of 1614 would answer neither the purpose of the then Government nor of the Nation. As matters were at that time circumstanced it would have been too contentious to agree upon anything. The debates would have been endless upon privileges and exemptions, in which neither the wants of the Government nor the wishes of the Nation for a Constitution would have been attended to. But as he did not choose to take the decision upon himself, he summoned again the *Assembly of the Notables* and referred it to them. This body was in general interested in the decision, being chiefly of the Aristocracy and the high-paid Clergy, and they decided in favour of the mode of 1614. This decision was against the sense of the Nation, and also against the wishes of the Court; for the Aristocracy opposed itself to both and contended for privileges independent of either. The subject was then taken up by the Parliament, who recommended that the number of the Commons should be equal to the other two: and they should all sit in one house and vote in one body. The number finally determined on was 1200; 600 to be chosen by the Commons (and this was less than their proportion ought to have been when their worth and consequence is considered on a national scale), 300 by the Clergy, and 300 by the Aristocracy; but with respect to the mode of assembling themselves, whether together or apart, or the manner in which they should vote, these matters were referred.

The election that followed was not a contested election, but an animated one. The candidates were not men, but principles. Societies were formed in Paris, and committees of correspondence and communication established throughout the Nation, for the purpose of enlightening the people, and explaining to them the principles of civil Government; and so orderly was the election conducted, that it did not give rise even to the rumour of tumult.

The States-General were to meet at Versailles in April, 1789, but did not assemble till May. They situated themselves in three separate chambers, or rather the Clergy and the Aristocracy withdrew each into a separate chamber.

The majority of the Aristocracy claimed what they called the privilege of voting as a separate body, and of giving their consent or their negative in that manner; and many of the Bishops and the high-beneficed Clergy claimed the same privilege on the part of their Order.

The *Tiers Etat* (as they were then called) disowned any knowledge of artificial Orders and artificial privileges; and they were not only resolute on this point, but somewhat disdainful. They began to consider Aristocracy as a kind of fungus growing out of the corruption of society, that could not be admitted even as a branch of it; and from the disposition the Aristocracy had shown by upholding *Lettres de Cachet* and in sundry other instances, it was manifest that no Constitution could be formed by admitting men in any other character than as National Men.

After various altercations on this head, the *Tiers Etat* or Commons (as they were then called) declared themselves (on a motion made for that purpose by the Abbé Sieyes) "The Representatives of the Nation; and that the two Orders could be considered but as deputies of corporations, and could only have a deliberate voice when they assembled in a national character with the national representatives."

This proceeding extinguished the stile of *Etats Généraux,* or States-General, and erected it into the stile it now bears, that of *L'Assemblée Nationale,* or National Assembly.

This motion was not made in a precipitate manner. It was the result of cool deliberation, and concerted between the national representatives and the patriotic members of the two chambers, who saw into the folly, mischief and injustice of artificial privileged distinctions.

It was become evident, that no Constitution, worthy of being called by that name, could be established on anything less than a national ground. The Aristocracy had hitherto opposed the despotism of the Court, and affected the language of patriotism; but it opposed it as its rival (as the English Barons opposed King John), and it now opposed the nation from the same motives.

On carrying this motion, the national representatives, as had been concerted, sent an invitation to the two chambers, to unite with them in a National character, and proceed to business.

A majority of the Clergy, chiefly of the parish priests, withdrew from the clerical chamber, and joined the Nation; and forty-five from the other chamber joined in like manner.

There is a sort of secret history belonging to this last circumstance, which is necessary to its explanation; it was not judged prudent that all the patriotic members of the chamber stiling itself the Nobles, should quit it at once; and in consequence of this arrangement, they drew off by degrees, always leaving some, as well to reason the case, as to watch the suspected.

In a little time the numbers increased from forty-five to eighty, and soon after to a greater number; which, with the majority of the clergy, and the whole of the national representatives, put the malcontents in a very diminutive condition.

The King, who, very different from the general class called by that name, is a man of a good heart, showed himself disposed to recommend a union of the three chambers, on the ground the National Assembly had taken; but the malcontents exerted themselves to prevent it, and began now to have another project in view.

Their numbers consisted of a majority of the aristocratical chamber and a minority of the clerical chamber, chiefly of Bishops and high-beneficed Clergy; and these men were determined to put everything to issue, as well by strength as by stratagem.

They had no objection to a Constitution; but it must be such a one as themselves should dictate, and suited to their own views and particular situations.

On the other hand, the Nation disowned knowing anything of them but as citizens, and was determined to shut out all such upstart pretensions. The more Aristocracy appeared, the more it was despised; there was a visible imbecility and want of intellects in the majority—a sort of *je ne sais quoi,* that while it affected to be more than citizen, was less than man. It lost ground from contempt more than from hatred; and was rather jeered at as an ass than dreaded as a lion. This is the general character of Aristocracy, or what are called Nobles or Nobility, or rather No-ability, in all countries.

The plan of the malcontents consisted now of two things; either to deliberate and vote by chambers (or orders), more especially on all questions respecting a Constitution (by which the aristocratical chamber would have had a negative on any article of the Constitution); or, in case they could not accomplish this object, to overthrow the National Assembly entirely.

To effect one or other of these objects they began now to cultivate a friendship with the despotism they had hitherto attempted to rival, and the Count D'Artois became their chief.

The King (who has since declared himself deceived into their measures) held, according to the old form, a *Bed of Justice,* in which he accorded to the deliberation and vote *par tête* (by head) upon several subjects; but reserved the deliberation and vote upon all questions respecting a Constitution to the three chambers separately.

This declaration of the King was made against the advice of M. Neckar, who now began to perceive that he was growing out of fashion at Court, and that another Minister was in contemplation.

As the form of sitting in separate chambers was yet apparently kept up, though essentially destroyed, the national representatives immediately after this declaration of the King resorted to their own chambers to consult on a protest against it; and the minority of the chamber (calling itself the Nobles), who had joined the national cause, retired to a private house to consult in like manner.

The malcontents had by this time concerted their measures with the Court, which Count D'Artois undertook to conduct; and as they saw from the discontent which the declaration excited, and the opposition making against it, that they could not obtain a control over the intended Constitution by a separate vote, they prepared themselves for their final object—that of conspiring against the National Assembly, and overthrowing it.

The next morning the door of the chamber of the National Assembly was shut against them, and guarded by troops; and the members were refused admittance. On this they withdrew to a tennis-ground in the neighbourhood of Versailles, as the most convenient place they could find, and, after renewing their session, took an oath never to separate from each other, under any circumstance whatever, death excepted, until they had established a Constitution. As the experiment of shutting up the house had no other effect than that of producing a closer connection in the members, it was opened again the next day, and the public business recommenced in the usual place.

We now are to have in view the forming of the new Ministry, which was to accomplish the overthrow of the National Assembly. But as force would be necessary, orders were issued to assemble thirty thousand troops, the command of which was given to Broglio, one of the new-intended Ministry, who was recalled from the country for this purpose. But as some management was necessary to keep this plan concealed till the moment it should be ready for execution, it is to this policy that a declaration made by Count D'Artois must be attributed, and which is here proper to be introduced.

It could not but occur, while the malcontents continued to resort to their chambers separate from the National Assembly, that more jealousy would be excited than if they were mixed with it, and that the plot might be suspected. But as they had taken their ground, and wanted a pretence for quitting it, it was necessary that one should be devised. This was effectually accomplished by a declaration made by the Count D'Artois: "That if they took not a part in the National Assembly, the life of the King would be endangered;" on which they quitted their chambers, and mixed with the Assembly, in one body.

At the time this declaration was made, it was generally treated as a piece of absurdity in Count D'Artois, and calculated merely to relieve the outstanding members of the two chambers from the diminutive situation they were put in; and if nothing more had followed, this conclusion would have been good. But as things best explain themselves by their events, this apparent union was only a cover to the machinations which were secretly going on; and the declaration accommodated itself to answer that purpose. In a little time the National Assembly found itself surrounded by troops, and thousands more were daily arriving. On this a very strong declaration was made by the National Assembly to the King, remonstrating on the impropriety of the measure, and demanding the reason. The King, who was not in the secret of this business, as himself afterwards declared, gave substantially for answer, that he had no other object in view than to preserve the public tranquillity, which appeared to be much disturbed.

But in a few days from this time the plot unravelled itself. M. Neckar and the Ministry were displaced, and a new one formed of the enemies of the Revolution; and Broglio, with between twenty-five and thirty thousand foreign troops, was arrived to support them. The mask was now thrown off, and matters were come to a crisis. The event was that in a space of three days the new Ministry and their abettors found it prudent to fly the Nation; the Bastille was taken, and Broglio and his foreign troops dispersed, as is already related in the former part of this work.

There are some curious circumstances in the history of this short-lived Ministry, and this short-lived attempt at a counter-revolution. The Palace of Versailles, where the Court was sitting, was not more than four hundred yards distant from the hall where the National Assembly was sitting. The two places were at this moment like the separate headquarters of two combatant armies; yet the Court was as perfectly ignorant of the information which had arrived from Paris to the National Assembly, as if it had resided at a hundred miles distance. The then Marquis de la Fayette, who (as has been already mentioned) was chosen to preside in the National Assembly on this particular occasion, named by order of the Assembly three successive deputations to the King, on the day and up to the evening on which the Bastille was taken, to inform and confer with him on the state of affairs; but the Ministry, who knew not so much as that it was attacked, precluded all communication, and were solacing themselves how dexterously they had succeeded; but in a few hours the accounts arrived so thick and fast that they had to start from their desks and run. Some set off in one disguise, and some in another, and none in their own character. Their anxiety now was to outride the news, lest they should be stopped, which, though it flew fast, flew not so fast as themselves.

It is worth relating that the National Assembly neither pursued those fugitive conspirators, nor took any notice of them, nor sought to retaliate in any shape whatever.

Occupied with establishing a Constitution founded on the Rights of Man and the Authority of the People, the only authority on which Government has a right to exist in any country, the National Assembly felt none of those mean passions which mark the character of impertinent Governments, founding themselves on their own authority, or on the absurdity of hereditary succession. It is the faculty of the human mind to become what it contemplates, and to act in unison with its object.

The conspiracy being thus dispersed, one of the first works of the National Assembly, instead of vindictive proclamations, as has been the case with other Governments, published a Declaration of the Rights of Man, as the basis on which the new Constitution was to be built, and which is here subjoined.

Declaration of the Rights of Man and of Citizens by the National Assembly of France

The representatives of the people of France, formed into a National Assembly, considering that ignorance, neglect, or contempt of human rights, are the sole causes of public misfortunes and corruptions of Government, have resolved to set forth in a solemn declaration, these natural, imprescriptible, and inalienable rights; that this declaration being constantly present to the minds of the members of the body social, they may be ever kept attentive to their rights and their duties; that the acts of the legislative and executive powers of Government, being capable of being every moment compared with the end of political institutions, may be more respected; and also, that the future claims of the citizens, being directed by simple and incontestable principles, may always tend to the maintenance of the Constitution, and the general happiness.

For these reasons the National Assembly doth recognise and declare, in the presence of the Supreme Being, and with the hope of his blessing and favour, the following *sacred* rights of men and of citizens:

I. Men are born, and always continue, free and equal in respect of their rights. Civil distinctions, therefore, can be founded only on public utility.

II. The end of all political associations is the preservation of the natural and imprescriptible rights of man; and these rights are Liberty, Property, Security, and Resistance of Oppression.

III. The Nation is essentially the source of all sovereignty; nor can any individual, or any body of men, be entitled to any authority which is not expressly derived from it.

IV. Political Liberty consists in the power of doing whatever does not injure another. The exercise of the natural rights of every man, has no other limits than those which are necessary to secure to every *other* man the free exercise of the same rights; and these limits are determinable only by the law.

V. The law ought to prohibit only actions hurtful to society. What is not prohibited by the law should not be hindered; nor should any one be compelled to that which the law does not require.

VI. The law is an expression of the will of the community. All citizens have a right to concur, either personally or by their representatives, in its formation. It should be the same to all, whether it protects or punishes; and all being equal in its sight, are equally eligible to all honours, places, and employments, according to their different abilities, without any other distinction than that created by their virtues and talents.

VII. No man should be accused, arrested, or held in confinement, except in cases determined by the law, and according to the forms which it has prescribed. All who promote, solicit, execute, or cause to be executed, arbitrary orders, ought to be punished, and every citizen called upon, or apprehended by virtue of the law, ought immediately to obey, and renders himself culpable by resistance.

VIII. The law ought to impose no other penalties but such as are absolutely and evidently necessary; and no one ought to be punished, but in virtue of a law promulgated before the offence, and legally applied.

IX. Every man being presumed innocent till he has been convicted, whenever his detention becomes indispensable, all rigour to him, more than is necessary to secure his person, ought to be provided against by the law.

X. No man ought to be molested on account of his opinions, not even on account of his religious opinions, provided his avowal of them does not disturb the public order established by the law.

XI. The unrestrained communication of thoughts

and opinions being one of the most precious Rights of Man, every citizen may speak, write, and publish freely, provided he is responsible for the abuse of this liberty, in cases determined by the law.

XII. A public force being necessary to give security to the Rights of Men and of citizens, that force is instituted for the benefit of the community and not for the particular benefit of the persons with whom it is intrusted.

XIII. A common contribution being necessary for the support of the public force, and for defraying the other expenses of Government, it ought to be divided equally among the members of the community, according to their abilities.

XIV. Every citizen has a right, either by himself or his representative, to a free voice in determining the necessity of public contributions, the appropriation of them, and their amount, mode of assessment, and duration.

XV. Every community has a right to demand of all its agents an account of their conduct.

XVI. Every community in which a separation of powers and a security of rights is not provided for, wants a Constitution.

XVII. The right of property being inviolable and sacred, no one ought to be deprived of it, except in cases of evident public necessity, legally ascertained, and on condition of a previous just indemnity.

Observations on the Declaration of Rights

The first three articles comprehend in general terms the whole of a Declaration of Rights; all the succeeding articles either originate from them or follow as elucidations. The 4th, 5th, and 6th define more particularly what is only generally expressed in the 1st, 2nd, and 3rd.

The 7th, 8th, 9th, 10th, and llth articles are declaratory of principles upon which laws shall be constructed, conformable to rights already declared.

But it is questioned by some very good people in France, as well as in other countries, whether the 10th article sufficiently guarantees the right it is intended to accord with; besides which it takes off from the divine dignity of religion, and weakens its operative force upon the mind, to make it a subject of human laws. It then presents itself to man like light intercepted by a cloudy medium, in which the source of it is obscured from his sight, and he sees nothing to reverence in the dusky ray.

The remaining articles, beginning with the twelfth, are substantially contained in the principles of the preceding articles; but in the particular situation which France then was, having to undo what was wrong, as well as to set up what was right, it was proper to be more particular than what in another condition of things would be necessary.

While the Declaration of Rights was before the National Assembly some of its members remarked that if a Declaration of Rights was published it should be accompanied by a declaration of duties. The observation discovered a mind that reflected, and it only erred by not reflecting far enough. A Declaration of Rights is, by reciprocity, a declaration of duties also. Whatever is my right as a man is also the right of another; and it becomes my duty to guarantee as well as to possess.

The first three articles are the basis of Liberty, as well individual as national; nor can any country be called free whose Government does not take its beginning from the principles they contain, and continue to preserve them pure; and the whole of the Declaration of Rights is of more value to the world, and will do more good, than all the laws and statutes that have yet been promulgated.

In the declaratory exordium which prefaces the Declaration of Rights we see the solemn and majestic spectacle of a Nation opening its commission, under the auspices of its Creator, to establish a Government, a scene so new, and so transcendently unequalled by anything in the European world, that the name of a Revolution is diminutive of its character, and it rises into a REGENERATION OF MAN. What are the present Governments of Europe but a scene of iniquity and oppression? What is that of England? Do not its own inhabitants say it is a market where every man has his price, and where corruption is common traffic at the expence of a deluded people? No wonder, then, that the French Revolution is traduced. Had it confined itself merely to the destruction of flagrant despotism perhaps Mr. Burke and some others had been silent. Their cry now is, "It has gone too far"—that is, it has gone too far for them. It stares corruption in the face, and the venal tribe are all alarmed. Their fear discovers itself in their outrage, and they are but publishing the groans of a wounded vice. But from such opposition the French Revolution, instead of suffering, receives an homage. The more it is struck the more sparks it will emit; and the fear is it will not be struck enough. It has nothing to dread from attacks: Truth has given it an establishment, and Time will record it with a name as lasting as his own.

Having now traced the progress of the French Revolution through most of its principal stages, from its commencement to the taking of the Bastille, and its establishment by the Declaration of Rights, I will close the subject with the energetic apostrophe of M. de la Fayette— MAY THIS GREAT MONUMENT, RAISED TO LIBERTY, SERVE AS A LESSON TO THE OPPRESSOR, AND AN EXAMPLE TO THE OPPRESSED!

Miscellaneous Chapter

To prevent interrupting the argument in the preceding part of this work, or the narrative that follows it, I reserved some observations to be thrown together into a miscellaneous chapter; by which variety might not be censured for confusion.

Mr. Burke's book is *all* miscellany. His intention was to make an attack on the French Revolution; but instead of proceeding with an orderly arrangement, he has stormed it with a mob of ideas tumbling over and destroying one another.

But this confusion and contradiction in Mr. Burke's book is easily accounted for. When a man in a long cause attempts to steer his course by anything else than some polar truth or principle, he is sure to be lost. It is beyond the compass of his capacity to keep all the parts of an argument together, and make them unite in one issue, by any other means than having this guide always in view. Neither memory nor invention will supply the want of it. The former fails him, and the latter betrays him.

Notwithstanding the nonsense, for it deserves no better name, that Mr. Burke has asserted about hereditary succession, and that a Nation has not a right to form a Government for itself; it happened to fall in his way to give some account of what Government is.

"Government," says he, "is a contrivance of human wisdom."

Admitting that Government is a contrivance of human *wisdom,* it must necessarily follow, that hereditary succession and hereditary rights (as they are called), can make no part of it, because it is impossible to make wisdom hereditary; and on the other hand, that cannot be a wise contrivance, which in its operation may commit the Government of a Nation to the wisdom of an idiot.

The ground which Mr. Burke now takes is fatal to every part of his cause. The argument changes from hereditary rights to hereditary wisdom; and the question is, Who is the wisest man?

He must now shew that every one in the line of hereditary succession was a Solomon, or his title is not good to be a King.

What a stroke has Mr. Burke now made! To use a sailor's phrase, he has swabbed the deck, and scarcely left a name legible in the list of Kings; and he has mowed down and thinned the House of Peers, with a scythe as formidable as Death and Time.

But Mr. Burke appears to have been aware of this retort; and he has taken care to guard against it, by making Government to be not only a contrivance of human wisdom, but a monopoly of wisdom.

He puts the Nation as fools on one side, and places his Government of wisdom, all wise men of Gotham, on the other side; and he then proclaims and says that "Men have a RIGHT that their WANTS should be provided for by this wisdom." Having thus made proclamation, he next proceeds to explain to them what their *wants* are, and also what their *rights* are.

In this he has succeeded dexterously, for he makes their wants to be a *want* of wisdom; but as this is but cold comfort, he then informs them, that they have a *right*—not to any of the wisdom, but to be governed by it; and in order to impress them with a solemn reverence for this monopoly-government of wisdom, and of its vast capacity for all purposes, possible or impossible, right or wrong, he proceeds with astrological mysterious importance, to tell them its powers in these words: "The rights of men in Government are their advantages; and these are often in balance between differences of good; and in compromises sometimes between *good* and *evil* and sometimes between *evil* and *evil*. Political reason is a *computing principle;*

adding—subtracting—multiplying—and dividing, morally and not metaphysically or mathematically, true moral demonstrations.''

As the wondering audience, whom Mr. Burke supposes himself talking to, may not understand all this learned jargon, I will undertake to be its interpreter. The meaning, then, good people, of all this, is, That Government is governed by no principle whatever; that it can make evil good, or good evil, just as it pleases. In short, that Government is *arbitrary power*.

But there are some things which Mr. Burke has forgotten.

First, he has not shewn where the wisdom originally came from.

And *Secondly,* he has not shewn by what authority it first began to act.

In the manner he introduces the matter, it is either Government stealing wisdom, or wisdom stealing Government. It is without an origin, and its powers without authority. In short, it is usurpation.

Whether it be from a sense of shame, or from a consciousness of some radical defect in a Government necessary to be kept out of sight, or from both, or from any other cause, I undertake not to determine, but so it is, that a monarchical reasoner never traces Government to its source, or from its source. It is one of the *shibboleths* by which he may be known. A thousand years hence, those who shall live in America or in France, will look back with contemplative pride on the origin of their Governments, and say, *This was the work of our glorious ancestors!* But what can a monarchical talker say? What has he to exult in? Alas! he has nothing. A certain something forbids him to look back to a beginning, lest some robber, or some Robin Hood, should rise from the long obscurity of time and say, *I am the origin.* Hard as Mr. Burke laboured the Regency Bill and hereditary succession two years ago, and much as he dived for precedents, he still had not boldness enough to bring up William of Normandy, and say, *There is the head of the list, there is the fountain of honour;* the son of a prostitute and the plunderer of the English Nation.

The opinions of men with respect to Government are changing fast in all countries. The Revolutions in America and France have thrown a beam of light over the world, which reaches into man. The enormous expense of Governments has provoked people to think, by making them feel; and when once the veil begins to rend, it admits not of repair. Ignorance is of a peculiar nature: and once dispelled, it is impossible to re-establish it. It is not originally a thing of itself, but is only the absence of knowledge; and though man may be *kept* ignorant, he cannot be *made* ignorant.

The mind, in discovering truth, acts in the same manner as it acts through the eye in discovering objects; when once any object has been seen, it is impossible to put the mind back to the same condition it was in before it saw it.

Those who talk of a counter-revolution in France, show how little they understand of man. There does not exist in the compass of language an arrangement of words to express so much as the means of effecting a counter-revolution. The means must be an obliteration of knowledge; and it has never yet been discovered how to make man *unknow* his knowledge, or *unthink* his thoughts.

Mr. Burke is labouring in vain to stop the progress of knowledge; and it comes with the worse grace from him, as there is a certain transaction known in the city which renders him suspected of being a pensioner in a fictitious name. This may account for some strange doctrine he has advanced in his book, which though he points it at the Revolution Society, is effectually directed against the whole Nation.

"The King of England," says he, "holds *his* Crown" (for it does not belong to the Nation, according to Mr.

Burke) "in *contempt* of the choice of the Revolution Society, who have not a single vote for a King among them either *individually* or *collectively*; and his Majesty's heirs each in their time and order, will come to the Crown *with the same contempt* of their choice with which his Majesty has succeeded to that which he now wears."

As to who is King in England or elsewhere, or whether there is any King at all, or whether the people choose a Cherokee chief, or a Hessian hussar for a King, it is not a matter that I trouble myself about, be that to themselves; but with respect to the doctrine, so far as it relates to the rights of Men and Nations, it is as abominable as anything ever uttered in the most enslaved country under heaven. Whether it sounds worse to my ear, by not being accustomed to hear such despotism, than what it does to the ear of another person, I am not so well a judge of; but of its abominable principle I am at no loss to judge.

It is not the Revolution Society that Mr. Burke means; it is the Nation, as well in its *original* as in its *representative* character; and he has taken care to make himself understood, by saying that they have not a vote either *collectively* or *individually*. The Revolution Society is composed of citizens of all denominations, and of members of both the Houses of Parliament; and consequently, if there is not a right to a vote in any of the characters, there can be no right to any either in the Nation or in its Parliament. This ought to be a caution to every country how it imports foreign families to be Kings. It is somewhat curious to observe, that although the people of England have been in the habit of talking about Kings, it is always a foreign house of Kings, hating foreigners yet governed by them. It is now the House of Brunswick, one of the petty tribes of Germany.

It has hitherto been the practice of the English Parliaments to regulate what was called the succession (taking it for granted that the Nation then continued to accord to the form of annexing a monarchical branch to its Government; for without this the Parliament could not have had authority to have sent either to Holland or to Hanover, or to impose a King upon the Nation against its will). And this must be the utmost limit to which Parliament can go upon the case; but the right of the Nation goes to the *whole* case, because it has the right of changing its *whole* form of Government. The right of a Parliament is only a right in trust, a right by delegation, and that but from a very small part of the Nation; and one of its Houses has not even this. But the right of the Nation is an original right, as universal as taxation. The Nation is the paymaster of everything, and everything must conform to its general will.

I remember taking notice of a speech in what is called the English House of Peers, by the then Earl of Shelburne, and I think it was at the time he was Minister, which is applicable to this case. I do not directly charge my memory with every particular; but the words and the purport, as nearly as I remember, were these: *That the form of a Government was a matter wholly at the will of a Nation at all times, that if it chose a monarchical form, it had a right to do so; and if it afterwards chose to be a Republic, it had a right to be a Republic, and to say to a King, "We have no longer any occasion for you."*

When Mr. Burke says that "his Majesty's heirs and successors, each in their time and order, will come to the Crown with the *same contempt* of their choice with which his Majesty has succeeded to that he wears," it is saying too much even to the humblest individual in the country, part of whose daily labour goes towards making up the million sterling a-year, which the country gives the person it stiles a King. Government with insolence is despotism; but when contempt is added it becomes worse; and to pay for contempt is the excess of slavery. This species of Government comes from Germany; and reminds me of what one of the Brunswick soldiers told me, who was taken prisoner by the Americans in the late war: "Ah!" said he, "America is a fine free country, it is worth the people's fighting for; I know the difference by knowing my own; in my country, if the prince says eat straw, we eat straw." God help that country, thought I, be it England or elsewhere, whose liberties are to be protected by German principles of Government, and Princes of Brunswick!

As Mr. Burke sometimes speaks of England, sometimes of France, and sometimes of the world, and of Government in general, it is difficult to answer his book without apparently meeting him on the same ground. Although principles of Government are general subjects, it is next to impossible, in many cases, to separate them from the idea of place and circumstance, and the more so when circumstances are put for arguments, which is frequently the case with Mr. Burke.

In the former part of his book, addressing himself to the people of France, he says: "No experience has taught us (meaning the English), that in any other course or method than that of a *hereditary crown,* can our liberties be regularly perpetuated and preserved sacred as our *hereditary right.*" I asked Mr. Burke, Who is to take them away? M. de la Fayette, in speaking to France, says: "For a Nation to be free, it is sufficient that she wills it." But Mr. Burke represents England as wanting capacity to take care of itself, and that its liberties must be taken care of by a King holding it in "contempt." If England is sunk to this, it is preparing itself to eat straw, as in Hanover, or in Brunswick. But besides the folly of the declaration, it happens that the facts are all against Mr. Burke. It was by the Government *being hereditary,* that the liberties of the people were endangered. Charles I. and

James II. are instances of this truth; yet neither of them went so far as to hold the Nation in contempt.

As it is sometimes of advantage to the people of one country to hear what those of other countries have to say respecting it, it is possible that the people of France may learn something from Mr. Burke's book, and that the people of England may also learn something from the answers it will occasion. When Nations fall out about freedom, a wide field of debate is opened. The argument commences with the rights of war, without its evils; and as knowledge is the object contended for, the party that sustains the defeat obtains the prize.

Mr. Burke talks about what he calls an hereditary crown, as if it were some production of Nature; or as if, like time, it had a power to operate, not only independently, but in spite of man; or as if it were a thing or a subject universally consented to. Alas! it has none of those properties, but is the reverse of them all. It is a thing in imagination, the propriety of which is more than doubted, and the legality of which in a few years will be denied.

But, to arrange this matter in a clearer view than what general expression can convey, it will be necessary to state the distinct heads under which (what is called) an hereditary crown, or more properly speaking, an hereditary succession to the Government of a Nation, can be considered; which are—

First, the right of a particular Family to establish itself.

Secondly, the right of a Nation to establish a particular Family.

With respect to the first of these heads, that of a Family establishing itself with hereditary powers on its own authority, and independent of the consent of a Nation, all men will concur in calling it despotism, and it would be trespassing on their understanding to attempt to prove it.

But the second head, that of a Nation establishing a particular Family with hereditary powers, does not present itself as despotism on the first reflection; but if men will permit a second reflection to take place, and carry that reflection forward but one remove out of their own persons to that of their offspring, they will then see that hereditary succession becomes in its consequences the same despotism to others, which they reprobated for themselves. It operates to preclude the consent of the succeeding generations; and the preclusion of consent is despotism. When the person who at any time shall be in possession of a Government, or those who stand in succession to him, shall say to a Nation, I hold this power in "contempt" of you, it signifies not on what authority he pretends to say it. It is no relief, but an aggravation to a person in slavery, to reflect that he was sold by his parent; and as that which heightens the criminality of an act cannot be produced to prove the legality of it, hereditary succession cannot be established as a legal thing.

In order to arrive at a more perfect decision on this head, it will be proper to consider the generation which undertakes to establish a family with hereditary powers, apart and separate from the generations which are to follow; and also to consider the character in which the first generation acts with respect to succeeding generations.

The generation which first selects a person, and puts him at the head of its Government, either with the title of King, or any other distinction, acts its own choice, be it wise or foolish, as a free agent for itself.

The person so set up is not hereditary, but selected and appointed; and the generation who sets him up, does not live under an hereditary Government, but under a Government of its own choice and establishment.

Were the generation who sets him up, and the person so set up, to live for ever, it never could become hereditary succession; and of consequence hereditary succession can only follow on the death of the first parties.

As, therefore, hereditary succession is out of the question with respect to the *first* generation, we have now to consider the character in which *that* generation acts with respect to the commencing generation, and to all succeeding ones.

It assumes a character, to which it has neither right nor title. It changes itself from a legislator to a testator, and affects to make its WILL, which is to have operation after the demise of the makers, to bequeath the Government: and it not only attempts to bequeath, but to establish on the succeeding generation, a new and different form of Government under which itself lived. Itself, as already observed, lived not under a hereditary Government, but under a Government of its own choice and establishment; and it now attempts, by virtue of a will and testament (and which it has not authority to make), to take from the commencing generation, and all future ones, the rights and free agency by which itself acted.

But, exclusive of the right which any generation has to act collectively as a testator, the objects to which it applies itself in this case, are not within the compass of any law, or of any will or testament.

The rights of men in society, are neither devisable or transferable, nor annihilable, but are descendable only, and it is not in the power of any generation to intercept finally, and cut off the descent.

If the present generation, or any other, are disposed to be slaves, it does not lessen the right of the succeeding generation to be free. Wrongs cannot have a legal descent.

When Mr. Burke attempts to maintain that the English Nation did at the Revolution of 1688, most solemnly renounce and abdicate their rights for themselves, and for all their posterity for ever, he speaks a language that merits not reply, and which can only excite contempt for his prostitute principles, or pity for his ignorance.

In whatever light hereditary succession, as growing out of the will and testament of some former generation, presents itself, it is an absurdity. A cannot make a will to take from B the property of B, and give it to C; yet this is the manner in which (what is called) hereditary succession by law operates. A certain former generation made a will to take away the rights of the commencing generation, and all future ones, and convey those rights to a third person, who afterwards comes forward, and tells them, in Mr. Burke's language, that they have *no rights,* that their rights are already bequeathed to him and that he will govern in *contempt* of them. From such principles, and such ignorance, Good Lord deliver the world!

But, after all, what is the metaphor called a Crown, or rather what is Monarchy? Is it a thing, or is it a name, or is it a fraud? Is it a "contrivance of human wisdom," or of human craft to obtain money from a Nation under specious pretenses? Is it a thing necessary to a Nation? If it is, in what does that necessity consist, what services does it perform, what is its business, and what are its merits? Does the virtue consist in the metaphor, or in the man? Doth the goldsmith that makes the crown, make the virtue also? Doth it operate like Fortunatus's wishing-cap, or Harlequin's wooden sword? Doth it make a man a conjuror? In fine, what is it? It appears to be a something going much out of fashion, falling into ridicule, and rejected in some countries both as unnecessary and expensive. In America it is considered as an absurdity; and in France it has so far declined, that the goodness of the man and the respect for his personal character, are the only things that preserve the appearance of its existence.

If Government be what Mr. Burke describes it, "a

contrivance of human wisdom," I might ask him, if wisdom was at such a low ebb in England, that it was become necessary to import it from Holland and from Hanover? But I will do the country the justice to say, that was not the case; and even if it was, it mistook the cargo. The wisdom of every country, when properly exerted, is sufficient for all its purposes; and there could exist no more real occasion in England to have sent for a Dutch stadtholder, or a German elector, than there was in America to have done a similar thing. If a country does not understand its own affairs, how is a foreigner to understand them, who knows neither its laws, its manners, nor its language? If there existed a man so transcendently wise above all others, that his wisdom was necessary to instruct a Nation, some reason might be offered for Monarchy; but when we cast our eyes about a country, and observe how every part understands its own affairs; and when we look around the world, and see that of all men in it, the race of Kings are the most insignificant in capacity, our reason cannot fail to ask us—What are those men kept for?

If there be anything in Monarchy which we people of America do not understand, I wish Mr. Burke would be so kind as to inform us. I see in America, a Government extending over a country ten times as large as England, and conducted with regularity, for a fortieth part of the expence which Government costs in England. If I ask a man in America if he wants a King, he retorts, and asks me if I take him for an idiot? How is it that this difference happens? are we more or less wise than others? I see in America the generality of people living in a stile of plenty unknown in monarchical countries; and I see that the principle of its Government, which is that of the *equal Rights of Man,* is making a rapid progress in the world.

If Monarchy is a useless thing, why is it kept up anywhere? and if a necessary thing, how can it be dispensed with? That *civil Government* is necessary, all civilised Nations will agree: but civil Government is republican Government. All that part of the Government of England which begins with the office of constable, and proceeds through the department of magistrate, quarter-sessions, and general assize, including trial by jury, is republican Government. Nothing of Monarchy appears in any part of it, except the name which William the Conqueror imposed upon the English, that of obliging them to call him "Their Sovereign Lord the King."

It is easy to conceive that a band of interested men, such as placemen, pensioners, lords of the bedchamber, lords of the kitchen, lords of the necessary-house, and the Lord knows what besides, can find as many reasons for Monarchy as their salaries, paid at the expence of the country, amount to; but if I ask the farmer, the manufacturer, the merchant, the tradesman, and down through all the occupations of life to the common labourer, what service Monarchy is to him? he can give me no answer. If I ask him what Monarchy is, he believes it is something like a sinecure.

Notwithstanding the taxes of England amount to almost seventeen millions a year said to be for the expences of Government, it is still evident that the sense of the nation is left to govern itself, and does govern itself, by magistrates and juries, almost at its own charge, on republican principles, exclusive of the expence of taxes. The salaries of the judges are almost the only charge that is paid out of the revenue. Considering that all the internal Government is executed by the people, the taxes of England ought to be the lightest of any nation in Europe; instead of which, they are the contrary. As this cannot be counted on the score of civil Government, the subject necessarily extends itself to the Monarchical part.

When the people of England sent for George the

First, (and it would puzzle a wiser man than Mr. Burke to discover for what he could be wanted, or what service he could render) they ought at least to have conditioned for the abandonment of Hanover. Besides the endless German intrigues that must follow from a German Elector being King of England, there is a natural impossibility of uniting in the same person the principles of freedom and the principles of despotism, or as it is usually called in England arbitrary power. A German Elector is in his electorate a despot; how then could it be expected that he should be attached to principles of liberty in one country while his interest in another was to be supported by despotism? The union cannot exist; and it might easily have been foreseen that German electors would make German Kings, or in Mr. Burke's words, would assume Government with "contempt." The English have been in the habit of considering a King of England only in the character in which he appears to them; whereas the same person, while the connection lasts, has a home-seat in another country, the interest of which is different to their own, and the principles of the Governments in opposition to each other. To such a person England will appear as a town-residence, and the electorate as the estate. The English may wish, as I believe they do, success to the principles of liberty in France, or in Germany; but a German Elector trembles for the fate of despotism in his electorate; and the Dutchy of Mecklenburg, where the present Queen's family governs, is under the same wretched state of arbitrary power, and the people in slavish vassalage.

There never was a time when it became the English to watch continental intrigues more circumspectly than at the present moment, and to distinguish the politics of the electorate from the politics of the Nation. The Revolution of France has entirely changed the ground with respect to England and France, as Nations; but the German despots, with Prussia at their head, are combining against Liberty; and the fondness of Mr. Pitt for office, and the interest which all his family connections have obtained, do not give sufficient security against this intrigue.

As everything which passes in the world becomes matter for history, I will now quit this subject, and take a concise review of the state of parties and politics in England, as Mr. Burke has done in France.

Whether the present reign commenced with contempt, I leave to Mr. Burke; certain, however, it is that it had strongly that appearance. The animosity of the English Nation, it is very well remembered, ran high; and, had the true principles of Liberty been as well understood then as they now promise to be, it is probable the Nation would not have patiently submitted to so much. George the First and Second were sensible of a rival in the remains of the Stuarts; and as they could not but consider themselves as standing on their good behaviour, they had prudence to keep their German principles of Government to themselves; but as the Stuart family wore away, the prudence became less necessary.

The contest between rights, and what were called prerogatives, continued to heat the Nation till some time after the conclusion of the American War—when all at once it fell a calm—execration exchanged itself for applause, and Court popularity sprang up like a mushroom in a night.

To account for this sudden transition, it is proper to observe that there are two distinct species of popularity; the one excited by merit, and the other by resentment. As the Nation had formed itself into two parties, and each was extolling the merits of its parliamentary champions for and against prerogative, nothing could operate to give a more general shock than an immediate coalition of the champions themselves. The partisans of each being thus suddenly left in the lurch, and mutually heated with disgust at the measure, felt no other relief than uniting in a common execration against both. A higher stimulus of resentment being thus excited than what the contest on prerogatives occasioned, the Nation quitted all former objects of rights and wrongs, and sought only that of gratification. The indignation at the Coalition so effectually superseded the indignation against the Court as to extinguish it; and without any change of principles on the part of the Court, the same people who had reprobated its despotism united with it to revenge themselves on the Coalition Parliament. The case was not, which they liked best, but which they hated most; and the least hated passed for love. The dissolution of the Coalition Parliament, as it afforded the means of gratifying the resentment of the Nation, could not fail to be popular: and from hence arose the popularity of the Court.

Transitions of this kind exhibit a Nation under the Government of temper, instead of a fixed and steady principle; and having once committed itself, however rashly, it feels itself urged along to justify, by continuance, its first proceeding. Measures which at other times it would censure, it now approves, and acts persuasion upon itself to suffocate its judgment.

On the return of a new Parliament, the new Minister, Mr. Pitt, found himself in a secure majority; and the Nation gave him credit, not out of regard to himself, but because it had resolved to do it out of resentment to another. He introduced himself to public notice by a proposed reform of Parliament, which in its operation would have amounted to a public justification of corruption. The Nation was to be at the expence of buying up the rotten boroughs, whereas it ought to punish the persons who deal in the traffic.

Passing over the two bubbles of the Dutch business and the million a-year to sink the national debt, the matter which most presents itself, is the affair of the

Regency. Never, in the course of my observation, was delusion more successfully acted, nor a Nation more completely deceived. But, to make this appear, it will be necessary to go over the circumstances.

Mr. Fox had stated in the House of Commons, that the Prince of Wales, as heir in succession, had a right in himself to assume the Government. This was opposed by Mr. Pitt; and, so far as the opposition was confined to the doctrine, it was just. But the principles which Mr. Pitt maintained on the contrary side were as bad, or worse in their extent, than those of Mr. Fox; because they went to establish an Aristocracy over the Nation, and over the small representation it has in the House of Commons.

Whether the English form of Government be good or bad, it is not in this case the question; but, taking it as it stands, without regard to its merits or demerits, Mr. Pitt was farther from the point than Mr. Fox.

It is supposed to consist of three parts: while therefore the Nation is disposed to continue this form, the parts have a *national standing*, independent of each other, and are not the creatures of each other. Had Mr. Fox passed through Parliament, and said that the person alluded to claimed on the ground of the Nation, Mr. Pitt must then have contended (what he called) the right of the Parliament against the right of the Nation.

By the appearance which the contest made, Mr. Fox took the hereditary ground, and Mr. Pitt the parliamentary ground; but the fact is, they both took hereditary ground, and Mr. Pitt took the worse of the two.

What is called the Parliament is made up of two Houses, one of which is more hereditary, and more beyond the controul of the Nation than what the Crown (as it is called) is supposed to be. It is an hereditary Aristocracy, assuming and asserting indefeasible, irrevocable rights and authority, wholly independent of the Nation. Where, then, was the merited popularity of exalting this hereditary power over another hereditary power less independent of the Nation than what itself assumed to be, and of absorbing the rights of the Nation into a House over which it has neither election nor controul?

The general impulse of the Nation was right; but it acted without reflection. It approved the opposition made to the right set up by Mr. Fox, without perceiving that Mr. Pitt was supporting another indefeasible right more remote from the Nation in opposition to it.

With respect to the House of Commons, it is elected but by a small part of the Nation; but were the election as universal as taxation, which it ought to be, it would still be only the organ of the Nation, and cannot possess inherent rights. When the National Assembly of France resolves a matter, the resolve is made in right of the Nation; but Mr. Pitt, on all national questions, so far as they refer to the House of Commons, absorbs the rights of the nation into the organ, and makes the organ into a Nation, and the Nation itself into a cypher.

In a few words, the question on the Regency was a question of a million a-year, which is appropriated to the executive department; and Mr. Pitt could not possess himself of any management of this sum, without setting up the supremacy of Parliament; and when this was accomplished, it was indifferent who should be Regent, as he must be Regent at his own cost. Among the curiosities which this contentious debate afforded, was that of making the Great Seal into a King, the affixing of which to an act was to be royal authority. If, therefore, Royal Authority is a Great Seal, it consequently is in itself nothing; and a good Constitution would be of infinitely more value to the Nation than what the three nominal powers, as they now stand, are worth.

The continual use of the word *Constitution* in the English Parliament shews there is none; and that the whole is merely a form of Government without a Constitution, and constituting itself with what powers it pleases. If there were a Constitution it certainly could be referred to; and the debate on any constitutional point would terminate by producing the Constitution. One member says this is constitution, and another says that is constitution—to-day it is one thing, to-morrow it is something else—while the maintaining the debate proves there is none. Constitution is now the cant word of Parliament, tuning itself to the ear of the Nation. Formerly it was the *universal supremacy of Parliament—the omnipotence of Parliament:* but since the progress of Liberty in France, those phrases have a despotic harshness in their note; and the English Parliament have catched the fashion from the National Assembly, but without the substance, of speaking of *Constitution.*

As the present generation of people in England did not make the Government, they are not accountable for any of its defects; but, that sooner or later, it must come into their hands to undergo a constitutional reformation, is as certain as that the same thing has happened in France. If France, with a revenue of nearly twenty-four millions sterling, with an extent of rich and fertile country above four times larger than England, with a population of twenty-four millions of inhabitants to support taxation, with upwards of ninety millions sterling of gold and silver circulating in the Nation, and with a debt less than the present debt of England—still found it necessary, from whatever cause, to come to a settlement of its affairs, it solves the problem of funding for both countries.

It is out of the question to say how long what is called the English Constitution has lasted, and to argue from thence how long it is to last; the question is, how long can the funding system last? It is a thing but of modern invention, and has not yet continued beyond the life of a man; yet in that short space it has so far accumulated, that, together with the current expences, it requires an amount of taxes at least equal to the whole landed rental of the Nation in acres to defray the annual expenditure. That a Government could not have always gone on by the same system which has been followed for the last seventy years, must be evident to every man; and for the same reason it cannot always go on.

The funding system is not money; neither is it, properly speaking, credit. It, in effect, creates upon paper the sum which it appears to borrow, and lays on a tax to keep the imaginary capital alive by the payment of interest and sends the annuity to market, to be sold for paper already in circulation. If any credit is given, it is to the disposition of the people to pay the tax, and not to the government, which lays it on. When this disposition expires, what is supposed to be the credit of Government expires with it. The instance of France under the former Government, shews that it is impossible to compel the payment of taxes by force, when a whole Nation is determined to take its stand upon that ground.

Mr. Burke, in his review of the finances of France, states the quantity of gold and silver in France, at about eighty-eight millions sterling. In doing this, he has, I presume, divided by the difference of exchange, instead of the standard of twenty-four livres to a pound sterling; for M. Neckar's statement, from which Mr. Burke's is taken, is *two thousand two hundred millions of livres*, which is upwards of ninety-one million and a half sterling.

M. Neckar in France, and Mr. George Chalmers of the Office of Trade and Plantation in England, of which Lord Hawkesbury is president, published nearly about the same time (1786) an account of the quantity of money in each Nation, from the returns of the Mint of each Nation. Mr. Chalmers, from the returns of the English Mint at the Tower of London, states the quantity of money in England, including Scotland and Ireland, to be twenty millions sterling.

M. Neckar says that the amount of money in France, recoined from the old coin which was called in, was two thousand five hundred millions of livres (upwards of one hundred and four millions sterling); and, after deducting for waste, and what may be in the West Indies and other possible circumstances, states the circulation quantity at home to be ninety-one millions and a half sterling; but taking it as Mr. Burke has put it, it is sixty-eight millions more than the national quantity in England.

That the quantity of money in France cannot be under this sum, may at once be seen from the state of the French Revenue, without referring to the records of the French Mint for proofs. The Revenue of France, prior to the Revolution, was nearly twenty-four millions sterling; and as paper had then no existence in France the whole revenue was collected in gold and silver; and it would have been impossible to have collected such a quantity of revenue upon a less national quantity than M. Neckar has stated. Before the establishment of paper in England, the revenue was about a fourth part of the national amount of gold and silver, as may be known by referring to the revenue prior to King William and the quantity of money stated to be in the Nation at that time, which was nearly as much as it is now.

It can be of no real service to a Nation, to impose upon itself, or to permit itself to be imposed upon; but the prejudices of some, and the imposition of others, have always represented France as a Nation possessing but little money—whereas the quantity is not only more than four times what the quantity is in England, but is considerably greater on a proportion of numbers. To account for this deficiency on the part of England, some reference should be had to the English system of funding. It operates to multiply paper, and to substitute it in the room of money, in various shapes; and the more paper is multiplied, the more opportunities are afforded to export the specie; and it admits of a possibility (by extending it to small notes) of increasing paper till there is no money left.

I know this is not a pleasant subject to English readers; but the matters I am going to mention, are so important in themselves, as to require the attention of men interested in money transactions of a public nature. There is a circumstance stated by M. Neckar, in his treatise on the administration of the finances, which has never been attended to in England, but which forms the only basis whereon to estimate the quantity of money (gold and silver) which ought to be in every Nation in Europe, to preserve a relative proportion with other nations.

Lisbon and Cadiz are the two ports into which money, gold and silver, from South America are imported, and which afterwards divide and spread themselves over Europe by means of commerce, and increase the quantity of money in all parts of Europe. If, therefore, the amount of the annual importation into Europe can be known, and the relative proportion of the foreign commerce of the several nations by which it can be distributed can be ascertained, they give a rule sufficiently true, to ascertain the quantity of money which ought to be found in any Nation, at any given time.

M. Neckar shows from the registers of Lisbon and Cadiz, that the importation of gold and silver into Europe, is five millions sterling annually. He has not taken it on a single year, but on an average of fifteen succeeding years, from 1763 to 1777, both inclusive; in which time the amount was one thousand eight hundred million livres, which is seventy-five millions sterling.

From the commencement of the Hanover succession in 1714 to the time Mr. Chalmers published is seventy-two years; and the quantity imported into Europe, in that time, would be three hundred and sixty millions sterling.

If the foreign commerce of Great Britain be stated at a sixth part of what the whole foreign commerce of Europe amounts to (which is probably an inferior estimation to what the gentlemen at the exchange would allow) the proportion which Britain should draw by commerce of this sum, to keep herself on a proportion with the rest of Europe, would be also a sixth part, which is sixty millions sterling; and if the same allowance for waste and accident be made for England which M. Neckar makes for France, the quantity remaining after these deductions would be fifty-two millions; and this sum ought to have been in the Nation (at the time Mr. Chalmers published), in addition to the sum which was in the Nation at the commencement of the Hanover succession, and to have made in the whole at least sixty-six millions sterling; instead of which there were but twenty millions, which is forty-six millions below its proportionate quantity.

As the quantity of gold and silver imported into Lisbon and Cadiz is more exactly ascertained than that of any commodity imported into England, and as the quantity of money coined at the Tower of London is still more positively known, the leading facts do not admit of controversy. Either, therefore, the commerce of England is unproductive of profit, or the gold and silver which it brings in leak continually away by unseen means at the average rate of about three-quarters of a million a year, which, in the course of seventy-two years, accounts for the deficiency; and its absence is supplied by paper.

The Revolution of France is attended with many novel circumstances, not only in the political sphere, but in the circle of money transactions. Among others, it shews that a Government may be in a state of insolvency and a Nation rich. So far as the fact is confined to the late Government of France, it was insolvent; because the Nation would no longer support its extravagance, and therefore it could no longer support itself—but with respect to the Nation all the means existed. A Government may be said to be insolvent every time it applies to the Nation to discharge its arrears. The insolvency of the late Government of France and the present Government of England differed in no other respect than as the disposition of the people differ. The people of France refused their aid to the old Government; and the people of England submit to taxation without enquiry. What is called the Crown in England has been insolvent several times; the last of which, publicly known, was in May, 1777, when it applied to the nation to discharge upwards of £600,000 private debts, which otherwise it could not pay.

It was the error of Mr. Pitt, Mr. Burke, and all those who were unacquainted with the affairs of France, to confound the French Nation with the French Government. The French Nation, in effect, endeavoured to render the late Government insolvent for the purpose of taking Government into its own hands: and it reserved its means for the support of the new Government. In a country of such vast extent and population as France the natural means cannot be wanting; and the political means appear the instant the Nation is disposed to permit them. When Mr. Burke, in a speech last winter in the British Parliament, *cast his eyes over the map of Europe, and saw a chasm that once was France,* he talked like a dreamer of dreams. The same natural France existed as before, and all the natural means existed with it. The only chasm was that which the extinction of despotism had left, and which was to be filled up with a Constitution more formidable in resources than the power which had expired.

Although the French Nation rendered the late Government insolvent, it did not permit the insolvency to act towards the creditors; and the creditors, considering the Nation as the real pay-master, and the Government only as the agent, rested themselves on the Nation, in preference to the Government. This appears greatly to disturb Mr. Burke, as the precedent is fatal to the policy by which Governments have supposed themselves secure. They have contracted debts, with a view of attaching what is called the monied interest of a Nation to their support; but the example in France shews that the permanent security of the creditor is in the Nation, and not in the Government; and that in all possible Revolutions that may happen in Governments, the means are always with the Nation, and the Nation always in existence. Mr. Burke argues that the creditors ought to have abided the fate of the Government which they trusted; but the National Assembly considered them as the creditors of the Nation, and not of the Government—of the master, and not of the steward.

Notwithstanding the late Government could not discharge the current expences, the present Government has paid off a great part of the capital. This has been accomplished by two means; the one by lessening the expences of Government, and the other by the sale of the monastic and ecclesiastical landed estates. The devotees and penitent debauchees, extortioners and misers of former days, to ensure themselves a better world than that which they were about to leave, had bequeathed immense property in trust to the priesthood, for *pious uses*; and the priesthood kept it for themselves. The National Assembly has ordered it to be sold for the good of the whole Nation, and the priesthood to be decently provided for.

In consequence of the Revolution, the annual interest of the debt of France will be reduced at least six millions sterling, by paying off upwards of one hundred millions of the capital; which, with lessening the former expences of Government at least three millions, will place France in a situation worthy the imitation of Europe.

Upon a whole review of the subject, how vast is the contrast! While Mr. Burke has been talking of a general bankruptcy in France, the National Assembly has been paying off the capital of its debt; and while taxes have increased near a million a year in England, they have lowered several millions a year in France. Not a word has either Mr. Burke or Mr. Pitt said about the French affairs, or the state of the French finances, in the present session of Parliament. The subject begins to be too well understood, and imposition serves no longer.

There is a general enigma running through the whole of Mr. Burke's book. He writes in a rage against the National Assembly; but what is he enraged about? If his assertions were as true as they are groundless, and that France, by her Revolution, had annihilated her power, and become what he calls a *chasm,* it might excite the grief of a Frenchman (considering himself as a national man), and provoke his rage against the National Assembly; but why should it excite the rage of Mr. Burke? Alas! it is not the Nation of France that Mr. Burke means, but the COURT; and every Court in Europe, dreading the same fate, is in mourning. He writes neither in the character of a Frenchman nor an Englishman, but in the fawning character of that creature known in all countries, and a friend to none, a COURTIER. Whether it be the Court of Versailles, or the Court of St. James, or of Carlton House, or the Court in expectation, signifies not; for the caterpillar principle of all courts and courtiers are alike. They form a common policy throughout Europe, detached and separate from the interest of Nations; and while they appear to quarrel, they agree to plunder. Nothing can be more terrible to a Court or courtier than the Revolution of France. That which is a blessing to Nations is bitterness to them: and as their existence depends on the duplicity of a country, they tremble at the approach of principles, and dread the precedent that threatens their overthrow.

Conclusion

REASON and Ignorance, the opposite of each other, influence the great bulk of mankind. If either of these can be rendered sufficiently extensive in a country, the machinery of Government goes easily on. Reason obeys itself; and Ignorance submits to whatever is dictated to it.

The two modes of Government which prevail in the world, are—

First, Government by election and representation.

Secondly, Government by hereditary succession.

The former is generally known by the name of Republic; the latter by that of Monarchy and Aristocracy.

Those two distinct and opposite forms erect themselves on the two distinct and opposite bases of Reason and Ignorance.

As the exercise of Government requires talents and abilities, and as talents and abilities cannot have hereditary descent, it is evident that hereditary succession requires a belief from man to which his reason cannot subscribe, and which can only be established upon his ignorance; and the more ignorant any country is, the better it is fitted for this species of Government.

On the contrary, Government, in a well-constituted Republic, requires no belief from man beyond what his reason can give.

He sees the *rationale* of the whole system, its origin and its operation; and as it is best supported when best understood, the human faculties act with boldness, and acquire under this form of Government a gigantic manliness.

As, therefore, each of those forms acts on a different base, the one moving freely by the aid of reason, the other by ignorance, we have next to consider, what it is that gives motion to the species of Government which is called Mixed Government, or, as it is sometimes ludicrously stiled, a *Government of this, that and t'other*.

The moving power in this species of Government is of necessity Corruption. However imperfect election and representation may be in Mixed Governments, they still give exercise to a greater portion of reason than is convenient to the hereditary part; and therefore it becomes necessary to buy the reason up.

A Mixed Government is an imperfect everything, cementing and soldering the discordant parts together by corruption, to act as a whole. Mr. Burke appears highly disgusted that France, since she had resolved on a Revolution, did not adopt what he calls *"A British Constitution;"* and the regretful manner in which he expresses himself on this occasion implies a suspicion that the British Constitution needed something to keep its defects in countenance.

In Mixed Governments there is no responsibility: the parts cover each other till responsibility is lost; and the Corruption which moves the machine, contrives at the same time its own escape. When it is laid down as a maxim, that *a King can do no wrong*, it places him in a state of similar security with that of idiots and persons insane, and responsibility is out of the question with respect to himself.

It then descends upon the Minister, who shelters himself under a majority in Parliament, which by places, pensions, and corruption, he can always command; and that majority justifies itself by the same authority with which it protects the Minister. In this rotary motion, responsibility is thrown off from the parts, and from the whole.

When there is part in a Government which can do no wrong, it implies that it does nothing; and is only the machine of another power, by whose advice and direction it acts.

What is supposed to be the King in a Mixed Government is the Cabinet; and as the Cabinet is always a part of the Parliament, and the members justifying in one character what they advise and act in another, a Mixed Government becomes a continual enigma; entailing upon a country, by the quantity of corruption necessary to solder the parts, the expence of supporting all the forms of Government at once, and finally resolving them into a Government by committee; in which the advisers, the actors, the approvers, the justifiers, the persons responsible, and the persons not responsible, are the same persons.

By this pantomimical contrivance, and change of scene and character, the parts help each other out in matters which neither of them singly would assume to act.

When money is to be obtained, the mass of variety apparently dissolves, and a profusion of parliamentary praises passes between the parts. Each admires with astonishment, the wisdom, the liberality, and disinterestedness of the other; and all of them breathe a pitying sigh at the burdens of the Nation.

But in a well-constituted Republic, nothing of this soldering, praising, and pitying, can take place; the representation being equal throughout the country, and compleat in itself, however it may be arranged into legislative and executive, they have all one and the same natural source. The parts are not foreigners to each other, like Democracy, Aristocracy, and Monarchy. As there are no discordant distinctions, there is nothing to corrupt by compromise, nor confound by contrivance. Public measures appeal of themselves to the understanding of the Nation, and resting on their own merits, disown any flattering applications to vanity. The continual whine of lamenting the burden of taxes, however successfully it may be practised in Mixed Governments, is inconsistent with the sense and spirit of a Republic. If taxes are necessary, they are of course advantageous, but if they require an apology, the apology itself implies an impeachment. Why, then, is man imposed upon, or why does he impose upon himself?

When men are spoken of as Kings and subjects, or when Government is mentioned under the distinct or combined heads of Monarchy, Aristocracy, and Democracy, what is it that *reasoning* man is to understand by the terms? If there really existed in the world two or more distinct and separate *elements* of human power, we should then see the several origins to which those terms would descriptively apply; but as there is but one species of man, there can be but one element of human power, and that element is man himself. Monarchy, Aristocracy, and Democracy, are but creatures of imagination; and a thousand such may be contrived as well as three.

From the Revolutions of America and France, and the symptoms that have appeared in other countries, it is evident that the opinion of the world is changed with respect to systems of Government, and that Revolutions are not within the compass of political calculations.

The progress of time and circumstances, which men assign to the accomplishment of great changes, is too mechanical to measure the force of the mind, and the rapidity of reflection, by which Revolutions are generated: All the old Governments have received a shock from those that already appear, and which were once more improbable, and are a greater subject of wonder, than a general Revolution in Europe would be now.

When we survey the wretched condition of Man, under the monarchical and hereditary systems of Government, dragged from his home by one power, or driven by another, and impoverished by taxes more than by enemies, it becomes evident that those systems are bad, and that a general Revolution in the principle and construction of Governments is necessary.

What is Government more than the management of the affairs of a Nation? It is not, and from its nature cannot be, the property of any particular man or family, but of the whole community, at whose expence it is supported; and though by force and contrivance it has been usurped into an inheritance, the usurpation cannot alter the right of things. Sovereignty, as a matter of right, appertains to the Nation only, and not to any individual; and a Nation has at all times an inherent, indefeasible right to abolish any form of Government it finds inconvenient, and to establish such as accords with its interest, disposition, and happiness. The romantic and barbarous distinction of men into Kings and subjects, though it may suit the conditions of courtiers, cannot that of citizens; and is exploded by the principle upon which Governments are now founded. Every citizen is a member of the sovereignty; and, as such, can acknowledge no personal subjection: and his obedience can be only to the laws.

When men think of what Government is, they must necessarily suppose it to possess a knowledge of all the objects and matters upon which its authority is to be exercised. In this view of Government, the Republican system, as established by America and France, operates to embrace the whole of a Nation; and the knowledge necessary to the interest of all the parts, is to be found in the centre, which the parts by representation form; but the old Governments are on a construction that excludes knowledge as well as happiness; Government by monks, who know nothing of the world beyond the walls of a convent, is as inconsistent as Government by Kings.

What we formerly called Revolutions, were little more than a change of persons, or an alteration of local circumstances. They rose and fell like things of course, and had nothing in their existence or their fate that could influence beyond the spot that produced them. But what we now see in the world, from the Revolutions of America and France, are a renovation of the natural order of things, a system of principles as universal as truth and the existence of man, and combining moral with political happiness and national prosperity.

"I. *Men are born, and always continue, free and equal in respect of their rights. Civil distinctions, therefore, can be founded only on public utility.*

II. *The end of all political associations is the preservation of the natural and imprescriptible rights of man; and these rights are liberty, property, security, and resistance of oppression.*

III. *The Nation is essentially the source of all sovereignty; nor can* ANY INDIVIDUAL, *or* ANY BODY OF MEN, *be entitled to any authority which is not expressly derived from it.*"

In these principles there is nothing to throw a Nation into confusion by inflaming ambition. They are calculated to call forth wisdom and abilities, and to exercise them for the public good, and not for the emolument or aggrandisement of particular descriptions of men or families. Monarchical sovereignty, the enemy of mankind, and the source of misery, is abolished; and sovereignty itself is restored to its natural and original place, the Nation. Were this the case throughout Europe, the cause of wars would be taken away.

It is attributed to Henry the Fourth of France, a

man of enlarged and benevolent heart, that he proposed, about the year 1610, a plan for abolishing war in Europe: the plan consisted in constituting an European Congress, or as the French authors stile it, a Pacific Republic, by appointing delegates from the several Nations who were to act as a Court of Arbitration in any disputes that might arise between Nation and Nation.

Had such a plan been adopted at the time it was proposed, the taxes of England and France, as two of the parties, would have been at least ten millions sterling annually to each nation less than they were at the commencement of the French Revolution.

To conceive a cause why such a plan has not been adopted (and that instead of a Congress for the purpose of *preventing* war, it has been called only to *terminate* a war, after a fruitless expence of several years), it will be necessary to consider the interest of Governments as a distinct interest to that of Nations.

Whatever is the cause of taxes to a Nation, becomes also the means of revenue to a Government. Every war terminates with an addition of taxes, and consequently with an addition of revenue; and in any event of war, in the manner they are now commenced and concluded, the power and interest of Governments are increased. War, therefore, from its productiveness, as it easily furnishes the pretence of necessity for taxes and appointments to places and offices, becomes a principal part of the system of old Governments; and to establish any mode to abolish war, however advantageous it might be to Nations, would be to take from such Government the most lucrative of its branches. The frivolous matters upon which war is made shew the disposition and avidity of Governments to uphold the system of war, and betray the motives upon which they act.

Why are not Republics plunged into war, but because the nature of their Government does not admit of an interest distinct from that of the Nation? Even Holland, though an ill-constructed Republic, and with a commerce extending over the world, existed nearly a century without war; and the instant the form of Government was changed in France the republican principles of peace and domestic prosperity and economy arose with the new Government; and the same consequences would follow the same causes in other nations.

As war is the system of Government on the old construction, the animosity which Nations reciprocally entertain is nothing more than what the policy of their Governments excites to keep up the spirit of the system. Each Government accuses the other of perfidy, intrigue, and ambition, as a means of heating the imagination of their respective Nations, and incensing them to hostilities. Man is not the enemy of Man, but through the medium of a false system of Government. Instead, therefore, of exclaiming against the ambition of Kings, the exclamation should be directed against the principle of such Governments; and instead of seeking to reform the individual, the wisdom of a Nation should apply itself to reform the system.

Whether the forms and maxims of Governments which are still in practice were adapted to the condition of the world at the period they were established is not in this case the question. The older they are the less correspondence can they have with the present state of things.

Time, and change of circumstances and opinions, have the same progressive effect in rendering modes of Government obsolete as they have upon customs and manners. Agriculture, commerce, manufactures, and the tranquil arts, by which the prosperity of Nations is best promoted, require a different system of Government, and a different species of knowledge to direct its operations, than what might have been required in the former condition of the world.

As it is not difficult to perceive, from the enlightened state of mankind, that hereditary Governments are verging to their decline, and that Revolutions on the broad basis of national sovereignty and Government by representation, are making their way in Europe, it would be an act of wisdom to anticipate their approach, and produce Revolutions by reason and accommodation, rather than commit them to the issue of convulsions.

From what we now see, nothing of reform in the political world ought to be held improbable. It is an age of Revolutions, in which everything may be looked for.

The intrigue of Courts, by which the system of war is kept up, may provoke a confederation of Nations to abolish it; and an European Congress to patronize the progress of free Government, and promote the civilisation of Nations with each other, is an event nearer in probability than once were the Revolutions and Alliance of France and America.

RIGHTS OF MAN

PART THE SECOND

COMBINING PRINCIPLES
AND PRACTICE

1792

To M. de la Fayette

After an acquaintance of nearly fifteen years in difficult situations in America, and various consultations in Europe, I feel a pleasure in presenting to you this small treatise in gratitude for your services to my beloved America, and as a testimony of my esteem for the virtues, public and private, which I know you to possess.

The only point upon which I could ever discover that we differed was not as to principles of Government, but as to time. For my own part I think it equally as injurious to good principles to permit them to linger, as to push them on too fast. That which you suppose accomplishable in fourteen or fifteen years I may believe practicable in a much shorter period. Mankind, as it appears to me, are always ripe enough to understand their true interest, provided it be presented clearly to their understanding, and that in a manner not to create suspicion by anything like self-design, nor offend by assuming too much. Where we would wish to reform we must not reproach.

When the American Revolution was established I

felt a disposition to sit serenely down and enjoy the calm. It did not appear to me that any object could afterwards arise great enough to make me quit tranquillity and feel as I had felt before. But when principle, and not place, is the energetic cause of action, a man, I find, is everywhere the same.

I am now once more in the public world; and as I have not a right to contemplate on so many years of remaining life as you have, I am resolved to labour as fast as I can; and as I am anxious for your aid and your company, I wish you to hasten your principles and overtake me.

If you make a campaign the ensuing spring, which it is most probable there will be no occasion for, I will come and join you. Should the campaign commence, I hope it will terminate in the extinction of German despotism, and in establishing the freedom of all Germany. When France shall be surrounded with Revolutions she will be in peace and safety, and her taxes, as well as those of Germany, will consequently become less.

Your sincere,
Affectionate friend,
THOMAS PAINE.

London, February 9, 1792.

Preface

When I began the chapter entitled the *Conclusion* in the former part of RIGHTS OF MAN, published last year, it was my intention to have extended it to a greater length; but in casting the whole matter in my mind which I wish to add, I found that it must either make the work too bulky, or contract my plan too much. I therefore brought it to a close as soon as the subject would admit, and reserved what I had further to say to another opportunity.

Several other reasons contributed to produce this determination. I wished to know the manner in which a work, written in a style of thinking and expression different to what had been customary in England, would be received before I proceeded farther. A great field was opening to the view of mankind by means of the French Revolution. Mr. Burke's outrageous opposition thereto brought the controversy into England. He attacked principles which he knew (from information) I would contest with him, because they are principles I believe to be good, and which I have contributed to establish, and conceive myself bound to defend. Had he not urged the controversy, I had most probably been a silent man.

Another reason for deferring the remainder of the

work was, that Mr. Burke promised in his first publication to renew the subject at another opportunity, and to make a comparison of what he called the English and French Constitutions. I therefore held myself in reserve for him. He has published two works since, without doing this: which he certainly would not have omitted, had the comparison been in his favour.

In his last work, his *"Appeal from the new to the old Whigs,"* he has quoted about ten pages from the *Rights of Man,* and having given himself the trouble of doing this, says he shall "not attempt in the smallest degree to refute them," meaning the principles therein contained. I am enough acquainted with Mr. Burke to know that he would if he could. But instead of contesting them, he immediately after consoles himself with saying that "he has done his part." He has not done his part. He has not performed his promise of a comparison of Constitutions. He started the controversy, he gave the challenge and has fled from it; and he is now a *case in point* with his own opinion that *"the age of chivalry is gone!"*

The title as well as the substance of his last work, his *"Appeal,"* is his condemnation. Principles must stand on their own merits, and if they are good they certainly will. To put them under the shelter of other men's authority, as Mr. Burke has done, serves to bring them into suspicion. Mr. Burke is not very fond of dividing his honours, but in this case he is artfully dividing the disgrace.

But who are those to whom Mr. Burke has made his appeal? A set of childish thinkers, and half-way politicians born in the last century, men who went no farther with any principle than as it suited their purpose as a party; the Nation was always left out of the question; and this has been the character of every party from that day to this. The Nation sees nothing in such works, or such politics, worthy its attention. A little matter will move a party, but it must be something great that moves a Nation.

Though I see nothing in Mr. Burke's *Appeal* worth taking much notice of, there is, however, one expression upon which I shall offer a few remarks. After quoting largely from the *Rights of Man,* and declining to contest the principles contained in that work, he says: "This will most probably be done (*if such writings shall be thought to deserve any other refutation than that of criminal justice*) by others, who may think with Mr. Burke and with the same zeal."

In the first place, it has not yet been done by anybody. Not less, I believe, than eight or ten pamphlets intended as answers to the former part of the *Rights of Man* have been published by different persons, and not one of them to my knowledge has extended to a second edition, nor are even the titles of them so much as generally remembered. As I am averse to unnecessarily multiplying publications, I have answered none of them. And as I believe that a man may write himself out of reputation when nobody else can do it, I am careful to avoid that rock.

But as I would decline unnecessary publications on the one hand, so would I avoid everything that might appear like sullen pride on the other. If Mr. Burke, or any person on his side of the question, will produce an answer to the *Rights of Man* that shall extend to a half, or even to a fourth part of the number of copies to which the *Rights of Man* extended, I will reply to his work. But until this be done, I shall so far take the sense of the public for my guide (and the world knows I am not a flatterer) that what they do not think worth while to read, is not worth mine to answer. I suppose the number of copies to which the first part of the *Rights of Man* extended, taking England, Scotland, and Ireland, is not less than between forty and fifty thousand.

I now come to remark on the remaining part of the quotation I have made from Mr. Burke.

"If," says he, "such writing shall be thought to deserve any other refutation than that of *criminal* justice."

Pardoning the pun, it must be *criminal* justice indeed that should condemn a work as a substitute for not being able to refute it. The greatest condemnation that could be passed upon it would be a refutation. But in proceeding by the method Mr. Burke alludes to, the condemnation would, in the final event, pass upon the criminality of the process and not upon the work, and in this case, I had rather be the author, than be either the judge or the jury that should condemn it.

But to come at once to the point. I have differed from some professional gentlemen on the subject of prosecutions, and I since find they are falling into my opinion, which I will here state as fully, but as concisely as I can.

I will first put a case with respect to any law, and then compare it with a Government, or with what in England is, or has been, called a Constitution.

It would be an act of despotism, or what in England is called arbitrary power, to make a law to prohibit investigating the principles, good or bad, on which such a law, or any other, is founded.

If a law be bad it is one thing to oppose the practice of it, but it is quite a different thing to expose its errors, to reason on its defects, and to shew cause how it should be repealed, or why another ought to be substituted in its place. I have always held it an opinion (making it also my practice) that it is better to obey a bad law, making use at the same time of every argument to show its errors and procure its repeal, than forcibly to violate it; because the precedent of breaking a bad law might weaken the force, and lead to a discretionary violation of those which are good.

The case is the same with respect to principles and

forms of Government, or to what are called Constitutions and the parts of which they are composed.

It is for the good of Nations and not for the emolument or aggrandisement of particular individuals, that Government ought to be established, and that mankind are at the expence of supporting it. The defects of every Government and Constitution, both as to principle and form, must on a parity of reasoning, be as open to discussion as the defects of a law, and it is a duty which every man owes to society to point them out. When those defects, and the means of remedying them, are generally seen by a Nation, that Nation will reform its Government or its Constitution in the one case, as the Government repealed or reformed the law in the other. The operation of Government is restricted to the making and the administering of laws; but it is to a Nation that the right of forming or reforming, generating or regenerating, Constitutions and Governments belong; and consequently those subjects, as subjects of investigation, are always before a country *as a matter of right,* and cannot, without invading the general rights of that country, be made subjects for prosecution. On this ground I will meet Mr. Burke whenever he pleases. It is better that the whole argument should come out than to seek to stifle it. It was himself that opened the controversy, and he ought not to desert it.

I do not believe that Monarchy and Aristocracy will continue seven years longer in any of the enlightened countries in Europe. If better reasons can be shewn for them than against them, they will stand; if the contrary, they will not. Mankind are not now to be told they shall not think or they shall not read; and publications that go no further than to investigate principles of Government, to invite men to reason and to reflect and to shew the errors and excellencies of different systems, have a right to appear. If they do not excite attention, they are not worth the trouble of a prosecution, and if they do the prosecution will amount to nothing, since it cannot amount to a prohibition of reading. This would be a sentence on the public instead of the author, and would also be the most effectual mode of making or hastening Revolutions.

On all cases that apply universally to a Nation with respect to systems of Government, a jury of *twelve* men is not competent to decide. Where there are no witnesses to be examined, no facts to be proved, and where the whole matter is before the whole public, and the merits or demerits of it resting on their opinion; and where there is nothing to be known in a court, but what everybody knows out of it, any twelve men is equally as good a jury as the other, and would most probably reverse another's verdict; or, from the variety of their opinions, not be able to form one. It is one case whether a Nation approve a work or a plan: but it is quite another case whether it will commit to any such jury the power of determining whether that Nation have a right to or shall reform its Government or not. I mention those cases that Mr. Burke may see I have not written on Government without reflecting on what is Law, as well as on what are Rights. The only effectual jury in such cases would be a convention of the whole Nation fairly elected; for in all such cases the whole Nation is the vicinage. If Mr. Burke will propose such a jury I will waive all privileges of being the citizen of another country, and, defending its principles, abide the issue, provided he will do the same; for my opinion is that his work and his principles would be condemned instead of mine.

As to the prejudices which men have from education and habit, in favour of any particular form or system of Government, those prejudices have yet to stand the test of reason and reflection. In fact, such prejudices are nothing. No man is prejudiced in favour of a thing knowing it to be wrong. He is attached to it on the belief of its being right, and when he sees it is not so, the prejudice will be gone. We have but a defective idea of what prejudice is. It might be said that until men think for themselves the whole is prejudice, and *not opinion:* for that only is opinion which is the result of reason and reflection. I offer this remark that Mr. Burke may not confide too much in what have been the customary prejudices of the country.

I do not believe that the people of England have ever been fairly and candidly dealt by. They have been imposed on by parties and by men assuming the character of leaders. It is time that the Nation should rise above those trifles. It is time to dismiss that inattention which has so long been the encouraging cause of stretching taxation to excess. It is time to dismiss all those songs and toasts which are calculated to enslave, and operate to suffocate reflection. On all such subjects men have but to think and they will neither act wrong nor be misled. To say that any people are not fit for freedom is to make poverty their choice, and to say that they had rather be loaded with taxes than not. If such a case could be proved it would equally prove that those who govern are not fit to govern them, for they are a part of the same national mass.

But admitting Governments to be changed all over Europe; it certainly may be done without convulsion or revenge. It is not worth making changes or Revolutions, unless it be for some great national benefit: and when this shall appear to a Nation the danger will be as in America and France, to those who oppose; and with this reflection I close my preface.

THOMAS PAINE.

London, February 9, 1792.

Introduction

What Archimedes said of the mechanical powers may be applied to reason and liberty. *"Had we,"* said he, *"a place to stand upon, we might raise the world."*

The Revolution of America presented in politics what was only theory in mechanics. So deeply rooted were all the Governments of the old world, and so effectually had the tyranny and the antiquity of habit established itself over the mind, that no beginning could be made in Asia, Africa, or Europe, to reform the political condition of man. Freedom had been hunted round the globe; reason was considered as rebellion; and the slavery of fear had made men afraid to think.

But such is the irresistible nature of truth that all it asks, and all it wants, is the liberty of appearing. The sun needs no inscription to distinguish him from darkness; and no sooner did the American Governments display themselves to the world than despotism felt a shock and man began to contemplate redress.

The Independence of America, considered merely as a separation from England, would have been a matter of but little importance, had it not been accompanied by a Revolution in the principles and practice of Governments. She made a stand, not for herself only, but for the world, and looked beyond the advantages herself could receive. Even the Hessian, though hired to fight against her, may live to bless his defeat; and England, condemning the viciousness of its Government, rejoice in its miscarriage.

As America was the only spot in the political world where the principles of universal reformation could begin, so also was it the best in the natural world. An assemblage of circumstances conspired not only to give birth, but to add gigantic maturity to its principles. The scene which that country presents to the eye of a spectator has something in it which generates and encourages great ideas. Nature appears to him in magnitude. The mighty objects he beholds act upon his mind by enlarging it, and he partakes of the greatness he contemplates. Its first settlers were emigrants from different European Nations, and of diversified professions of religion, retiring from the governmental persecutions of the old world, and meeting in the new, not as enemies, but as brothers. The wants which necessarily accompany the cultivation of a wilderness produced among them a state of society which countries long harassed by the quarrels and intrigues of Governments had neglected to cherish. In such a situation man becomes what he ought. He sees his species, not with the inhuman idea of a natural enemy, but as kindred; and the example shows to the artificial world that man must go back to nature for information.

From the rapid progress which America makes in every species of improvement, it is rational to conclude that, if the Governments of Asia, Africa, and Europe had begun on a principle similar to that of America, or had not been very early corrupted therefrom, those countries must by this time have been in a far superior condition to what they are. Age after age has passed away, for no other purpose than to behold their wretchedness. Could we suppose a spectator who knew nothing of the world, and who was put into it merely to make his observations, he would take a great part of the old world to be new, just struggling with the difficulties and hardships of an infant settlement. He could not suppose that the hordes of miserable poor with which old countries abound could be any other than those who had not yet had time to provide for themselves. Little would he think they were the consequence of what in such countries is called Government.

If, from the more wretched parts of the old world,

we look at those which are in an advanced stage of improvement, we still find the greedy hand of Government thrusting itself into every corner and crevice of industry, and grasping the spoil of the multitude. Invention is continually exercised to furnish new pretences for revenue and taxation. It watches prosperity as its prey, and permits none to escape without a tribute.

As Revolutions have begun (and as the probability is always greater against a thing beginning than of proceeding after it has begun), it is natural to expect that other Revolutions will follow. The amazing and still increasing expences with which old Governments are conducted, the numerous wars they engage in or provoke, the embarrassments they throw in the way of universal civilization and commerce, and the oppression and usurpation they practise at home, have wearied out the patience and exhausted the property of the world. In such a situation and with the examples already existing, Revolutions are to be looked for. They are become subjects of universal conversation, and may be considered as the *Order of the Day*.

If systems of Government can be introduced less expencive and more productive of general happiness than those which have existed, all attempts to oppose their progress will in the end be fruitless. Reason, like time, will make its own way, and prejudice will fall in a combat with interest. If universal peace, civilization, and commerce are ever to be the happy lot of man, it cannot be accomplished but by a Revolution in the system of Governments. All the monarchical Governments are military. War is their trade, plunder and revenue their objects. While such Governments continue, peace has not the absolute security of a day. What is the history of all monarchical Governments but a disgustful picture of human wretchedness, and the accidental respite of a few years' repose? Wearied with war, and tired with human butchery, they sat down to rest, and called it peace. This certainly is not the condition that heaven intended for man; and if *this be Monarchy,* well might Monarchy be reckoned among the sins of the Jews.

The Revolutions which formerly took place in the world had nothing in them that interested the bulk of mankind. They extended only to a change of persons and measures, but not of principles, and rose or fell among the common transactions of the moment. What we now behold may not improperly be called a *"counter Revolution."* Conquest and tyranny, at some early period, dispossessed man of his rights, and he is now recovering them. And as the tide of all human affairs has its ebb and flow in directions contrary to each other, so also is it in this. Government founded on a *moral theory, on a system of universal peace, on the indefeasible hereditary Rights of Man,* is now revolving from west to east by a stronger impulse than the Government of the sword revolved from east to west. It interests not particular individuals, but Nations in its progress, and promises a new era to the human race.

The danger to which the success of Revolutions is most exposed is that of attempting them before the principles on which they proceed, and the advantages to result from them, are sufficiently seen and understood. Almost everything appertaining to the circumstances of a Nation, has been absorbed and confounded under the general and mysterious word *Government.* Though it avoids taking to its account the errors it commits, and the mischiefs it occasions, it fails not to arrogate to itself whatever has the appearance of prosperity. It robs industry of its honours, by pedanticly making itself the cause of its effects; and purloins from the general character of man, the merits that appertain to him as a social being.

It may therefore be of use in this day of Revolutions to discriminate between those things which are the

effect of Government, and those which are not. This
will best be done by taking a review of society and
civilisation, and the consequences resulting therefrom,
as things distinct from what are called Governments.
By beginning with this investigation, we shall be able
to assign effects to their proper cause and analyze the
mass of common errors.

Chapter I
Of Society and Civilisation

Great part of that order which reigns among mankind
is not the effect of Government. It has its origin in
the principles of society and the natural constitution
of man. It existed prior to Government, and would
exist if the formality of Government was abolished.
The mutual dependence and reciprocal interest which
man has upon man, and all the parts of a civilised
community upon each other, create that great chain
of connection which holds it together. The landholder,
the farmer, the manufacturer, the merchant, the
tradesman, and every occupation, prospers by the aid
which each receives from the other, and from the
whole. Common interest regulates their concerns, and
forms their law; and the laws which common usage
ordains, have a greater influence than the laws of Government. In fine, society performs for itself almost everything which is ascribed to Government.

To understand the nature and quantity of Government proper for man, it is necessary to attend to his
character. As nature created him for social life, she
fitted him for the station she intended. In all cases
she made his natural wants greater than his individual
powers. No one man is capable, without the aid of
society, of supplying his own wants; and those wants,
acting upon every individual, impel the whole of them
into society, as naturally as gravitation acts to a centre.

But she has gone further. She has not only forced man into society by a diversity of wants which the reciprocal aid of each other can supply, but she has implanted in him a system of social affections, which, though not necessary to his existence, are essential to his happiness. There is no period in life when this love for society ceases to act. It begins and ends with our being.

If we examine with attention the composition and constitution of man, the diversity of his wants and talents in different men for reciprocally accommodating the wants of each other, his propensity to society, and consequently to preserve the advantages resulting from it, we shall easily discover that a great part of what is called Government is mere imposition.

Government is no farther necessary than to supply the few cases to which society and civilisation are not conveniently competent; and instances are not wanting to show, that everything which Government can usefully add thereto, has been performed by the common consent of society, without Government.

For upwards of two years from the commencement of the American War, and to a longer period in several of the American States, there were no established forms of Government. The old Governments had been abolished, and the country was too much occupied in defence to employ its attention in establishing new Governments; yet during this interval order and harmony were preserved as inviolate as in any country in Europe. There is a natural aptness in man, and more so in society, because it embraces a greater variety of abilities and resources, to accommodate itself to whatever situation it is in. The instant formal Government is abolished, society begins to act: a general association takes place, and common interest produces common security.

So far is it from being true, as has been pretended, that the abolition of any formal Government is the dissolution of society, that it acts by a contrary impulse, and brings the latter the closer together. All that part of its organization which it had committed to its Government, devolves again upon itself, and acts through its medium. When men, as well from natural instinct as from reciprocal benefits, have habituated themselves to social and civilised life, there is always enough of its principles in practice to carry them through any changes they may find necessary or convenient to make in their Government. In short, man is so naturally a creature of society that it is almost impossible to put him out of it.

Formal Government makes but a small part of civilised life; and when even the best that human wisdom can devise is established, it is a thing more in name and idea than in fact. It is to the great and fundamental principles of society and civilisation—to the common usage universally consented to, and mutually and reciprocally maintained—to the unceasing circulation of interest, which passing through its million channels, invigorates the whole mass of civilised man—it is to these things, infinitely more than to anything which even the best instituted Government can perform, that the safety and prosperity of the individual and of the whole depends.

The more perfect civilisation is, the less occasion has it for Government, because the more it does regulate its own affairs, and govern itself; but so contrary is the practice of old Governments to the reason of the case, that the expences of them increase in the proportion they ought to diminish. It is but few general laws that civilised life requires, and those of such common usefulness, that whether they are enforced by the forms of government or not, the effect will be nearly the same. If we consider what the principles are that first condense men into society, and what the motives that regulate their mutual intercourse afterwards, we shall find, by the time we arrive at what is called Government, that nearly the whole of the business is performed by the natural operation of the parts upon each other.

Man, with respect to all those matters, is more a creature of consistency than he is aware, or that Governments would wish him to believe. All the great laws of society are laws of nature. Those of trade and commerce, whether with respect to the intercourse of individuals or of nations, are laws of mutual and reciprocal interests. They are followed and obeyed, because it is the interest of the parties so to do, and not on account of any formal laws their Governments may impose or interpose.

But how often is the natural propensity to society disturbed or destroyed by the operations of Government! When the latter, instead of being ingrafted on the principles of the former, assumes to exist for itself, and acts by partialities of favour and oppression, it becomes the cause of the mischiefs it ought to prevent.

If we look back to the riots and tumults which at various times have happened in England, we shall find that they did not proceed from the want of a Government, but that Government was itself the generating cause: instead of consolidating society it divided it; it deprived it of its natural cohesion, and engendered discontents and disorders which otherwise would not have existed. In those associations, which men promiscuously form for the purpose of trade, or of any concern in which Government is totally out of the question, and in which they act merely on the principles of society, we see how naturally the various parties unite; and this shows, by comparison, that Governments, so far from being always the cause or means of order, are often the destruction of it. The riots of 1780 had no other source than the remains of those prejudices which the Government of itself had encouraged. But with respect to England there are also other causes.

Excess and inequality of taxation, however disguised in the means, never fail to appear in their effects. As a great mass of the community are thrown thereby into poverty and discontent, they are constantly on the brink of commotion; and deprived, as they unfortunately are, of the means of information, are easily heated to outrage. Whatever the apparent cause of any riots may be, the real one is always want of happiness. It shows that something is wrong in the system of Government that injures the felicity by which society is to be preserved.

But as fact is superior to reasoning, the instance of America presents itself to confirm these observations. If there is a country in the world where concord, according to common calculation, would be least expected, it is America. Made up as it is of people from different nations, accustomed to different forms and habits of Government, speaking different languages, and more different in their modes of worship, it would appear that the union of such a people was impracticable; but by the simple operation of constructing Government on the principles of Society and the rights of man, every difficulty retires, and all the parts are brought into cordial unison. There the poor are not oppressed, the rich are not privileged. Industry is not mortified by the splendid extravagance of a Court rioting at its expence. Their taxes are few, because their Government is just: and as there is nothing to render them wretched, there is nothing to engender riots and tumults.

A metaphysical man, like Mr. Burke, would have tortured his invention to discover how such a people could be governed. He would have supposed that some must be managed by fraud, others by force, and all by some contrivance; that genius must be hired to impose upon ignorance, and show and parade to fascinate the vulgar. Lost in the abundance of his researches, he would have resolved and re-resolved, and finally overlooked the plain and easy road that lay directly before him.

One of the great adventures of the American Revolution has been, that it led to a discovery of the principles, and laid open the imposition, of Governments. All the Revolutions till then had been worked within the small sphere of a Court, and never on the great floor of a Nation. The parties were always of the class of courtiers; and whatever was their rage for reformation, they carefully preserved the fraud of the profession.

In all cases they took care to represent Government as a thing made up of mysteries, which only themselves understood; and they hid from the understanding of the Nation the only thing that was beneficial to know, namely, *that Government is nothing more than a national association acting on the principles of society.*

Having thus endeavoured to show that the social and civilised state of man is capable of performing within itself almost everything necessary to its protection and Government, it will be proper, on the other hand, to take a review of the present old Governments, and examine whether their principles and practice are correspondent thereto.

Chapter II
Of the Origin of the Present Old Governments

It is impossible that such Governments as have hitherto existed in the world, would have commenced by any other means than a total violation of every principle, sacred and moral. The obscurity in which the origin of all the present old Governments is buried, implies the iniquity and disgrace with which they began. The origin of the present Government of America and France will ever be remembered, because it is honourable to record it; but with respect to the rest, even flattery has consigned them to the tomb of time, without an inscription.

It could have been no difficult thing in the early and solitary ages of the world, while the chief employment of men was that of attending flocks and herds, for a banditti of ruffians to overrun a country and lay it under contributions. Their power being thus established the chief of the band contrived to lose the name of Robber in that of Monarch; and hence the origin of Monarchy and Kings.

The origin of the Government of England, so far as relates to what is called its line of Monarchy, being one of the latest, is perhaps the best recorded. The hatred which the Norman invasion and tyranny begat, must have been deeply rooted in the nation, to have outlived the contrivance to obliterate it. Though not a courtier will talk of the curfeu-bell, not a village in England has forgotten it.

Those bands of robbers having parcelled out the world, and divided it into dominions, began, as is naturally the case, to quarrel with each other. What at first was obtained by violence was considered by others as lawful to be taken, and a second plunderer succeeded the first. They alternately invaded the dominions which each had assigned to himself, and the brutality with which they treated each other explains the original character of monarchy. It was ruffian torturing ruffian. The conqueror considered the conquered, not as his prisoner, but his property. He led him in triumph rattling in chains, and doomed him, at pleasure, to slavery or death. As time obliterated the history of their beginning, their successors assumed new appearances, to cut off the entail of their disgrace, but their principles and objects remained the same. What at first was plunder, assumed the softer name of revenue; and the power originally usurped, they affected to inherit.

From such beginning of Governments, what could

be expected but a continual system of war and extortion? It has established itself into a trade. The vice is not peculiar to one more than to another, but is the common principle of all. There does not exist within such Governments sufficient stamina whereon to engraft reformation; and the shortest, easiest, and most effectual remedy is to begin anew on the ground of the oration.

What scenes of horror, what perfection in iniquity, present themselves in contemplating the character and reviewing the history of such Governments! If we would delineate human nature with a baseness of heart and hypocrisy of countenance that reflection would shudder at and humanity disown, it is Kings, Courts, and Cabinets that must sit for the portrait. Man, naturally as he is, with all his faults about him, is not up to the character.

Can we possibly suppose that if Governments had originated in a right principle, and had not an interest in pursuing a wrong one, the world could have been in the wretched and quarrelsome condition we have seen it? What inducement has the farmer, while following the plough, to lay aside his peaceful pursuits, and go to war with the farmer of another country? or what inducement has the manufacturer? What is dominion to them, or to any class of men in a nation? Does it add an acre to any man's estate, or raise its value? Are not conquest and defeat each of the same price, and taxes the never-failing consequence? Though this reasoning may be good to a Nation, it is not so to a Government. War is the Pharo table of Governments, and Nations the dupes of the games.

If there is anything to wonder at in this miserable scene of Governments more than might be expected, it is the progress which the peaceful arts of agriculture, manufacture and commerce have made beneath such a long accumulating load of discouragement and oppression. It serves to show that instinct in animals does not act with stronger impulse than the principles of society and civilization operate in man. Under all discouragements, he pursues his object, and yields to nothing but impossibilities.

Chapter III
Of the Old and New Systems of Government

Nothing can appear more contradictory than the principles on which the old Governments began, and the condition to which society, civilization and commerce are capable of carrying mankind. Government, on the old system, is an assumption of power, for the aggrandizement of itself; on the new a delegation of power for the common benefit of society. The former supports itself by keeping up a system of war; the latter promotes a system of peace, as the true means of enriching a Nation. The one encourages national prejudices; the other promotes universal society, as the means of universal commerce. The one measures its prosperity by the quantity of revenue it extorts; the other proves its excellence by the small quantity of taxes it requires.

Mr. Burke has talked of old and new whigs. If he can amuse himself with childish names and distinctions, I shall not interrupt his pleasure. It is not to him, but to the Abbé Sieyes, that I address this chapter. I am already engaged to the latter gentleman to discuss the subject of monarchical Government; and as it naturally occurs in comparing the old and new systems, I make this the opportunity of presenting to him my observations. I shall occasionally take Mr. Burke in my way.

Though it might be proved that the system of Government now called the NEW is the most ancient in principle of all that have existed, being founded on the original inherent Rights of Man; yet, as tyranny and the sword have suspended the exercise of those rights for many centuries past, it serves better the purpose of distinction to call it the *new* than to claim the right of calling it the old.

The first general distinction between those two systems is that the one now called the old is *hereditary,* either in whole or in part; and the new is entirely *representative.* It rejects all hereditary Government:

First, As being an imposition on mankind.

Secondly, As inadequate to the purposes for which Government is necessary.

With respect to the first of these heads—It cannot be proved by what right hereditary Government could begin; neither does there exist within the compass of mortal power a right to establish it. Man has no authority over posterity in matters of personal right; and, therefore, no man or body of men had, or can have, a right to set up hereditary Government. Were even ourselves to come again into existence, instead of being succeeded by posterity, we have not now the right of taking from ourselves the rights which would then be ours. On what ground, then, do we pretend to take them from others?

All hereditary Government is in its nature tyranny. An heritable crown, or an heritable throne, or by what other fanciful name such things may be called, have no other significant explanation than that mankind are heritable property. To inherit a Government, is to inherit the people, as if they were flocks and herds.

With respect to the second head, that of being inadequate to the purposes for which Government is necessary, we have only to consider what Government essentially is, and compare it with the circumstances to which hereditary succession is subject.

Government ought to be a thing always in full maturity. It ought to be so constructed as to be superior to all the accidents to which individual man is subject; and, therefore, hereditary succession, by being *subject*

to them all, is the most irregular and imperfect of all
the systems of Government.

We have heard the *Rights of Man* called a *levelling*
system; but the only system to which the word *levelling*
is truly applicable, is the hereditary monarchical system.
It is a system of *mental levelling.* It indiscriminately
admits every species of character to the same authority.
Vice and virtue, ignorance and wisdom, in short, every
quality, good or bad, is put on the same level. Kings
succeed each other, not as rationals, but as animals. It
signifies not what their mental or moral characters are.
Can we then be surprised at the abject state of the
human mind in monarchical countries, when the Government itself is formed on such an abject levelling system? It has no fixed character. To-day it is one thing;
to-morrow it is something else. It changes with the temper of every succeeding individual, and is subject to all
the varieties of each. It is Government through the medium of passions and accidents. It appears under all the
various characters of childhood, decrepitude, dotage; a
thing at nurse, in leading-strings, or in crutches. It reverses the wholesome order of nature. It occasionally
puts children over men, and the conceits of nonage over
wisdom and experience. In short, we cannot conceive a
more ridiculous figure of Government, than hereditary
succession, in all its cases, presents.

Could it be made a decree in nature, or an edict
registered in heaven, and man could know it, that virtue and wisdom should invariably appertain to hereditary succession, the objections to it would be removed;
but when we see that nature acts as if she disowned
and sported with the hereditary system; that the mental characters of successors, in all countries, are below
the average of human understanding; that one is a
tyrant, another an idiot, a third insane, and some all
three together, it is impossible to attach confidence to
it, when reason in man has power to act.

It is not to the Abbé Sieyes that I need apply this

reasoning; he has already saved me that trouble by giving his own opinion upon the case. "If it be asked," says he, "what is my opinion with respect to hereditary right, I answer, without hesitation, that, in good theory, an hereditary transmission of any power or office, can never accord with the laws of a true representation. Hereditaryship is, in this sense, as much an attaint upon principle, as an outrage upon society. But let us," continues he, "refer to the history of all elective monarchies and principalities: is there one in which the elective mode is not worse than the hereditary succession?"

As to debating on which is the worse of the two, it is admitting both to be bad: and herein we are agreed. The preference which the Abbé has given is a condemnation of the thing that he prefers. Such a mode of reasoning on such a subject is inadmissible, because it finally amounts to an accusation upon Providence, as if she had left to man no other choice with respect to Government than between two evils, the best of which he admits to be "an attaint upon principle, and an outrage upon society."

Passing over for the present all the evils and mischiefs which monarchy has occasioned in the world, nothing can more effectually prove its uselessness in a state of *civil government,* than making it hereditary. Would we make any office hereditary that required wisdom and abilities to fill it? and where wisdom and abilities are not necessary, such an office, whatever it may be, is superfluous or insignificant.

Hereditary succession is a burlesque upon monarchy. It puts it in the most ridiculous light, by presenting it as an office which any child or idiot may fill. It requires some talents to be a common mechanic; but to be a King requires only the animal figure of man—a sort of breathing automaton. This sort of superstition may last a few years more, but it cannot long resist the awakened reason and interest of man.

As to Mr. Burke, he is a stickler for monarchy, not altogether as a pensioner, if he is one, which I believe, but as a political man. He has taken up a contemptible opinion of mankind, who, in their turn, are taking up the same of him. He considers them as a herd of beings that must be governed by fraud, effigy, and show; and an idol would be as good a figure of monarchy with him as a man. I will, however, do him the justice to say that, with respect to America, he has been very complimentary. He always contended, at least in my hearing, that the people of America were more enlightened than those of England, or of any country in Europe; and that therefore the imposition of shew was not necessary in their Governments.

Though the comparison between hereditary and elective monarchy, which the Abbé has made, is unnecessary to the case, because the representative system rejects both; yet, were I to make the comparison, I should decide contrary to what he has done.

The civil wars which have originated from contested hereditary claims are more numerous, and have been more dreadful, and of longer continuance, than those which have been occasioned by election. All the civil wars in France arose from the hereditary system; they were either produced by hereditary claims, or by the imperfection of the hereditary form, which admits of regencies, or monarchy at nurse. With respect to England, its history is full of the same misfortunes. The contests for succession between the houses of York and Lancaster, lasted a whole century; and others of a similar nature have renewed themselves since that period. Those of 1715 and 1745 were of the same kind. The succession war for the crown of Spain embroiled almost half Europe. The disturbances in Holland are generated from the hereditaryship of the Stadtholder. A Government calling itself free, with an hereditary office, is like a thorn in the flesh, that produces a fermentation which endeavours to discharge it.

But I might go further, and place also foreign wars, of whatever kind, to the same cause. It is by adding the evil of hereditary succession to that of monarchy, that a permanent family interest is created, whose constant objects are dominion and revenue. Poland, though an elective monarchy, has had fewer wars than those which are hereditary; and it is the only Government that has made a voluntary essay, though but a small one, to reform the condition of the country.

Having thus glanced at a few of the defects of the old, or hereditary systems of Government, let us compare it with the new, or representative system.

The representative system takes society and civilisation for its basis; nature, reason, and experience for its guide.

Experience, in all ages and in all countries, has demonstrated that it is impossible to controul nature in her distribution of mental powers. She gives them as she pleases. Whatever is the rule by which she, apparently to us, scatters them among mankind, that rule remains a secret to man. It would be as ridiculous to attempt to fix the hereditaryship of human beauty as of wisdom. Whatever wisdom constituently is, it is like a seedless plant; it may be reared when it appears, but it cannot be voluntarily produced. There is always a sufficiency somewhere in the general mass of society for all purposes; but with respect to the parts of society, it is continually changing its place. It rises in one to-day, in another to-morrow, and has most probably visited in rotation every family of the earth, and again withdrawn.

As this is in the order of nature, the order of Government must necessarily follow it, or Government will, as we see it does, degenerate into ignorance. The hereditary system, therefore, is as repugnant to human wisdom as to human rights; and is as absurd as it is unjust.

As the republic of letters brings forward the best

literary productions, by giving to genius a fair and universal chance; so the representative system of Government is calculated to produce the wisest laws, by collecting wisdom from where it can be found. I smile to myself when I contemplate the ridiculous insignificance into which literature and all the sciences would sink, were they made hereditary; and I carry the same idea into Governments. An hereditary governor is as inconsistent as an hereditary author. I know not whether Homer or Euclid had sons; but I will venture an opinion that if they had, and had left their works unfinished, those sons could not have completed them.

Do we need a stronger evidence of the absurdity of hereditary Government than is seen in the descendants of those men, in any line of life, who once were famous? Is there scarcely an instance in which there is not a total reverse of the character? It appears as if the tide of mental faculties flowed as far as it could in certain channels, and then forsook its course and arose in others. How irrational then is the hereditary system, which establishes channels of power, in company with which wisdom refuses to flow! By continuing this absurdity, man is perpetually in contradiction with himself; he accepts, for a King, or a chief magistrate, or a legislator, a person whom he would not elect for a constable.

It appears to general observation that Revolutions create genius and talents; but those events do no more than bring them forward. There is existing in man a mass of sense lying in a dormant state, and which, unless something excites to action, will descend with him, in that condition, to the grave. As it is to the advantage of society that the whole of the faculties should be employed, the construction of Government ought to be such as to bring forward by a quiet and regular operation, all that extent of capacity which never fails to appear in Revolutions.

This cannot take place in the insipid state of hereditary Government, not only because it prevents, but because it operates to benumb. When the mind of a Nation is bowed down by any political superstition in its Government, such as hereditary succession is, it loses a considerable portion of its powers on all other subjects and objects. Hereditary succession requires the same obedience to ignorance as to wisdom; and when once the mind can bring itself to pay this indiscriminate reverence, it descends below the stature of mental manhood. It is fit to be great only in little things. It acts a treachery upon itself, and suffocates the sensations that urge to detection.

Though the ancient Governments present to us a miserable picture of the condition of man, there is one which above all others exempts itself from the general description. I mean the democracy of Athenians. We see more to admire, and less to condemn, in that great, extraordinary people than in anything which history affords.

Mr. Burke is so little acquainted with constituent principles of Government, that he confounds democracy and representation together. Representation was a thing unknown in the ancient democracies. In those the mass of the people met and enacted laws (grammatically speaking) in the first person. Simple democracy was no other than the common hall of the ancients. It signifies the *form* as well as the public principle of the Government. As those democracies increased in population, and the territory extended, the simple democratical form became unwieldy and impracticable; and as the system of representation was not known, the consequence was, they either degenerated convulsively into monarchies or became absorbed into such as then existed. Had the system of representation been then understood, as it now is, there is no reason to believe that those forms of Government now called monarchical or aristocratical would ever have taken place. It was the want of some method to consolidate the parts of society after it became too populous and too extensive for the simple democratical form, and also the lax and solitary condition of shepherds and herdsmen in other parts of the world, that afforded opportunities to those unnatural modes of Government to begin.

As it is necessary to clear away the rubbish of errors into which the subject of Government has been thrown, I shall proceed to remark on some others.

It has always been the political craft of courtiers and court-governments to abuse something which they called republicanism; but what republicanism was or is they never attempt to explain. Let us examine a little into this case.

The only forms of Government are the democratical, the aristocratical, the monarchical, and what is now called the representative.

What is called a *Republic* is not any *particular form* of Government. It is wholly characteristical of the purport, matter or object for which Government ought to be instituted, and on which it is to be employed: RES-PUBLICA, the public affairs, or the public good; or, literally translated, the *public thing*. It is a word of a good original, referring to what ought to be the character and business of Government; and in this sense it is naturally opposed to the word *monarchy*, which has a base original signification. It means arbitrary power in an individual person; in the exercise of which, *himself*, and not the *res-publica*, is the object.

Every Government that does not act on the principle of a *Republic*, or, in other words, that does not make the *res-publica* its whole and sole object, is not a good Government. Republican Government is no other than Government established and conducted for the interest of the public, as well individually as collectively. It is not necessarily connected with any particular form, but it most naturally associates with the representative form, as being best calculated to secure the end for which a Nation is at the expense of supporting it.

Various forms of Government have affected to stile themselves a Republic. Poland calls itself a Republic which is an hereditary Aristocracy, with what is called an elective Monarchy. Holland calls itself a Republic which is chiefly aristocratical, with an hereditary stadtholdership. But the Government of America, which is wholly on the system of representation, is the only real Republic, in character and in practice, that now exists. Its Government has no other object than the public business of the Nation, and therefore it is properly a Republic; and the Americans have taken care that THIS, and no other, shall always be the object of their Government, by their rejecting everything hereditary, and establishing Government on the system of representation only.

Those who have said that a Republic is not a *form* of Government calculated for countries of great extent, mistook, in the first place, the *business* of a Government, for a *form* of Government; for the *respublica* equally appertains to every extent of territory and population. And, in the second place, if they meant anything with respect to *form*, it was the simple democratical form, such as was the mode of Government in the ancient democracies, in which there was no representation. The case, therefore, is not that a Republic cannot be extensive, but that it cannot be extensive on the simple democratical form; and the question naturally presents itself, *what is the best form of Government for conducting the* RES-PUBLICA, *or the* PUBLIC BUSINESS *of a nation, after it becomes too extensive and populous for the simple democratical form?*

It cannot be Monarchy, because Monarchy is subject to an objection of the same amount to which the simple democratical form was subject.

It is possible that an individual may lay down a system of principles, on which Government shall be constitutionally established to any extent of territory. This is no more than an operation of the mind, acting by its own powers. But the practice upon those principles, as applying to the various and numerous circumstances of a Nation, its agriculture, manufacture, trade, commerce, etc., etc., requires a knowledge of a different kind, and which can be had only from the various parts of society. It is an assemblage of practical knowledge, which no one individual can possess; and therefore the monarchical form is as much limited, in useful practice, from the incompetency of knowledge, as was the democratical form from the multiplicity of population. The one degenerates, by extension, into confusion; the other into ignorance and incapacity, of which all the great monarchies are an evidence. The monarchical form, therefore, could not be a substitute for the democratical, because it has equal inconveniences.

Much less could it when made hereditary. This is the most effectual of all forms to preclude knowledge. Neither could the high democratical mind have voluntarily yielded itself to be governed by children and idiots, and all the motley insignificance of character which attends such a mere animal system, the disgrace and the reproach of reason and of man.

As to the aristocratical form, it has the same vices and defects with the monarchical, except that the chance of abilities is better from the proportion of numbers, but there is still no security for the right use and application of them.

Referring then to the original simple Democracy, it affords the true data from which Government on a large scale can begin. It is incapable of extension, not from its principle, but from the inconvenience of its form; and Monarchy and Aristocracy, from their incapacity. Retaining, then, Democracy as the ground, and rejecting the corrupt systems of Monarchy and Aristocracy, the representative system naturally presents itself; remedying at once the defects of the simple Democracy as to form, and the incapacity of the other two with respect to knowledge.

Simple Democracy was society governing itself without the aid of secondary means. By ingrafting representation upon Democracy, we arrive at a system of Government capable of embracing and confederating all the various interests and every extent of territory and population; and that also with advantages as much superior to hereditary Government, as the Republic of Letters is to hereditary literature.

It is on this system that the American Government is founded. It is representation ingrafted upon Democracy. It has fixed the form by a scale parallel in all cases to the extent of the principle. What Athens was in miniature, America will be in magnitude. The one was the wonder of the ancient world; the other is becoming the admiration, the model of the present. It is the easiest of all the forms of Government to be understood and the most eligible in practice, and excludes at once the ignorance and insecurity of the hereditary mode, and the inconvenience of the simple Democracy.

It is impossible to conceive a system of Government capable of acting over such an extent of territory, and such a circle of interests, as is immediately produced by the operation of representation. France, great and populous as it is, is but a spot in the capaciousness of the system. It is preferable to simple Democracy even in small territories. Athens, by representation, would have outrivalled her own Democracy.

That which is called Government, or rather that which we ought to conceive Government to be, is no more than some common centre, in which all the parts of society unite. This cannot be accomplished by any method so conducive to the various interests of the community as by the representative system. It concentrates the knowledge necessary to the interest of the parts, and of the whole. It places Government in a

state of constant maturity. It is, as has already been
observed, never young, never old. It is subject neither
to nonage nor dotage. It is never in the cradle nor
on crutches. It admits not of a separation between
knowledge and power, and is superior, as Government
always ought to be, to all the accidents of individual
man, and is therefore superior to what is called
Monarchy.

A Nation is not a body, the figure of which is to be
represented by the human body, but is like a body
contained within a circle, having a common centre in
which every radius meets; and that centre is formed by
representation. To connect representation with what is
called Monarchy is eccentric Government. Representation is of itself the delegated Monarchy of a Nation,
and cannot debase itself by dividing it with another.

Mr. Burke has two or three times, in his parliamentary speeches, and in his publication, made use of a
jingle of words that convey no ideas. Speaking of Government, he says: "It is better to have Monarchy for
its basis, and Republicanism for its corrective, than
Republicanism for its basis, and Monarchy for its corrective." If he means that it is better to correct folly
with wisdom than wisdom with folly, I will not otherwise contend with him, than that it would be much
better to reject the folly entirely.

But what is this thing which Mr. Burke calls Monarchy? Will he explain it? All men can understand what
representation is; and that it must necessarily include
a variety of knowledge and talents. But what security
is there for the same qualities on the part of Monarchy? Or, when this Monarchy is a child, where then
is the wisdom? What does it know about Government? Who then is the Monarch, or where is the Monarchy? If it is to be performed by Regency, it proves
to be a farce. A Regency is a mock species of Republic, and the whole of Monarchy deserves no better
description. It is a thing as various as imagination can

paint. It has none of the stable character that Government ought to possess. Every succession is a Revolution, and every regency a counter-revolution. The whole of it is a scene of perpetual court cabal and intrigue, of which Mr. Burke is himself an instance. To render Monarchy consistent with Government, the next in succession should not be born a child, but a man at once, and that man a Solomon. It is ridiculous that Nations are to wait and Government be interrupted till boys grow to be men.

Whether I have too little sense to see, or too much to be imposed upon; whether I have too much or too little pride, or of anything else, I leave out of the question; but certain it is, that what is called Monarchy always appears to me a silly contemptible thing. I compare it to something kept behind a curtain, about which there is a great deal of bustle and fuss, and a wonderful air of seeming solemnity; but when, by an accident, the curtain happens to be opened, and the company see what it is, they burst into laughter.

In the representative system of Government, nothing of this can happen. Like the Nation itself, it possesses a perpetual stamina, as well of body as of mind, and presents itself on the open theatre of the world in a fair and manly manner. Whatever are its excellencies or defects, they are visible to all. It exists not by fraud and mystery; it deals not in cant and sophistry; but inspires a language that, passing from heart to heart, is felt and understood.

We must shut our eyes against reason, we must basely degrade our understanding, not to see the folly of what is called Monarchy. Nature is orderly in all her works; but this is a mode of Government that counteracts nature. It turns the progress of the human faculties upside down. It subjects age to be governed by children, and wisdom by folly.

On the contrary, the representative system is always parallel with the order and immutable laws of nature, and meets the reason of man in every part. For example:—

In the American federal Government, more power is delegated to the President of the United States than to any other individual member of Congress. He cannot, therefore, be elected to this office under the age of thirty-five years. By this time the judgment of man becomes matured, and he has lived long enough to be acquainted with man and things, and the country with him. But on the monarchical plan (exclusive of the numerous chances there are against every man born into the world, of drawing a prize in the lottery of human faculties), the next in succession, whatever he may be, is put at the head of a Nation, and of a Government, at the age of eighteen years. Does this appear like an act of wisdom? Is it consistent with the proper dignity and manly character of a Nation? Where is the propriety of calling such a lad the father of the people? In all other cases, a person is a minor until the age of twenty-one years. Before this period, he is not entrusted with the management of an acre of land, or with the heritable property of a flock of sheep or an herd of swine; but wonderful to tell! he may at the age of eighteen years be trusted with a Nation.

That Monarchy is all a bubble, a mere court artifice to procure money, is evident (at least to me) in every character in which it can be viewed. It would be impossible, on the rational system of representative Government, to make out a bill of expences to such an enormous amount as this deception admits. Government is not of itself a very chargeable institution. The whole expence of the federal Government of America, founded, as I have already said, on the system of representation, and extending over a country nearly ten times as large as England, is but six hundred thousand dollars, or one hundred and thirty-five thousand pounds sterling.

I presume that no man in his sober sense will compare the character of the Kings of Europe with that of General Washington. Yet in France, and also in England, the expence of the civil list only, for the support of one man, is eight times greater than the whole expence of the federal Government in America. To assign a reason for this appears almost impossible. The generality of the people of America, especially the poor, are more able to pay taxes than the generality of people either in France or England.

But the case is, that the representative system diffuses such a body of knowledge throughout a Nation, on the subject of Government, as to explode ignorance and preclude imposition. The craft of courts cannot be acted on that ground. There is no place for mystery; nowhere for it to begin. Those who are not in the representation know as much of the nature of business as those who are. An affectation of mysterious importance would there be scouted. Nations can have no secrets; and the secrets of courts, like those of individuals, are always their defects.

In the representative system, the reason for everything must publicly appear. Every man is a proprietor in Government, and considers it a necessary part of his business to understand. It concerns his interest, because it affects his property. He examines the cost, and compares it with the advantages; and above all, he does not adopt the slavish custom of following what in other Governments are called LEADERS.

It can only be by blinding the understanding of man, and making him believe that Government is some wonderful mysterious thing, that excessive revenues are obtained. Monarchy is well calculated to ensure this end. It is the popery of Government, a thing kept up to amuse the ignorant and quiet them into taxes.

The Government of a free country, properly speaking, is not in the persons, but in the laws. The enacting of those requires no great expence; and when they are administered the whole of civil Government is performed—the rest is all court contrivance.

Chapter IV
Of Constitutions

That men mean distinct and separate things when they speak of Constitutions and of Governments, is evident; or why are those terms distinctly and separately used? A Constitution is not the act of a Government, but of a people constituting a Government; and Government without a Constitution is power without a right.

All power exercised over a Nation must have some beginning. It must either be delegated or assumed. There are no other sources. All delegated power is trust, and all assumed power is usurpation. Time does not alter the nature and quality of either.

In viewing this subject, the case and circumstances of America present themselves as in the beginning of a world; and our enquiry into the origin of Government is shortened by referring to the facts that have arisen in our own day. We have no occasion to roam for information into the obscure field of antiquity, nor hazard ourselves upon conjecture. We are brought at once to the point of seeing Government begin, as if we had lived in the beginning of time. The real volume, not of history, but of fact, is directly before us, unmutilated by contrivance or the errors of tradition.

I will here concisely state the commencement of the American Constitutions: by which the difference between Constitutions and Governments will sufficiently appear.

It may not be improper to remind the reader that the United States of America consist of thirteen separate states, each of which established a Government for itself, after the Declaration of Independence, done the 4th of July, 1776. Each state acted independently of the rest, in forming its Government; but the same general principle pervades the whole. When the several state Governments were formed, they proceeded to form the federal Government that acts over the whole in all matters which concern the interest of the whole, or which relate to the intercourse of the several states with each other, or with foreign Nations. I will begin with giving an instance from one of the state Governments (that of Pennsylvania), and then proceed to the federal Government.

The state of Pennsylvania, though nearly of the same extent of territory as England, was then divided into only twelve counties. Each of these counties had elected a committee at the commencement of the dispute with the English Government; and as the city of Philadelphia, which also had its committee, was the most central for intelligence, it became the centre of communication to the several county committees. When it became necessary to proceed to the formation of a Government, the committee of Philadelphia proposed a conference of all the committees, to be held in that city, and which met the latter end of July, 1776.

Though these committees had been elected by the people, they were not elected expressly for the purpose, nor invested with the authority, of forming a Constitution; and as they could not, consistently with the American ideas of right, assume such a power, they could only confer upon the matter, and put it into a train of operation. The conferees, therefore, did no more than state the case, and recommend to the several counties to elect six representatives for each county, to meet in convention at Philadelphia, with powers to form a Constitution, and propose it for public consideration.

This convention, of which Benjamin Franklin was President, having met and deliberated, and agreed upon a Constitution, they next ordered it to be published, not as a thing established, but for the consideration of the whole people, their approbation or rejection, and then adjourned to a stated time. When the time of adjournment was expired, the convention re-assembled, and as the general opinion of the people in approbation of it was then known, the Constitution was signed, sealed, and proclaimed, on the *authority of the people,* and the original instrument deposited as a public record. The convention then appointed a day for the general election of the representatives who were to compose the Government, and the time it should commence; and having done this they dissolved, and returned to their several homes and occupations.

In this Constitution were laid down, first, a declaration of rights; then followed the form which the Government should have, and the powers which it should possess—the authority of the courts of judicature and of juries—the manner in which elections should be conducted, and the proportion of representatives to the number of electors—the time which each succeeding assembly should continue, which was one year—the mode of levying, and the accounting for the expenditure, of public money—of appointing public officers, etc., etc.

No article of this Constitution could be altered or infringed at the discretion of the Government that was to ensue. It was to the Government a law. But as it would have been unwise to preclude the benefit of experience, and in order also to prevent the accumulation of errors, if any should be found, and to preserve a unison of Government with the circumstances of the state to all times, the Constitution provided that at the expiration of every seven years, a convention should be elected for the express purpose of revising the Constitution and making alterations, additions, or abolitions therein, if any such should be found necessary.

Here we see a regular process—a Government issuing out of a Constitution, formed by the people in their original character; and that Constitution serving not only as an authority, but as a law of controul to the Government. It was the political Bible of the state. Scarcely a family was without it. Every member of the Government had a copy; and nothing was more common when any debate arose on the principle of a bill, or on the extent of any species of authority, than for the members to take the printed Constitution out of their pocket and read the chapter with which such matter in debate was connected.

Having thus given an instance from one of the states, I will show the proceedings by which the federal Constitution of the United States arose and was formed.

Congress, at its first two meetings, in September, 1774, and May, 1775, was nothing more than a deputation from the legislatures of the several provinces, afterwards states; and had no other authority than what arose from common consent, and the necessity of its acting as a public body. In everything which related to the internal affairs of America, Congress went no further than to issue recommendations to the several provincial assemblies, who at discretion adopted them or not. Nothing on the part of Congress was compulsive; yet in this situation, it was more faithfully and affectionately obeyed than was any Government in Europe. This instance, like that of the National Assembly of France, sufficiently shews, that the strength of Government does not consist of anything *within* itself, but in the attachment of a Nation, and the interest which the people feel in supporting it. When this is lost Government is but a child in power, and though like the old Government of France it may harass individuals for a while, it but facilitates its own fall.

After the Declaration of Independence it became consistent with the principle on which representative

Government is founded, that the authority of Congress should be defined and established. Whether that authority should be more or less than Congress then discretionarily exercised, was not the question. It was merely the rectitude of the measure.

For this purpose, the act called the Act of Confederation (which was a sort of imperfect federal Constitution) was proposed, and after long deliberation was concluded in the year 1781. It was not the Act of Congress, because it is repugnant to the principles of representative Government that a body should give power to itself. Congress first informed the several states of the powers which it conceived were necessary to be invested in the union, to enable it to perform the duties and services required from it; and the states severally agreed with each other, and concentrated in Congress those powers.

It may not be improper to observe that in both those instances (the one of Pennsylvania, and the other of the United States) there is no such thing as an idea of a compact between the people on one side and the Government on the other. The compact was that of the people with each other to produce and constitute a Government. To suppose that any Government can be a party in a compact with the whole people is to suppose it to have existence before it can have a right to exist. The only instance in which a compact can take place between the people and those who exercise the Government is, that the people shall pay them while they choose to employ them.

Government is not a trade which any man, or any body of men, has a right to set up and exercise for his own emolument, but is altogether a trust in right of those by whom the trust is delegated, and by whom it is always resumable. It has of itself no rights; they are altogether duties.

Having thus given two instances of the original formation of a Constitution, I will shew the manner in which both have been changed since their first establishment.

The powers vested in the Governments of the several states, by the state Constitutions, were found upon experience to be too great, and those vested in the federal Government by the Act of Confederation, too little. The defect was not in the principle but in the distribution of power.

Numerous publications, in pamphlets and in newspapers, appeared on the propriety and necessity of new modelling the federal Government. After some time of public discussion, carried on through the channel of the press, and in conversations, the state of Virginia, experiencing some inconvenience with respect to commerce, proposed holding a continental conference; in consequence of which, a deputation from five or six of the state assemblies met at Annapolis, in Maryland, 1786. This meeting, not conceiving itself sufficiently authorised to go into business of a reform, did no more than state their general opinions of the propriety of the measure, and recommend that a convention of all the states should be held the year following.

The convention met at Philadelphia in May, 1787, of which General Washington was elected President. He was not at that time connected with any of the state Governments, or with Congress. He delivered up his commission when the war ended, and since then had lived a private citizen.

The convention went deeply into all the subjects; and having, after a variety of debate and investigation, agreed among themselves upon the several parts of a federal Constitution, the next question was, the manner of giving it authority and practice.

For this purpose they did not, like a cabal of courtiers, send for a Dutch Stadtholder, or a German Elector; but they referred the whole matter to the sense and interests of the country.

They first directed that the proposed Constitution should be published. Secondly, that each state should elect a convention expressly for the purpose of taking it into consideration, and of ratifying or rejecting it; and that as soon as the approbation and ratification of any nine states should be given, that those states should proceed to the election of their proportion of members to the new federal Government; and that the operation of it should then begin, and the federal Government cease.

The several states proceeded accordingly to elect their conventions. Some of those conventions ratified the Constitution by very large majorities, and two or three unanimously. In others there were much debate and division of opinion. In the Massachusetts convention, which met at Boston, the majority was not above nineteen or twenty in about three hundred members; but such is the nature of representative Government, that it quietly decides all matters by majority. After the debate in the Massachusetts convention was closed, and the vote taken, the objecting members rose and declared: *"That though they had argued and voted against it because certain parts appeared to them in a different light to what they appeared to other members; yet, as the vote had decided in favour of the Constitution as proposed, they should give it the same practical support as if they had voted for it."*

As soon as nine states had concurred (and the rest followed in the order their conventions were elected), the old fabric of the federal Government was taken down, and the new erected, of which General Washington is President. In this place I cannot help remarking that the character and services of this gentleman are sufficient to put all those men called Kings to shame. While they are receiving from the sweat and labours of mankind a prodigality of pay, to which neither their abilities nor their services can entitle them, he is rendering every service in his power, and refusing every pecuniary reward. He accepted no pay as commander-in-chief; he accepts none as President of the United States.

After the new federal Constitution was established, the state of Pennsylvania, conceiving that some parts of its own Constitution required to be altered, elected a convention for that purpose. The proposed alterations were published, and the people concurring therein, they were established.

In forming those Constitutions, or in altering them, little or no inconvenience took place. The ordinary course of things was not interrupted, and the advantages have been much. It is always the interest of a far greater number of people in a Nation to have things right than to let them remain wrong; and when public matters are open to debate, and the public judgment free, it will not decide wrong, unless it decides too hastily.

In the two instances of changing the Constitutions, the Governments then in being were not actors either way. Government has no right to make itself a party in any debate respecting the principles or modes of forming, or of changing, Constitutions. It is not for the benefit of those who exercise the powers of Government that Constitutions, and the Governments issuing from them, are established. In all those matters the right of judging and acting are in those who pay, and not in those who receive.

A Constitution is the property of a Nation, and not of those who exercise the Government. All the Constitutions of America are declared to be established on the authority of the people. In France, the word Nation is used instead of the people; but in both cases a Constitution is a thing antecedent to the Government, and always distinct therefrom.

In England it is not difficult to perceive that everything has a Constitution, except the Nation. Every society and association that is established first agreed upon a number of original articles, digested into form, which are its Constitution. It then appointed its officers, whose powers and authorities are described in that Constitution, and the Government of that society then commenced. Those officers, by whatever name they are called, have no authority to add to, alter, or abridge the original articles. It is only to the constituting power that this right belongs.

From the want of understanding the difference between a Constitution and a Government, Dr. Johnson and all writers of his description have always bewildered themselves. They could not but perceive that there must necessarily be a *controuling* power existing somewhere, and they placed this in the discretion of the persons exercising the Government, instead of placing it in a Constitution formed by the Nation. When it is in a Constitution it has the Nation for its support, and the natural and the political controuling powers are together. The laws which are enacted by Governments controul men only as individuals, but the Nation, through its Constitution, controuls the whole Government, and has a natural ability so to do. The final controuling power, therefore, and the original constituting power, are one and the same power.

Dr. Johnson could not have advanced such a position in any country where there was a Constitution; and he is himself an evidence that no such thing as a Constitution exists in England. But it may be put as a question, not improper to be investigated, that if a Constitution does not exist how came the idea of its existence so generally established.

In order to decide this question, it is necessary to consider a Constitution in both its cases:—First, as creating a Government and giving it powers. Secondly, as regulating and restraining the powers so given.

If we begin with William of Normandy, we find that the Government of England was originally a tyranny, founded on an invasion and conquest of the country.

This being admitted, it will then appear that the exertion of the Nation at different periods to abate that tyranny and render it less intolerable, has been credited for a Constitution.

Magna Charta, as it was called (it is now like an almanack of the same date), was no more than compelling the Government to renounce a part of its assumptions. It did not create and give powers to Government in the manner a Constitution does; but was, as far as it went, of the nature of a re-conquest, and not a Constitution; for could the Nation have totally expelled the usurpation as France has done its despotism, it would then have had a Constitution to form.

The history of the Edwards and the Henries, and up to the commencement of the Stuarts, exhibits as many instances of tyranny as could be acted within the limits to which the Nation had restricted it. The Stuarts endeavoured to pass those limits, and their fate is well known. In all those instances we see nothing of a Constitution, but only of restrictions on assumed power.

After this, another William, descended from the same stock, and claiming from the same origin, gained possession; and of the two evils, *James* and *William*, the nation preferred what it thought the least; since, from circumstances, it must take one. The act, called the Bill of Rights, comes here into view. What is it but a bargain which the parts of the Government made with each other, to divide powers, profits, and privileges? You shall have so much, and I will have the rest; and with respect to the Nation, it said, for *your share* YOU *shall have the right of petitioning*. This being the case, the Bill of Rights is more properly the bill of wrongs and of insult. As to what is called the convention Parliament, it was a thing that made itself, and then made the authority by which it acted. A few persons got together, and called themselves by that name. Several of them had never been elected, and none of them for the purpose.

From the time of William a species of Government arose, issuing out of this coalition Bill of Rights; and more so since the corruption introduced at the Hanover succession, by the agency of Walpole, that can be described by no other name than a despotic legislation. Though the parts may embarrass each other, the whole has no bounds; and the only right it acknowledges out of itself is the right of petitioning. Where then is the Constitution that either gives or restrains power?

It is not because a part of the Government is elective, that makes it less a despotism, if the persons so elected possess afterwards, as a Parliament, unlimited powers. Election in this case becomes separated from representation, and the candidates are candidates for despotism.

I cannot believe that any Nation, reasoning on its own right, would have thought of calling those things *a Constitution,* if the cry of Constitution had not been set up by the Government. It has got into circulation like the words *bore* and *quiz,* by being chalked up in the speeches of Parliament, as those words were on window-shutters and door-posts; but whatever the Constitution may be in other respects, it has undoubtedly been *the most productive machine of taxation that was ever invented.* The taxes in France, under the new Constitution, are not quite thirteen shillings per head, and the taxes in England, under what is called its present Constitution, are forty-eight shillings and sixpence per head—men, women, and children—amounting to nearly seventeen millions sterling, besides the expence of collecting, which is upwards of a million more.

In a country like England, where the whole of the civil Government is executed by the people of every town and county by means of parish officers, magistrates, quarterly sessions, juries, and assize, without any trouble to what is called the Government or any other expence to the revenue than the salary of the judges, it is astonishing how such a mass of taxes can be employed. Not even the internal defence of the country is paid out of the revenue. On all occasions, whether real or contrived, recourse is continually had to new loans and new taxes. No wonder, then, that a machine of Government so advantageous to the advocates of a Court should be so triumphantly extolled. No wonder, that St. James' or St. Stephen's should echo with the continual cry of Constitution! No wonder that the French Revolution should be reprobated, and the *res-publica* treated with reproach! The *red book* of England, like the red book of France, will explain the reason.

I will now, by way of relaxation, turn a thought or two to Mr. Burke. I ask his pardon for neglecting him so long.

"America," says he (in his speech on the Canada Constitution Bill), "never dreamed of such absurd doctrine as the *Rights of Man*."

Mr. Burke is such a bold presumer, and advances his assertions and his premises with such a deficiency of judgment, that without troubling ourselves about the principles of philosophy or politics, the mere logical conclusions they produce are ridiculous. For instance:

If Governments, as Mr. Burke asserts, are not founded on the Rights of MAN, and are founded on *any rights* at all, they consequently must be founded on the right of *something* that is *not man*. What then is that something?

Generally speaking, we know of no other creatures that inhabit the earth than man and beast; and in all cases where only two things offer themselves, and one must be admitted, a negation proved on any one amounts to an affirmative on the other; and therefore,

Mr. Burke, by proving against the Rights of *Man* proves in behalf of the *beast;* and consequently, proves that Government is a beast; and as difficult things sometimes explain each other, we now see the origin of keeping wild beasts in the Tower; for they certainly can be of no other use than to shew the origin of the Government. They are in the place of a Constitution. O, John Bull, what honours thou has lost by not being a wild beast. Thou mightest, on Mr. Burke's system, have been in the Tower for life.

If Mr. Burke's arguments have not weight enough to keep one serious, the fault is less mine than his; and as I am willing to make an apology to the reader for the liberty I have taken, I hope Mr. Burke will also make his for giving the cause.

Having thus paid Mr. Burke the compliment of remembering him, I return to the subject.

From the want of a Constitution in England to restrain and regulate the wild impulse of power, many of the laws are irrational and tyrannical, and the administration of them vague and problematical.

The attention of the Government of England (for I rather chuse to call it by this name than the English Government) appears since its political connection with Germany to have been so completely engrossed and absorbed by foreign affairs, and the means of raising taxes, that it seems to exist for no other purposes. Domestic concerns are neglected; and with respect to regular law there is scarcely such a thing.

Almost every case now must be determined by some precedent, be that precedent good or bad, or whether it properly applies or not; and the practice is become so general as to suggest a suspicion that it proceeds from a deeper policy than at first sight appears.

Since the Revolution of America, and more so since that of France, this preaching up the doctrines of precedents, drawn from times and circumstances antecedent to those events, has been the studied practice of the English Government. The generality of those precedents are founded on principles and opinions, the reverse of what they ought; and the greater distance of time they are drawn from the more they are to be suspected. But by associating those precedents with a superstitious reverence for ancient things, as monks shew relics and call them holy, the generality of mankind are deceived into the design. Governments now act as if they were afraid to awaken a single reflection in man. They are softly leading him to the sepulchre of precedents to deaden his faculties and call attention from the scene of Revolutions. They feel that he is arriving at knowledge faster than they wish, and their policy of precedent is the barometer of their fears. This political popery, like the ecclesiastical popery of old, has had its day, and is hastening to its exit. The ragged relic and the antiquated precedent, the monk and the monarch, will moulder together.

Government by precedent, without any regard to the principle of the precedent, is one of the vilest systems that can be set up. In numerous instances the precedent ought to operate as a warning, and not as an example, and requires to be shunned instead of imitated; but instead of this, precedents are taken in the lump, and put at once for Constitution and for law.

Either the doctrine of precedents is policy to keep man in a state of ignorance, or it is a practical confession that wisdom degenerates in Governments as Governments increase in age, and can only hobble along by the stilts and crutches of precedents. How is it that the same persons who would proudly be thought wiser than their predecessors appear at the same time only as the ghosts of departed wisdom? How strangely is antiquity treated! To answer some purposes it is spoken of as the times of darkness and ignorance, and to answer others, it is put for the light of the world.

If the doctrine of precedents is to be followed, the

expences of Government need not continue the same. Why pay men extravagantly who have but little to do? If everything that can happen is already in precedent, legislation is at an end, and precedent, like a dictionary, determines every case. Either, therefore, Government has arrived at its dotage, and requires to be renovated, or all the occasions for exercising its wisdom have already occurred.

We now see all over Europe, and particularly in England, the curious phaenomenon of a nation looking one way, and the Government the other—the one forward and the other backward. If Governments are to go on by precedent, while Nations go on by improvement, they must at last come to a final separation; and the sooner, and the more civilly they determine this point, the better.

Having thus spoken of Constitutions generally, as things distinct from actual Governments, let us proceed to consider the parts of which a Constitution is composed.

Opinions differ more on this subject than with respect to the whole. That a Nation ought to have a Constitution, as a rule, for the conduct of its Government is a simple question in which all men not directly courtiers, will agree. It is only on the component parts that questions and opinions multiply.

But this difficulty, like every other, will diminish when put into a train of being rightly understood.

The first thing is, that a Nation has a right to establish a Constitution.

Whether it exercises this right in the most judicious manner at first is quite another case. It exercises it agreeably to the judgment it possesses; and by continuing to do so, all errors will at last be exploded.

When this right is established in a Nation, there is no fear that it will be employed to its own injury. A Nation can have no interest in being wrong.

Though all the Constitutions of America are on one general principle, yet no two of them are exactly alike in their component parts or in the distribution of the powers which they give to the actual Governments. Some are more, and others less complex.

In forming a Constitution, it is first necessary to consider what are the ends for which Government is necessary? Secondly, what are the best means, and the least expencive, for accomplishing those ends?

Government is nothing more than a national association; and the object of this association is the good of all, as well individually as collectively. Every man wishes to pursue his occupation, and to enjoy the fruits of his labours and the produce of his property in peace and safety, and with the least possible expence. When these things are accomplished, all the objects for which Government ought to be established are answered.

It has been customary to consider Government under three distinct general heads. The legislative, the executive, and the judicial.

But if we permit our judgment to act unencumbered by the habit of multiplied terms, we can perceive no more than two divisions of power, of which civil Government is composed, namely that of legislating or enacting laws, and that of executing or administering them. Everything, therefore, appertaining to civil Government, classes itself under one or other of these two divisions.

So far as regards the execution of the laws, that which is called the judicial power, is strictly and properly the executive power of every country. It is that power to which every individual has to appeal, and which causes the law to be executed; neither have we any other clear idea with respect to the official execution of the laws. In England, and also in America and France, this power begins with the magistrate, and proceeds up through all the courts of judicature.

I leave to courtiers to explain what is meant by

calling Monarchy the executive power. It is merely a name in which acts of Government are done; and any other, or none at all, would answer the same purpose. Laws have neither more or less authority on this account. It must be from the justness of their principles, and the interest which a Nation feels therein, that they derive support; if they require any other than this, it is a sign that something in the system of Government is imperfect. Laws difficult to be executed cannot be generally good.

With respect to the organization of the *legislative power,* different modes have been adopted in different countries. In America it is generally composed of two houses. In France it consists but of one, but in both countries it is wholly by representation.

The case is, that mankind (from the long tyranny of assumed power) have had so few opportunities of making the necessary trials on modes and principles of Government, in order to discover the best, *that Government is but now beginning to be known,* and experience is yet wanting to determine many particulars.

The objections against two houses are, first, that there is an inconsistency in any part of a whole legislature, coming to a final determination by vote on any matter, whilst *that matter,* with respect to *that whole,* is yet only in a train of deliberation, and consequently open to new illustrations.

Secondly. That by taking a vote on each, as a separate body, it always admits of the possibility, and is often the case in practice, that the minority governs the majority, and that in some instances to a degree of great inconsistency.

Thirdly. That two houses arbitrarily checking or controuling each other is inconsistent; because it cannot be proved on the principles of just representation, that either should be wiser or better than the other. They may check in the wrong as well as in the right—

and therefore to give the power where we cannot give the wisdom to use it, nor be assured of its being rightly used, renders the hazard at least equal to the precaution.

The objection against a single house is, that it is always in a condition of committing itself too soon. But it should at the same time be remembered, that when there is a Constitution which defines the power, and establishes the principles within which a legislature shall act, there is already a more effectual check provided, and more powerfully operating, than any other check can be. For example:

Were a Bill to be brought into any of the American legislatures similar to that which was passed into an act by the English Parliament, at the commencement of George the First, to extend the duration of the assemblies to a longer period than they now sit, the check is in the Constitution, which in effect says, *Thus far shalt thou go and no further.*

But in order to remove the objection against a single house, that of acting with too quick an impulse, and at the same time to avoid the inconsistencies, in some cases absurdities, arising from two houses, the following method has been proposed as an improvement upon both.

First, to have but one representation.

Secondly, to divide that representation, by lot, into two or three parts.

Thirdly, that every proposed Bill shall be first debated in those parts by succession, that they may become the hearers of each other, but without taking any vote. After which the whole representation to assemble for a general debate and determination by vote.

To this proposed improvement has been added another, for the purpose of keeping the representation in the state of constant renovation; which is that one-third of the representation of each country shall go out at the expiration of one year, and the number be replaced by new elections. Another third at the expiration of the second year replaced in like manner, and every third year to be a general election.

But in whatever manner the separate parts of a Constitution may be arranged there is *one* general principle that distinguishes freedom from slavery, which is, *that all hereditary* Government over a people is to them a species of slavery, and representative Government is freedom.

Considering Government in the only light in which it should be considered, that of a NATIONAL ASSOCIATION, it ought to be so constructed as not to be disordered by any accident happening among the parts; and, therefore, no extraordinary power, capable of producing such an effect, should be lodged in the hands of any individual. The death, sickness, absence or defection, of any one individual in a Government, ought to be a matter of no more consequence, with respect to the Nation, than if the same circumstances had taken place in a member of the English Parliament, or the French National Assembly.

Scarcely anything presents a more degrading character of national greatness, than its being thrown into confusion, by anything happening to or acted by any individual; and the ridiculousness of the scene is often increased by the natural insignificance of the person by whom it is occasioned. Were a Government so constructed, that it could not go on unless a goose or a gander were present in the senate, the difficulties would be just as great and as real, on the flight or sickness of the goose, or the gander, as if it were called a King. We laugh at individuals for the silly difficulties they make to themselves, without perceiving that the greatest of all ridiculous things are acted in Governments.

All the Constitutions of America are on a plan that excludes the childish embarrassments which occur in monarchical countries. No suspension of Government can there take place for a moment, from any circumstances whatever. The system of representation provides for everything, and is the only system in which Nations and Governments can always appear in their proper character.

As extraordinary power ought not to be lodged in the hands of any individual, so ought there to be no appropriations of public money to any person, beyond what his services in a state may be worth. It signifies not whether a man be called a president, a king, an emperor, a senator, or by any other name which propriety or folly may devise or arrogance assume, it is only a certain service he can perform in the state; and the service of any such individual in the routine of office, whether such office be called monarchical, presidential, senatorial, or by any other name or title, can never exceed the value of ten thousand pounds a year. All the great services that are done in the world are performed by volunteer characters, who accept nothing for them; but the routine of office is always regulated to such a general standard of abilities as to be within the compass of numbers in every country to perform, and therefore cannot merit very extraordinary recompence. *Government,* says Swift, *is a plain thing, and fitted to the capacity of many heads.*

It is inhuman to talk of a million sterling a year, paid out of the public taxes of any country, for the support of an individual, whilst thousands who are forced to contribute thereto, are pining with want, and struggling with misery. Government does not consist in a contrast between prisons and palaces, between poverty and pomp; it is not instituted to rob the needy of his mite, and increase the wretchedness of the wretched. But of this part of the subject I shall speak hereafter, and confine myself at present to political observations.

When extraordinary power and extraordinary pay

are allotted to any individual in a Government, he becomes the centre, round which every kind of corruption generates and forms. Give to any man a million a-year, and add thereto the power of creating and disposing of places, at the expence of a country, and the liberties of that country are no longer secure. What is called the splendour of a throne is no other than the corruption of the state. It is made up of a band of parasites living in luxurious indolence out of the public taxes.

When once such a vicious system is established it becomes the guard and protection of all inferior abuses. The man who is in the receipt of a million a year is the last person to promote a spirit of reform, lest, in the event, it should reach to himself. It is always his interest to defend inferior abuses, as so many outworks to protect the citadel; and on this species of political fortification, all the parts have such a common dependence that it is never to be expected that they will attack each other.

Monarchy would not have continued so many ages in the world had it not been for the abuses it protects. It is the master-fraud, which shelters all others. By admitting a participation of the spoil, it makes itself friends; and when it ceases to do this it will cease to be the idol of courtiers.

As the principle on which Constitutions are now formed rejects all hereditary pretensions to Government, it also rejects all that catalogue of assumptions known by the name of prerogatives.

If there is any Government where prerogatives might with apparent safety be entrusted to any individual, it is in the federal Government of America. The President of the United States of America is elected only for four years. He is not only responsible in the general sense of the word, but a particular mode is laid down in the Constitution for trying him. He cannot be elected under thirty-five years of age; and he must be a native of the country.

In a comparison of these cases with the Government of England, the difference when applied to the latter amounts to an absurdity. In England the person who exercises prerogative is often a foreigner; always half a foreigner, and always married to a foreigner. He is never in full natural or political connection with the country, is not responsible for anything, and becomes of age at eighteen years; yet such a person is permitted to form foreign alliances, without even the knowledge of the Nation, and to make war and peace without its consent.

But this is not all. Though such a person cannot dispose of the Government in the manner of a testator, he dictates the marriage connections, which, in effect, accomplish a great part of the same end. He cannot directly bequeath half the Government to Prussia, but he can form a marriage partnership that will produce the same thing. Under such circumstances, it is happy for England that she is not situated on the Continent, or she might, like Holland, fall under the dictatorship of Prussia. Holland, by marriage, is as effectually governed by Prussia, as if the whole tyranny of bequeathing the Government had been the means.

The presidency in America (or, as it is sometimes called, the executive) is the only office from which a foreigner is excluded, and in England it is the only one to which he is admitted. A foreigner cannot be a member of Parliament, but he may be what is called a King. If there is any reason for excluding foreigners, it ought to be from those offices where mischief can be most acted, and where, by uniting every bias of interest and attachment, the trust is best secured. But as Nations proceed in the great business of forming Constitutions, they will examine with more precision into the nature and business of that department which is called executive. What the legislative and judicial departments are every one can see; but with respect to what, in Europe, is called the executive, as distinct from these two, it is either a political superfluity or a chaos of unknown things.

Some kind of official department, to which reports shall be made from the different parts of a Nation, or from abroad, to be laid before the national representatives, is all that is necessary; but there is no consistency in calling this the executive; neither can it be considered in any other light than as inferior to the legislative. The sovereign authority in any country is the power of making laws, and everything else is an official department.

Next to the arrangement of the principles and the organization of the several parts of a Constitution, is the provision to be made for the support of the persons to whom the Nation shall confide the administration of the Constitutional powers.

A nation can have no right to the time and services of any person at his own expence, whom it may choose to employ or entrust in any department whatever; neither can any reason be given for making provision for the support of any one part of a Government and not for the other.

But admitting that the honour of being entrusted with any part of a Government is to be considered a sufficient reward, it ought to be so to every person alike. If the members of the legislature of any country are to serve at their own expence, that which is called the executive, whether monarchical or by any other name, ought to serve in like manner. It is inconsistent to pay the one, and accept the service of the other gratis.

In America, every department in the Government is decently provided for; but no one is extravagantly paid. Every member of Congress, and of the assemblies, is allowed a sufficiency for his expences. Whereas in England, a most prodigal provision is made for the support of one part of the Government and none for the other, the consequence of which is that the one is furnished with the means of corruption and the other is put into the condition of being corrupted. Less than a fourth part of such expence, applied as it is in America, would remedy a great part of the corruption.

Another reform in the American Constitutions is the exploding of all oaths of personality. The oath of allegiance in America is to the nation only. The putting any individual as a figure for a Nation is improper. The happiness of a Nation is the superior object, and therefore the intention of an oath of allegiance ought not to be obscured by being figuratively taken to, or in the name of, any person. The oath, called the civic oath, in France, viz., the *"Nation, the Law, and the King,"* is improper. If taken at all, it ought to be as in America, to the nation only. The law may or may not be good; but in this place it can have no other meaning than as being conducive to the happiness of the nation, and therefore is included in it. The remainder of the oath is improper on the ground that all personal oaths ought to be abolished. They are the remains of tyranny on one part and slavery on the other; and the name of the CREATOR ought not to be introduced to witness the degradation of his creation; or if taken, as is already mentioned, as figurative of the Nation, it is in this place redundant. But whatever apology may be made for oaths at the first establishment of a Government, they ought not to be permitted afterwards. If a Government requires the support of oaths, it is a sign that it is not worth supporting, and ought not to be supported. Make Government what it ought to be, and it will support itself.

To conclude this part of the subject:—One of the greatest improvements that has been made for the perpetual security and progress of constitutional liberty, is the provision which the new Constitutions make for occasionally revising, altering, and amending them.

The principle upon which Mr. Burke formed his political creed, that of *binding and controuling posterity to the end of time, and of renouncing and abdicating the rights of all posterity for ever,* is now become too detestable to be made a subject of debate; and therefore I pass it over with no other notice than exposing it.

Government is but now beginning to be known. Hitherto it has been the mere exercise of power which forbade all effectual enquiry into rights, and grounded itself wholly on possession. While the enemy of liberty was its judge, the progress of its principles must have been small indeed.

The Constitutions of America, and also that of France, have either affixed a period for their revision, or laid down the mode by which improvement shall be made. It is perhaps impossible to establish anything that combines principles with opinions and practice, which the progress of circumstances, through a length of years, will not in some measure derange, or render inconsistent; and, therefore, to prevent inconveniences accumulating, till they discourage reformations or provoke Revolutions, it is best to provide the means of regulating them as they occur. The Rights of Man are the rights of all generations of men, and cannot be monopolized by any. That which is worth following will be followed for the sake of its worth, and it is in this that its security lies, and not in any conditions with which it may be encumbered. When a man leaves property to his heirs, he does not connect it with an obligation that they shall accept it. Why, then, should we do otherwise with respect to Constitutions?

The best Constitution that could now be devised, consistent with the condition of the present moment, may be far short of that excellence which a few years may afford. There is a morning of reason rising upon man on the subject of Government that has not appeared before. As the barbarism of the present old Governments expires, the moral condition of Nations with respect to each other will be changed. Man will not be brought up with the savage idea of considering his species as his enemy, because the accident of birth gave the individuals existence in countries distinguished by different names; and as Constitutions have always some relation to external as well as to domestic circumstances, the means of benefiting by every change, foreign or domestic, should be a part of every Constitution.

We already see an alteration in the national disposition of England and France towards each other, which, when we look back to only a few years, is itself a Revolution. Who could have foreseen, or who would have believed, that a French National Assembly would ever have been a popular toast in England, or that a friendly alliance of the two Nations should become the wish of either? It shews that man, were he not corrupted by Governments, is naturally the friend of man, and that human nature is not of itself vicious. That spirit of jealousy and ferocity, which the Governments of the two countries inspired, and which they rendered subservient to the purpose of taxation, is now yielding to the dictates of reason, interest, and humanity. The trade of courts is beginning to be understood, and the affectation of mystery, with all the artificial sorcery by which they imposed upon mankind, is on the decline. It has received its death wound; and though it may linger, it will expire.

Government ought to be as much open to improvement as anything which appertains to man, instead of which it has been monopolized from age to age, by the most ignorant and vicious of the human race. Need we any other proof of their wretched management, than the excess of debts and taxes with which every nation groans, and the quarrels into which they have precipitated the world?

Just emerging from such a barbarous condition, it is too soon to determine to what extent of improvement Government may yet be carried. For what we can foresee, all Europe may form but one great Republic, and man be free of the whole.

Chapter V
Ways and Means of Improving the Condition of Europe, Interspersed with Miscellaneous Observations

In contemplating a subject that embraces with equatorial magnitude the whole region of humanity it is impossible to confine the pursuit in one single direction. It takes ground on every character and condition that appertains to man, and blends the individual, the nation, and the world.

From a small spark, kindled in America, a flame has arisen not to be extinguished. Without consuming, like the *Ultima Ratio Regum,* it winds its progress from Nation to Nation and conquers by a silent operation. Man finds himself changed, he scarcely perceives how. He acquires a knowledge of his rights by attending justly to his interest, and discovers in the event that the strength and powers of despotism consist wholly in the fear of resisting it, and that in order *"to be free it is sufficient that he wills it."*

Having in all the preceding parts of this work endeavoured to establish a system of principles as a basis on which Governments ought to be erected, I shall proceed in this to the ways and means of rendering them into practice. But in order to introduce this part of the subject with more propriety and stronger effect, some preliminary observations, deducible from, or connected with those principles, are necessary.

Whatever the form or Constitution of Government may be, it ought to have no other object than the *general* happiness. When instead of this it operates to create and increase wretchedness, in any of the parts of society, it is on a wrong system and reformation is necessary.

Customary language has classed the condition of man under the two descriptions of civilized and uncivilized life. To the one it has ascribed felicity and affluence: to the other hardship and want. But, however our imagination may be impressed by painting and comparison, it is nevertheless true, that a great portion of mankind, in what are called civilized countries, are in a state of poverty and wretchedness, far below the condition of an Indian. I speak not of one country, but of all. It is so in England, it is so all over Europe. Let us enquire into the cause.

It lies not in any natural defect in the principles of civilization, but in preventing those principles having an universal operation; the consequence of which is a perpetual system of war and expence, that drains the country and defeats the general felicity of which civilization is capable.

All the European Governments (France now excepted) are constructed not on the principle of universal civilization, but on the reverse of it. So far as those Governments relate to each other they are in the same condition as we conceive of savage uncivilized life, they put themselves beyond the law as well of GOD as of man, and are with respect to principle and reciprocal conduct like so many individuals in a state of nature.

The inhabitants of every country, under the civilization of laws, easily civilize together, but Governments being yet in an uncivilized state, and almost continually at war, they pervert the abundance which civilized life produces to carry on the uncivilized part to a greater extent. By thus engrafting the barbarism of

Government upon the internal civilization of a country, it draws from the latter, and more especially from the poor, a great portion of those earnings which should be applied to their own subsistence and comfort. Apart from all reflections of morality and philosophy, it is a melancholy fact that more than one-fourth of the labour of mankind is annually consumed by this barbarous system.

What has served to continue this evil is the pecuniary advantage which all the Governments of Europe have found in keeping up this state of uncivilization. It affords to them pretences for power and revenue, for which there would be neither occasion nor apology if the circle of civilization were rendered complete. Civil Government alone, or the Government of laws, is not productive of pretences for many taxes; it operates at home, directly under the eye of the country, and precludes the possibility of much imposition. But when the scene is laid in the uncivilized contention of Governments, the field of pretences is enlarged, and the country being no longer a judge, is open to every imposition which Governments please to act.

Not a thirtieth, scarcely a fortieth, part of the taxes which are raised in England are either occasioned by, or applied to, the purposes of civil Government. It is not difficult to see that the whole which the actual Government does in this respect is to enact laws, and that the country administers and executes them, at its own expense, by means of magistrates, juries, sessions, and assize, over and above the taxes which it pays.

In this view of the case, we have two distinct characters of Government; the one the civil Government, or the Government of laws, which operates at home, the other the Court or Cabinet Government, which operates abroad, on the rude plan of uncivilized life; the one attended with little charge, the other with boundless extravagance; and so distinct are the two, that if the latter were to sink, as it were, by a sudden opening of the earth, and totally disappear, the former would not be deranged. It would still proceed, because it is the common interest of the Nation that it should, and all the means are in practice.

Revolutions, then, have for their object a change in the moral condition of Governments, and with this change the burden of public taxes will lessen, and civilization will be left to the enjoyment of that abundance of which it is now deprived.

In contemplating the whole of this subject, I extend my views into the department of commerce. In all my publications, where the matter would admit, I have been an advocate for commerce, because I am a friend to its effects. It is a pacific system, operating to cordialise mankind, by rendering Nations, as well as individuals, useful to each other. As to the mere theoretical reformation, I have never preached it up. The most effectual process is that of improving the condition of man by means of his interest; and it is on this ground that I take my stand.

If commerce were permitted to act to the universal extent it is capable, it would extirpate the system of war, and produce a Revolution in the uncivilized state of Governments. The invention of commerce has arisen since those Governments began, and it is the greatest approach towards universal civilization that has yet been made by any means not immediately flowing from moral principles.

Whatever has a tendency to promote the civil intercourse of Nations by an exchange of benefits, is a subject as worthy of philosophy as of politics. Commerce is no other than the traffic of two individuals, multiplied on a scale of number; and the same rule that nature intended the intercourse of two, she intended for all. For this purpose she has distributed the materials of manufactures and commerce in various and distant parts of a Nation and of the world; and as they cannot be procured by war so cheaply or so commodiously as by commerce, she has rendered the latter the means of extirpating the former.

As the two are nearly the opposites of each other, consequently, the uncivilized state of the European Governments is injurious to commerce. Every kind of destruction or embarrassment serves to lessen the quantity, and it matters but little in what part of the commercial world the reduction begins. Like blood, it cannot be taken from any of the parts, without being taken from the whole mass in circulation, and all partake of the loss. When the ability in any Nation to buy is destroyed, it equally involves the seller. Could the Government of England destroy the commerce of all other Nations, she would most effectually ruin her own.

It is possible that a Nation may be the carrier for the world, but she cannot be the merchant. She cannot be the seller and buyer of her own merchandize. The ability to buy must reside out of herself; and, therefore, the prosperity of any commercial Nation is regulated by the prosperity of the rest. If they are poor she cannot be rich, and her condition, be it what it may, is an index of the height of the commercial tide in other Nations.

That the principles of commerce, and its universal operation, may be understood, without understanding the practice, is a position that reason will not deny; and it is on this ground only that I argue the subject. It is one thing in the counting-house, in the world it is another. With respect to its operation it must necessarily be contemplated as a reciprocal thing; that only one-half of its power resides within the Nation, and that the whole is as effectually destroyed by destroying the half that resides without, as if the destruction had been committed on that which is within; for neither can act without the other.

When in the last, as well as in the former wars, the commerce of England sunk, it was because the general quantity was lessened everywhere; and it now rises, because commerce is in a rising state in every Nation. If England, at this day, imports and exports more than at any former period, the Nation with which she trades must necessarily do the same; her imports are their exports, and *vice versa*.

There can be no such thing as a Nation flourishing alone in commerce; she can only participate; and the destruction of it in any part must necessarily affect all. When, therefore, Governments are at war, the attack is made upon the common stock of commerce, and the consequence is the same as if each had attacked his own.

The present increase of commerce is not to be attributed to ministers, or to any political contrivances, but to its own natural operations in consequence of peace. The regular markets had been destroyed, the channels of trade broken up, the high road of the seas infested with robbers of every Nation, and the attention of the world called to other objects. Those interruptions have ceased, and peace has restored the deranged condition of things to their proper order.

It is worth remarking, that every Nation reckons the balance of trade in its own favour; and therefore something must be irregular in the common ideas upon this subject.

The fact, however, is true, according to what is called a balance; and it is from this case that commerce is universally supported. Every Nation feels the advantage, or it would abandon the practice; but the deception lies in the mode of making up the accounts, and in attributing what are called profits to a wrong cause.

Mr. Pitt has sometimes amused himself, by showing what he called a balance of trade from the custom-house books. This mode of calculation, not only affords no rule that is true, but one that is false.

In the first place, Every cargo that departs from the

custom-house, appears on the books as an export; and according to the custom-house balance, the losses at sea, and by foreign failures, are all reckoned on the side of profit because they appear as exports.

Secondly, Because the importation by the smuggling trade does not appear on the custom-house books, to arrange against the exports.

No balance, therefore, as applying to superior advantages, can be drawn from those documents: and if we examine the natural operation of commerce, the idea is fallacious, and if true, would soon be injurious. The great support of commerce consists in the balance being a level of benefits among all Nations.

Two merchants of different Nations trading together, will both become rich, and each makes the balance in his own favour; consequently they do not get rich out of each other; and it is the same with respect to the Nations in which they reside. The case must be, that each Nation must get rich out of its own means, and encrease that riches by something which it procures from another in exchange.

If a merchant in England sends an article of English manufacture abroad which costs him a shilling at home and imports something which sells for two, he makes a balance of one shilling in his own favour; but this is not gained out of the foreign Nation or the foreign merchant, for he also does the same by the articles he receives, and neither has a balance of advantage upon the other. The original value of the two articles in their proper countries was but two shillings, but by changing their places, they acquire a new idea of value equal to double what they had at first, and that encreased value is equally divided.

There is no otherwise a balance on foreign than on domestic commerce. The merchants of London and Newcastle trade on the same principles, as if they resided in different Nations, and make their balances in the same manner; yet London does not get rich out of Newcastle, any more than Newcastle out of London; but coals, the merchandize of Newcastle, have an additional value at London, and London merchandize has the same at Newcastle.

Though the principle of all commerce is the same, the domestic, in a national view, is the part the most beneficial; because the whole of the advantages, on both sides, rests within the Nation; whereas, in foreign commerce, it is only participation of one-half.

The most unprofitable of all commerce is that connected with foreign dominion. To a few individuals it may be beneficial, merely because it is commerce; but to the Nation it is a loss. The expence of maintaining dominion more than absorbs the profits of any trade. It does not encrease the general quantity in the world, but operates to lessen it, and as a greater mass would be afloat by relinquishing dominion, the participation without the expence would be more valuable than a greater quantity with it.

But it is impossible to engross commerce by dominion; and therefore it is still more fallacious. It cannot exist in confined channels, and necessarily breaks out by regular or irregular means, that defeat the attempt; and to succeed would be still worse. France, since the Revolution, has been more than indifferent as to foreign possessions, and other Nations will become the same when they investigate the subject with respect to commerce.

To the expence of dominion is to be added that of navies, and when the amount of the two are subtracted from the profits of commerce, it will appear that what is called the balance of trade, even admitting it to exist, is not enjoyed by the Nation, but absorbed by the Government.

The idea of having navies for the protection of commerce is delusive. It is putting the means of destruction for the means of protection. Commerce needs no other protection than the reciprocal interest which every nation feels in supporting it—it is common stock—it exists by a balance of advantages to all; and the only interruption it meets, is from the present uncivilized state of Governments, and which it is common interest to reform.

Quitting this subject, I now proceed to other matters. As it is necessary to include England in the prospect of a general reformation, it is proper to enquire into the defects of its Government. It is only by each Nation reforming its own, that the whole can be improved, and the full benefit of reformation enjoyed. Only partial advantages can flow from partial reforms.

France and England are the only two countries in Europe where a reformation in Government could have successfully begun. The one secure by the ocean, and the other by the immensity of its internal strength, could defy the malignancy of foreign despotism. But it is with Revolutions as with commerce, the advantages increase by their becoming general, and double to either what each would receive alone.

As a new system is now opening to the view of the world, the European courts are plotting to counteract it. Alliances, contrary to all former systems, are agitating, and a common interest of Courts is forming against the common interest of man. This combination draws a line that runs throughout Europe, and presents a cause so entirely new as to exclude all calculations from former circumstances. While despotism warred with despotism, man had no interest in the contest; but in a cause that unites the soldier with the citizen, and Nation with Nation, the despotism of Courts, though it feels the danger, and meditates revenge, is afraid to strike.

No question has arisen within the records of history that pressed with the importance of the present. It is not whether this or that party shall be in or not, or Whig or Tory, or high or low shall prevail; but whether man shall inherit his rights, and universal civilization take place? Whether the fruits of his labours shall be enjoyed by himself or consumed by the profligacy of Governments? Whether robbery shall be banished from Courts, and wretchedness from countries?

When, in countries that are called civilized, we see age going to the workhouse and youth to the gallows, something must be wrong in the system of Government. It would seem, by the exterior appearances of such countries, that all was happiness; but there lies hidden from the eye of common observation, a mass of wretchedness that has scarcely any other chance, than to expire in poverty or infamy. Its entrance into life is marked with the presage of its fate; and until this is remedied, it is in vain to punish.

Civil Government does not consist in executions; but in making that provision for the instruction of youth and the support of age, as to exclude, as much as possible, profligacy from the one and despair from the other. Instead of this, the resources of a country are lavished upon kings, upon Courts, upon hirelings, imposters and prostitutes; and even the poor themselves, with all their wants upon them, are compelled to support the fraud that oppresses them.

Why is it that scarcely any are executed but the poor? The fact is a proof, among other things, of a wretchedness in their condition. Bred up without morals, and cast upon the world without a prospect, they are the exposed sacrifice of vice and legal barbarity. The millions that are superfluously wasted upon Governments are more than sufficient to reform those evils and to benefit the condition of every man in a Nation, not included within the purlieus of a Court. This I hope to make appear in the progress of this work.

It is the nature of compassion to associate with misfortune. In taking up this subject I seek no recompence—I fear no consequence. Fortified with that proud integrity that disdains to triumph or to yield, I will advocate the Rights of Man.

It is to my advantage that I have served an apprenticeship to life. I know the value of moral instruction, and I have seen the danger of the contrary.

At an early period, little more than sixteen years of age, raw and adventurous, and heated with the false heroism of a master who had served in a man-of-war, I began the carver of my own fortune, and entered on board the *Terrible* Privateer, Captain Death. From this adventure I was happily prevented by the affectionate and moral remonstrance of a good father, who, from his own habits of life, being of the Quaker profession, must begin to look upon me as lost. But the impression, much as it affected at the time, began to wear away, and I entered afterwards in the *King of Prussia* Privateer, Captain Mendez, and went with her to sea. Yet from such a beginning, and with all the inconvenience of early life against me, I am proud to say that with a perseverence undismayed by difficulties, a disinterestedness that compelled respect, I have not only contributed to raise a new empire in the world, founded on a new system of Government, but I have arrived at an eminence in political literature, the most difficult of all lines to succeed and excel in, which Aristocracy with all its aids has not been able to reach or to rival.

Knowing my own heart and feeling myself as I now do, superior to all the skirmish of party, the inveterancy of interested or mistaken opponents, I answer not to falsehood or abuse, but proceed to the defects of the English Government.

I begin with charters and corporations.

It is a perversion of terms to say that a charter gives rights. It operates by a contrary effect—that of taking rights away. Rights are inherently in all the inhabitants; but charters, by annulling those rights in the majority, leave the right, by exclusion, in the hands of a few. If charters were constructed so as to express in direct terms, *"that every inhabitant, who is not a member of a corporation, shall not exercise the right of voting,"* such charters would, in the face, be charters not of rights, but of exclusion. The effect is the same under the form they now stand; and the only persons on whom they operate are the persons whom they exclude. Those whose rights are guaranteed, by not being taken away, exercise no other rights than as members of the community they are entitled to without a charter; and, therefore, all charters have no other than an indirect negative operation. They do not give rights to A, but they make a difference in favour of A by taking away the right of B, and consequently are instruments of injustice.

But charters and corporations have a more extensive evil effect than what relates merely to elections. They are sources of endless contentions in the places where they exist, and they lessen the common rights of national society. A native of England, under the operation of these charters and corporations, cannot be said to be an Englishman in full sense of the word. He is not free of the Nation in the same manner that, a Frenchman is free of France, and an American of America. His rights are circumscribed to the town, and in some cases to the parish of his birth; and all other parts, though in his native land, are to him as a foreign country. To acquire a residence in these he must undergo a local naturalization by purchase, or he is forbidden or expelled the place. This species of feudality is kept up to aggrandize the corporations at the ruin of towns; and the effect is visible.

The generality of corporation towns are in a state of solitary decay, and prevented from further ruin only by some circumstance in their situation, such as a navigable river, or a plentiful surrounding country. As population is one of the chief sources of wealth (for without it land itself has no value), everything which operates to prevent it must lessen the value of property; and as corporations have not only this tendency, but directly this effect, they cannot be but injurious. If any policy were to be followed, instead of that of general freedom to every person to settle where he choose (as in France or America) it would be more consistent to give encouragement to new comers than to preclude their admission by exacting premiums from them.

The persons most immediately interested in the abolition of corporations are the inhabitants of the towns where corporations are extablished. The instances of Manchester, Birmingham, and Sheffield shew, by contrast, the injury which those Gothic institutions are to property and commerce. A few examples may be found, such as that of London, whose natural and commericial advantages, owing to its situation on the Thames, is capable of bearing up against the political evils of a corporation; but in almost all other cases the fatality is too visible to be doubted or denied.

Though the whole Nation is not so directly affected by the depression of property in corporation towns as the inhabitants themselves, it partakes of the consequence. By lessening the value of property, the quantity of national commerce is curtailed. Every man is a customer in proportion to his ability; and as all parts of the Nation trade with each other, whatever affects any of the parts must necessarily communicate to the whole.

As one of the houses of English Parliament is, in a great measure, made up of elections from these corporations; and as it is unnatural that a pure stream should flow from a foul fountain, its vices are but a continuation of the vices of its origin. A man of moral honour and good political principles cannot submit to the mean drudgery and disgraceful arts by which such elections are carried. To be a successful candidate he must be destitute of the qualities that constitute a just legislator; and being thus disciplined to corruption by the mode of entering into Parliament, it is not to be expected that the representative should be better than the man.

Mr. Burke, in speaking of the English representation, has advanced as bold a challenge as ever was given in the days of chivalry. "Our representation," says he, "has been found *perfectly adequate to all the purposes* for which a representation of the people can be desired or devised. I defy," continues he, "the enemies of our Constitution to shew the contrary." This declaration from a man who has been in constant opposition to all the measures of Parliament the whole of his political life, a year or two excepted, is most extraordinary; and, comparing him with himself, admits of no other alternative than that he acted against his judgment as a member, or has declared contrary to it as an author.

But it is not in the representation only that the defects lie, and therefore I proceed in the next place to the Aristocracy.

What is called the House of Peers is constituted on a ground very similar to that against which there is a law in other cases. It amounts to a combination of persons in one common interest. No reason can be given why a house of legislation should be composed entirely of men whose occupation consists in letting landed property, than why it should be composed of those who hire, or of brewers, or bakers, or any other separate class of men.

Mr. Burke calls this house *"the great ground and pillar of security to the landed interest."* Let us examine this idea.

What pillar of security does the landed interest require more than any other interest in the state, or what right has it to a distinct and separate representation from the general interest of a Nation? The only use to be made of this power (and which it has always

made) is to ward off taxes from itself, and throw the
burden upon such articles of consumption by which
itself would be least affected.

That this has been the consequence (and will always
be the consequence) of constructing Governments on
combinations, is evident with respect to England from
the history of its taxes.

Notwithstanding taxes have encreased and multiplied
upon every article of common consumption, the land-
tax, which more particularly affects this "pillar," has
diminished. In 1788 the amount of the land-tax was
£1,950,000, which is half-a-million less than it produced almost a hundred years ago, notwithstanding
the rentals are in many instances doubled since that
period.

Before the coming of the Hanoverians, the taxes
were divided in nearly equal proportions between the
land and articles of consumption, the land bearing
rather the largest share; but since that aera nearly thirteen millions annually of new taxes have been thrown
upon consumption; the consequence of which has been
a constant increase in the number and wretchedness
of the poor, and in the amount of the poor rates. Yet
here again the burden does not fall in equal proportions on the Aristocracy with the rest of the community. Their residences, whether in town or country, are
not mixed with the habitations of the poor. They live
apart from distress and the expence of relieving it. It
is in manufacturing towns and labouring villages that
those burdens press the heaviest, in many of which it
is one class of poor supporting another.

Several of the most heavy and productive taxes are
so contrived as to give an exemption to this pillar,
thus standing in its own defence. The tax upon beer
brewed for sale does not affect the Aristocracy, who
brew their own beer free of this duty. It falls only on
those who have not conveniency or ability to brew,
and who must purchase it in small quantities. But what

will mankind think of the justice of taxation when they know that this tax alone, from which the Aristocracy are from circumstances exempt, is nearly equal to the whole of the land-tax, being in the year 1788, and it is not less now, £1,666,152, and with its proportion of the taxes on malt and hops, it exceeds it. That a single article, thus partially consumed, and that chiefly by the working part, should be subject to a tax, equal to that on the whole rental of a Nation, is, perhaps, a fact not to be paralleled in the histories of revenues.

This is one of the consequences resulting from a house of legislation composed on the ground of a combination of common interest; for whatever their separate politics as to parties may be, in this they are united. Whether a combination acts to raise the price of any article for sale, or the rate of wages, or whether it acts to throw taxes from itself upon another class of the community, the principle and the effect are the same; and if the one be illegal, it will be difficult to shew that the other ought to exist.

It is to no use to say that taxes are first proposed in the House of Commons; for as the other House has always a negative it can always defend itself; and it would be ridiculous to suppose that its acquiescence in the measures to be proposed were not understood beforehand. Besides which it has obtained so much influence by borough-traffic, and so many of its relations and connections are distributed on both sides of the Commons, as to give it, besides an absolute negative in one House, a preponderancy in the other in all matters of common concern.

It is difficult to discover what is meant by the *landed interest,* if it does not mean a combination of aristocratical landholders opposing their own pecuniary interest to that of the farmer, and every branch of trade, commerce, and manufacture. In all other respects it is the only interest that needs no partial protection. It enjoys the general protection of the world. Every indi-

vidual, high or low, is interested in the fruits of the
earth; men, women, and children, of all ages and degrees, will turn out to assist the farmer, rather than a
harvest should not be got in; and they will not act thus
by any other property. It is the only one for which the
common prayer of mankind is put up, and the only
one that can never fail from the want of means. It is
the interest, not of the policy, but of the existence of
man, and when it ceases he must cease to be.

No other interest in a Nation stands on the same
united support. Commerce, manufactures, arts, sciences, and everything else, compared with this, are
supported but in parts. Their prosperity or their decay
has not the same universal influence. When the vallies
laugh and sing it is not the farmer only but all creation
that rejoices. It is a prosperity that excludes all envy;
and this cannot be said of anything else.

Why, then, does Mr. Burke talk of his House of
Peers as the pillar of the landed interest? Were that
pillar to sink into the earth, the same landed property
would continue, and the same ploughing, sowing, and
reaping would go on. The Aristocracy are not the
farmers who work the land and raise the produce, but
are the mere consumers of the rent; and when compared with the active world, are the drones, a seraglio
of males, who neither collect the honey nor form the
hive, but exist only for lazy employment.

Mr. Burke, in his first essay, called Aristocracy *"the
Corinthian capital of polished society."* Towards com-
pleating the figure he has now added the *pillar;* but
still the base is wanting: and whenever a Nation chuse
to act a Samson, not blind, but bold, down go the
temple of Dagon, the Lords and the Philistines.

If a house of legislation is to be composed of men
of one class for the purpose of protecting a distinct
interest, all the other interests should have the same.
The inequality as well as the burden of taxation arises
from admitting it in one case and not in all. Had there

been a house of farmers, there had been no game laws; or a house of merchants and manufacturers, the taxes had neither been so unequal nor so excessive. It is from the power of taxation being in the hands of those who can throw so great a part of it from their own shoulders, that it has raged without a check.

Men of small or moderate estates are more injured by the taxes being thrown on articles of consumption than they are eased by warding it from landed property for the following reasons:

First, They consume more of the productive taxable articles, in proportion to their property, than those of large estates.

Secondly, their residence is chiefly in towns, and their property in houses; and the encrease of the poor-rates, occasioned by taxes on consumption, is in much greater proportion than the land-tax has been favoured. In Birmingham, the poor-rates are not less than seven shillings in the pound. From this, as already observed, the Aristocracy are in a great measure exempt.

These are but a part of the mischiefs flowing from the wretched scheme of a House of Peers.

As a combination, it can always throw a considerable portion of taxes from itself; and as an hereditary house, accountable to nobody, it resembles a rotten borough, whose consent is to be courted by interest. There are but a few of its members, who are not in some mode or other participators, or disposers of the public money. One turns a candleholder, or a lord in waiting; another a lord of the bed-chamber, a groom of the stole, or any insignificant nominal office to which a salary is annexed, paid out of the public taxes, and which avoids the direct appearance of corruption. Such situations are derogatory to the character of man; and where they can be submitted to, honour cannot reside.

To all these are to be added the numerous dependents, the long list of younger branches and distant relations, who are to be provided for at the public expence; in short, were an estimation to be made of the charge of Aristocracy to a Nation, it will be found nearly equal to that of supporting the poor. The Duke of Richmond alone (and there are cases similar to his) takes away as much for himself as would maintain two thousand poor and aged persons. Is it, then, any wonder that under such a system of Government, taxes and rates have multiplied to their present extent?

In stating these matters, I speak an open and disengaged language dictated by no passion but that of humanity. To me, who have not only refused offers because I thought them improper; but have declined rewards I might with reputation have accepted; it is no wonder that meanness and imposition appear disgustful. Independence is my happiness, and I view things as they are, without regard to place or person; my country is the world, and my religion is to do good.

Mr. Burke, in speaking of the aristocratical law of primogeniture, says: "It is the standing law of our land inheritance; and which, without question, has a tendency, and I think," continues he, "a happy tendency, to preserve a character of weight and consequence."

Mr. Burke may call this law what he pleases, but humanity and impartial reflection will denounce it a law of brutal injustice. Were he not accustomed to the daily practice, and did we only hear of that as the law of some distant part of the world, we should conclude that the legislators of such countries had not yet arrived at a state of civilization.

As to its preserving a character of *weight and consequence,* the case appears to me directly the reverse. It is an attaint upon character; a sort of privateering on family property. It may have weight among dependent tenants, but it gives none on a scale of national, and much less of universal, character. Speaking for myself, my parents were not able to give me a shilling beyond what they gave me in education; and to do this they distressed themselves; yet I possess more of what is called consequence in the world, than any one in Mr. Burke's catalogue of aristocrats.

Having thus glanced at some of the defects of the two Houses of Parliament, I proceed to what is called the Crown, upon which I shall be very concise.

It signifies a nominal office of a million sterling a-year, the business of which consists in receiving the money. Whether the person be wise or foolish, sane or insane, a native or a foreigner, matters not. Every Ministry acts upon the same idea that Mr. Burke writes, namely, that the people must be hood-winked, and held in superstitious ignorance by some bugbear or other; and what is called the Crown answers this purpose, and therefore it answers all the purposes to be expected from it. This is more than can be said of the other two branches.

The hazard to which this office is exposed in all countries is not from anything that can happen to the man, but from what may happen to the Nation—the danger of its coming to its senses.

It has been customary to call the Crown the executive power, and the custom is continued, though the reason has ceased.

It was called the *executive,* because the person whom it signified used formerly to sit in the character of a judge, in administering or executing the laws. The tribunals were then a part of the Court. The power, therefore, which is now called the judicial, is what was called the executive; and, consequently, one or other of the terms is redundant, and one of the offices useless. We speak of the Crown now, it means nothing; it signifies neither a judge nor a general; besides which it is the laws that govern, and not the man. The old terms are kept up, to give an appearance of consequence to empty forms; and the only effect they have is that of encreasing expenses.

. . . The fraud, hypocrisy, and imposition of Governments, are now beginning to be too well understood to promise them any long career. The farce of Monarchy and Aristocracy in all countries is following that of chivalry, and Mr. Burke is dressing for the funeral. Let it then pass quietly to the tomb of all other follies, and the mourners be comforted.

The time is not very distant when England will laugh at itself for sending to Holland, Hanover, Zell, or Brunswick, for men, at the expence of a million a year, who understood neither her laws, her language, nor her interest, and whose capacities would scarcely have fitted them for the office of a parish constable. If Government could be trusted to such hands, it must be some easy and simple thing indeed, and materials fit for all the purposes may be found in every town and village in England.

When it shall be said in any country in the world my poor are happy; neither ignorance nor distress is to be found among them; my jails are empty of prisoners, my streets of beggars; the aged are not in want; the taxes are not oppressive; the rational world is my friend, because I am the friend of its happiness: When these things can be said, then may that country boast its Constitution and its Government.

Within the space of a few years we have seen two Revolutions, those of America and France. In the former the contest was long, and the conflict severe; in the latter the Nation acted with such a consolidated impulse, that, having no foreign enemy to contend with, the Revolution was complete in power the moment it appeared. From both those instances it is evident that the greatest forces that can be brought into the field of Revolutions are reason and common interest. Where these can have the opportunity of acting, opposition dies with fear, or crumbles away by conviction. It is a great standing which they have now universally obtained; and we may hereafter hope to see Revolutions, or changes in Governments, produced with the same quiet operation, by which any measure, determinable by reason and discussion, is accomplished.

When a Nation changes its opinion and habits of thinking it is no longer to be governed as before; but it would not only be wrong, but bad policy, to attempt by force what ought to be accomplished by reason. Rebellion consists in forcibly opposing the general will of a Nation, whether by a party or by a Government. There ought, therefore, to be in every Nation a method of occasionally ascertaining the state of public opinion with respect to Government. On this point the old Government of France was superior to the present Government of England, because, on extraordinary occasions, recourse could be had to what was then called the States-General. But in England there are no such occasional bodies; and as to those who are now called representatives, a great part of them are mere machines of the Court, placemen, and dependents.

I presume that though all the people of England pay taxes, not an hundredth part of them are electors, and the members of one of the Houses of Parliament represent nobody but themselves. There is, therefore, no power but the voluntary will of the people that has a right to act in any matter respecting a general reform; and by the same right that two persons can confer on such a subject, a thousand may. The object in all such preliminary proceedings, is to find out what the general sense of a Nation is and to be governed by it. If it prefer a bad or defective Government to a reform, or chuse to pay ten times more taxes than there is occasion for, it has a right so to do: and so long as the majority do not impose conditions on the minority, different from what they impose on themselves, though there may be much error, there is no injustice. Neither will the error continue long. Reason and discussion will soon bring things right, however wrong they may begin. By such a process no tumult is to be apprehended. The poor in all countries are naturally both peaceable and grateful in all reforms in which their interest and happiness is included. It is only by neglecting and rejecting them that they become tumultuous.

The objects that now press on the public attention are the French Revolution, and the prospect of a general Revolution in Governments. Of all Nations in Europe there is none so much interested in the French Revolution as England. Enemies for ages, and that at a vast expence, and without any rational object, the opportunity now presents itself of amicably closing the scene, and joining their efforts to reform the rest of Europe. By doing this they will not only prevent the further effusion of blood and increase of taxes, but be in a condition of getting rid of a considerable part of their present burdens, as has been already stated. Long experience, however, has shown that reforms of this kind are not those which old Governments wish to promote; and therefore it is to Nations, and not to such Governments, that these matters present themselves.

In the preceding part of this work I have spoken of an alliance between England, France and America, for purposes that were . to be afterwards mentioned. Though I have no direct authority on the part of America I have good reason to conclude that she is disposed to enter into a consideration of such a measure, provided that the Governments with which she might ally acted as national Governments, and not as Courts enveloped in intrigue and mystery. That France as a Nation, and a national Government, would prefer an alliance with England, is a matter of certainty. Nations, like individuals, who have long been enemies without knowing each other, or knowing why, become the better friends when they discover the errors and impositions under which they had acted.

Admitting, therefore, the probability of such a connection, I will state some matters by which such an alliance, together with that of Holland, might render service, not only to the parties immediately concerned, but to all Europe.

It is, I think, certain, that if the fleets of England, France and Holland were confederated they could propose, with effect, a limitation to, and a general dismantling of, all the navies of Europe, to a certain proportion to be agreed upon.

First, That no new ship of war shall be built by any power in Europe, themselves included.

Secondly, That all the navies now in existence shall be put back, suppose to one-tenth of their present force. This will save to France and England at least two millions sterling annually to each, and their relative force be in the same proportion as it is now. If men will permit themselves to think, as rational beings ought to think, nothing can appear more ridiculous and absurd, exclusive of all moral reflections, than to be at the expence of building navies, filling them with men, and then hauling them into the ocean, to try which can sink each other fastest. Peace, which costs nothing, is attended with infinitely more advantage than any victory with all its expence. But this, though it best answers the purpose of Nations, does not that of Court Governments, whose habited policy is pretence for taxation, places and offices.

It is, I think, also certain, that the above confederated powers, together with that of the United States of America, can propose with effect, to Spain, the independence of South America, and the opening those countries of immense extent and wealth to the general commerce of the world, as North America now is.

With how much more glory and advantage to itself

does a Nation act when it exerts its powers to rescue the world from bondage and to create itself friends, than when it employs those powers to increase ruin, desolation and misery. The horrid scene that is now acting by the English Government in the East Indies, is fit only to be told of Goths and Vandals, who, destitute of principle, robbed and tortured the world they were incapable of enjoying.

The opening of South America would produce an immense field of commerce, and a ready money market for manufactures, which the eastern world does not. The east is already a country full of manufactures, the importation of which is not only an injury to the manufactures of England, but a drain upon its specie. The balance against England by this trade is regularly upwards of half a million annually sent out in the East India ships in silver; and this is the reason, together with German intrigue and German subsidies, there is so little silver in England.

But any war is harvest to such Governments, however ruinous it may be to a nation. It serves to keep up deceitful expectations, which prevent a people looking into the defects and abuses of Government. It is the *lo here!* and the *lo there!* that amuses and cheats the multitude.

Never did so great an opportunity offer itself to England, and to all Europe, as is produced by the two Revolutions of America and France. By the former, freedom has a national champion in the western world; and by the latter, in Europe. When another Nation shall join France, despotism and bad Government will scarcely dare to appear. To use a trite expression, the iron is becoming hot all over Europe. The insulted German and the enslaved Spaniard, the Russ and the Pole, are beginning to think. The present age will hereafter merit to be called the Age of Reason, and the present generation will appear to the future as the Adam of a new world.

When all the Governments of Europe shall be established on the representative system, Nations will become acquainted, and the animosities and the prejudices fomented by the intrigue and artifice of Courts will cease. The oppressed soldier will become a freeman; and the tortured sailor, no longer dragged along the streets like a felon, will pursue his mercantile voyage in safety. It would be better that Nations should continue the pay of their soldiers during their lives, and give them their discharge, and restore them to freedom and their friends, and cease recruiting, than retain such multitudes at the same expence in a condition useless to society and themselves. As soldiers have hitherto been treated in most countries they might be said to be without a friend. Shunned by the citizens on an apprehension of being enemies to liberty, and too often insulted by those who commanded them, their condition was a double oppression. But where general principles of liberty pervade a people everything is restored to order; and the soldier, civilly treated, returns the civility.

In contemplating Revolutions, it is easy to perceive that they may arise from two distinct causes; the one, to avoid or get rid of some great calamity; the other, to obtain some great and positive good; and the two may be distinguished by the names of active and passive Revolutions. In those which proceed from the former cause, the temper becomes incensed and soured; and the redress, obtained by danger, is too often sullied by revenge. But in those which proceed from the latter, the heart, rather animated than agitated, enters serenely upon the subject. Reason and discussion, persuasion and conviction, become the weapons in the contest, and it is only when those are attempted to be suppressed that recourse is had to violence. When men unite in agreeing that a *thing is good,* could it be obtained, such as relief from a burden of taxes and the extinction of corruption, the object is more than half accomplished. What they approve as the end they will promote in the means.

Will any man say, in the present excess of taxation, falling so heavily on the poor, that a remission of five pounds annually of taxes to one hundred and four thousand poor families is not a *good thing?* Will he say that a remission of seven pounds annually to one hundred thousand other poor families, of eight pounds annually to another hundred thousand poor families, and of ten pounds annually to fifty thousand poor and widowed families, are not *good things?* And to proceed a step farther in this climax, will he say that to provide against the misfortunes to which all human life is subject, by securing six pounds annually for all poor, distressed, and reduced persons of the age of fifty and until sixty, and of ten pounds annually after sixty, is not a *good thing?*

Will he say that an abolition of two million of poor-rates, to the housekeepers, and of the whole of the house and window light tax, and of the commutation tax, is not a *good thing?* Or will he say that to abolish corruption is a *bad thing?*

If, therefore, the good to be obtained be worthy of a passive, rational, and costless Revolution, it would be bad policy to prefer waiting for a calamity that should force a violent one. I have no idea, considering the reforms which are now passing and spreading throughout Europe, that England will permit herself to be the last; and where the occasion and the opportunity quietly offer, it is better than to wait for a turbulent necessity. It may be considered as an honour to the animal faculties of man to obtain redress by courage and danger, but it is far greater honour to the rational faculties to accomplish the same object by reason, accommodation, and general consent.

As Reforms, or Revolutions, call them which you please, extend themselves among Nations, those Nations will form connections and conventions, and when a few are thus confederated, the progress will be rapid, till despotism and corrupt Government be totally expelled, at least out of two quarters of the world, Europe and America. The Algerine piracy may then be commanded to cease, for it is only by the malicious policy of old Governments, against each other, that it exists.

Throughout this work, various and numerous as the subjects are, which I have taken up and investigated, there is only a single paragraph upon religion, viz. *"that every religion is good, that teaches man to be good."*

I have carefully avoided to enlarge upon the subject, because I am inclined to believe, that what is called the present Ministry wish to see contentions about religion kept up, to prevent the Nation turning its attention to subjects of Government. It is, as if they were to say, *"Look that way, or any way, but this."*

But as religion is very improperly made a political machine, and the reality of it is thereby destroyed, I will conclude this work with stating in what light religion appears to me.

If we suppose a large family of children, who, on any particular day, or particular circumstance, made it a custom to present to their parent some token of their affection and gratitude, each of them would make a different offering, and most probably in a different manner. Some would pay their congratulations in themes of verse or prose; some by little devices, as their genius dictated, or according to what they thought would please; and, perhaps the least of all, not able to do any of those things, would ramble into the garden, or the field, and gather what it thought the prettiest flower it could find, though perhaps it might be but a simple weed. The parent would be more gratified by such variety than if the whole of them had acted on a concerted plan, and each had made exactly the same offering. This would have the cold appearance of contrivance, or the harsh one of controul. But of all unwelcome things nothing could more afflict the parent than to know that the whole of them had afterwards gotten together by the ears, boys and girls fighting, scratching, reviling, and abusing each other about which was the best or the worst present.

Why may we not suppose that the great Father of all is pleased with variety of devotion? and that the greatest offence we can act is that by which we seek to torment and render each other miserable? For my own part I am fully satisfied that what I am now doing, with an endeavour to conciliate mankind, to render their condition happy, to unite Nations that have hitherto been enemies, and to extirpate the horrid practice of war, and break the chains of slavery and oppression, is acceptable in his sight; and being the best service I can perform I act it cheerfully.

I do not believe that any two men, on what are called doctrinal points, think alike, who think at all. It is only those who have not thought that appear to agree. It is in this case as with what is called the British Constitution. It has been taken for granted to be good, and encomiums have supplied the place of proof. But when the Nation comes to examine into its principles and the abuses it admits, it will be found to have more defects than I have pointed out in this work and the former.

As to what are called national religions, we may with as much propriety talk of national Gods. It is either political craft or the remains of the Pagan system, when every Nation had its separate and particular deity. Among all the writers of the English Church clergy, who have treated on the general subject of religion, the present Bishop of Llandaff has not been excelled: and it is with much pleasure that I take the opportunity of expressing this token of respect.

I have now gone through the whole of the subject,

at least as far as it appears to me at present. It has been my intention for the five years I have been in Europe to offer an address to the people of England on the subject of Government; if the opportunity presented itself, before I returned to America. Mr. Burke has thrown it in my way and I thank him. On a certain occasion, three years ago, I pressed him to propose a national convention, to be fairly elected, for the purpose of taking the state of the Nation into consideration; but I found that however strongly the parliamentary current was then setting against the party he acted with, their policy was to keep everything within that field of corruption, and trust to accidents. Long experience had shewn that Parliaments would follow any change of ministers, and on this they rested their hopes and expectations.

Formerly, when divisions arose respecting Governments, recourse was had to the sword, and a civil war ensued. That savage custom is exploded by the new system; and reference is had to national conventions. Discussion and the general will arbitrate the question, and to this private opinion yields with a good grace, and order is preserved uninterrupted.

Some gentlemen have affected to call the principles upon which this work and the former part of the *Rights of Man* are founded "a new fangled doctrine." The question is not whether those principles are new or old, but whether they are right or wrong. Suppose the former, I will shew their effect by a figure easily understood.

It is now towards the middle of February. Were I to take a turn into the country the trees would present a leafless winterly appearance. As people are apt to pluck twigs as they walk along, I perhaps might do the same, and by chance might observe that a *single bud* on that twig had begun to swell. I should reason very unnaturally, or rather not reason at all, to suppose *this* was the *only* bud in England which had this appearance. Instead of deciding thus, I should instantly conclude that the same appearance was beginning, or about to begin, everywhere; and though the vegetable sleep will continue longer on some trees and plants than on others, and though some of them may not *blossom* for two or three years, all will be in leaf in the summer, except those which are *rotten*. What pace the political summer may keep with the natural, no human foresight can determine. It is, however, not difficult to perceive that the spring is begun. Thus wishing, as I sincerely do, freedom and happiness to all Nations, I close the SECOND PART.

THE AGE OF REASON

BEING AN INVESTIGATION OF TRUE AND
FABULOUS THEOLOGY

PART ONE (SELECTIONS)

1794

To My Fellow Citizens of the United States of America

I put the following work under your protection. It contains my opinion upon Religion. You will do me the justice to remember, that I have always strenuously supported the Right of every Man to his own opinion, however different that opinion might be to mine. He who denies to another this right, makes a slave of himself to his present opinion, because he precludes himself the right of changing it.

The most formidable weapon against errors of every kind is Reason. I have never used any other, and I trust I never shall.

Your affectionate friend and fellow-citizen,

Thomas Paine

Luxembourg, 8th Pluvôise.
Second year of the French Republic, one and indivisible.
January 27th, O. S., 1794

It has been my intention, for several years past, to publish my thoughts upon Religion. I am well aware of the difficulties that attend the subject; and, from that consideration, had reserved it to a more advanced period of life. I intended it to be the last offering I should make to my fellow citizens of all nations; and that at a time, when the purity of the motive that induced me to it, could not admit of a question, even by those who might disapprove the work.

The circumstance that has now taken place in France, of the total abolition of the whole national order of priesthood, and of every thing appertaining to compulsive systems of religion, and compulsive articles of faith, has not only precipitated my intention, but rendered a work of this kind exceedingly necessary; lest, in the general wreck of superstition, of false systems of government, and false theology, we lose sight of morality, of humanity, and of the theology that is true.

As several of my colleagues, and others of my fellow-citizens of France, have given me the example of making their voluntary and individual profession of faith, I also will make mine; and I do this with all that sincerity and frankness with which the mind of man communicates with itself.

I believe in one God, and no more; and I hope for happiness beyond this life.

I believe in the equality of man, and I believe that religious duties consist in doing justice, loving mercy, and endeavouring to make our fellow creatures happy.

But lest it should be supposed that I believe many other things in addition to these, I shall, in the progress of this work, declare the things I do not believe, and my reasons for not believing them.

I do not believe in the creed professed by the Jewish church, by the Roman church, by the Greek church, by the Turkish church, by the Protestant church, nor by any church that I know of. My own mind is my own church.

All national institutions of churches, whether Jewish, Christian, or Turkish, appear to me no other than human inventions set up to terrify and enslave mankind, and monopolize power and profit.

I do not mean by this declaration to condemn those who believe otherwise. They have the same right to their belief as I have to mine. But it is necessary to the happiness of man, that he be mentally faithful to himself. Infidelity does not consist in believing, or in disbelieving: it consists in professing to believe what he does not believe.

It is impossible to calculate the moral mischief, if I may so express it, that mental lying has produced in society. When a man has so far corrupted and prostituted the chastity of his mind, as to subscribe his professional belief to things he does not believe, he has prepared himself for the commission of every other crime. He takes up the trade of a priest for the sake of gain, and in order to *qualify* himself for that trade, he begins with a perjury. Can we conceive any thing more destructive to morality than this?

Soon after I had published the pamphlet COMMON-SENSE, in America, I saw the exceeding probability that a Revolution in the System of Government would be followed by a revolution in the system of religion. The adulterous connection of church and state, wherever it had taken place, whether Jewish, Christian, or Turkish, had so effectually prohibited, by pains and penalties, every discussion upon established creeds, and upon first principles of religion, that until the system of government should be changed, those subjects could not be brought fairly and openly before the world: but that whenever this should be done, a revolution in the system of religion would follow. Human inventions and priest-craft would be detected; and man would return to the pure, unmixed, and unadulterated belief of one God, and no more.

Every national church or religion has established itself by pretending some special mission from God communicated to certain individuals. The Jews have their Moses; the Christians their Jesus Christ, their apostles and saints; and the Turks their Mahomet; as if the way to God was not open to every man alike.

Each of those churches shows certain books, which they call *revelation*, or the word of God. The Jews say that their word of God was given by God to Moses face to face; the Christians say, that their word of God came by divine inspiration; and the Turks say, that their word of God (the Koran) was brought by an angel from heaven. Each of those churches accuses the other of unbelief; and, for my own part, I disbelieve them all.

As it is necessary to affix right ideas to words, I will, before I proceed further into the subject, offer some observations on the word *revelation*. Revelation, when applied to religion, means something communicated *immediately* from God to man.

No one will deny or dispute the power of the Almighty to make such a communication if he pleases. But admitting, for the sake of a case, that something has been revealed to a certain person, and not revealed to any other person, it is revelation to that person only. When he tells it to a second person, a second to a third, a third to a fourth, and so on, it ceases to be a revelation to all those persons. It is revelation to the first person only, and *hearsay* to every other, and, consequently, they are not obliged to believe it.

It is a contradiction in terms and ideas to call any thing a revelation that comes to us at second hand, either verbally or in writing. Revelation is necessarily limited to the first communication. After this, it is only an account of something which that person says was a revelation made to him; and though he may find himself obliged to believe it, it cannot be incumbent on me to believe it in the same manner, for it was not a revelation made to *me*, and I have only his word for it that it was made to *him*.

When Moses told the children of Israel that he received the two tables of the commandments from the hand of God, they were not obliged to believe him, because they had no other authority for it than his telling them so; and I have no other authority for it than some historian telling me so. The commandments carry no internal evidence of divinity with them. They contain some good moral precepts, such as any man qualified to be a law giver or a legislator could produce himself, without having recourse to supernatural intervention.

When I am told that the Koran was written in Heaven, and brought to Mahomet by an angel, the account comes to near the same kind of hearsay evidence, and second hand authority as the former. I did not see the angel myself, and therefore I have a right not to believe it.

When also I am told that a woman, called the Virgin Mary, said, or gave out, that she was with child without any cohabitation with a man, and that her betrothed husband, Joseph, said, that an angel told him so, I have a right to believe them or not: such a circumstance required a much stronger evidence than their bare word for it: but we have not even this; for neither Joseph nor Mary wrote any such matter themselves. It is only reported by others that *they said so*. It is hearsay upon hearsay, and I do not chuse to rest my belief upon such evidence.

It is, however, not difficult to account for the credit that was given to the story of Jesus Christ being the Son of God. He was born when the heathen mythology had still some fashion and repute in the world, and that mythology had prepared the people for the belief of such a story. Almost all the extraordinary men that lived under the heathen mythology were reputed to be the sons of some of their gods. It was not a new thing at that time to believe a man to have been celestially begotten: the intercourse of gods with women was then a matter of familiar opinion. Their Jupiter, according to their accounts, had cohabited with hundreds: the story therefore had nothing in it either new, wonderful, or obscene: it was conformable to the opinions that then prevailed among the people called Gentiles, or Mythologists, and it was those people only that believed it. The Jews, who had kept strictly to the belief of one God, and no more, and who had always rejected the heathen mythology, never credited the story.

It is curious to observe how the theory of what is called the Christian Church, sprung out of the tail of the heathen mythology. A direct incorporation took place in the first instance, by making the reputed founder to be celestially begotten. The trinity of gods that then followed was no other than a reduction of the former plurality, which was about twenty or thirty thousand. The statue of Mary succeeded the statue of Diana of Ephesus. The deification of heroes changed into the canonization of saints. The Mythologists had gods for everything; the Christian Mythologists had saints for every thing. The church became as crowded with the one, as the pantheon had been with the other; and Rome was the place of both. The Christian theory is little else than the idolatry of the ancient Mythologists, accommodated to the purposes of power and revenue; and it yet remains to reason and philosophy to abolish the amphibious fraud.

Nothing that is here said can apply, even with the most distant disrespect, to the *real* character of Jesus Christ. He was a virtuous and an amiable man. The morality that he preached and practised was of the most benevolent kind; and though similar systems of morality had been preached by Confucius, and by some of the Greek philosophers, many years before; by the Quakers since; and by many good men in all ages; it has not been exceeded by any.

Jesus Christ wrote no account of himself, of his

birth, parentage, or any thing else. Not a line of what is called the New Testament is of his writing. The history of him is altogether the work of other people; and as to the account given of his resurrection and ascension, it was the necessary counterpart to the story of his birth. His historians, having brought him into the world in a supernatural manner, were obliged to take him out again in the same manner, or the first part of the story must have fallen to the ground.

The wretched contrivance with which this latter part is told, exceeds everything that went before it. The first part, that of the miraculous conception, was not a thing that admitted of publicity; and therefore the tellers of this part of the story had this advantage, that though they might not be credited, they could not be detected. They could not be expected to prove it, because it was not one of those things that admitted of proof, and it was impossible that the person of whom it was told could prove it himself.

But the resurrection of a dead person from the grave, and his ascension through the air, is a thing very different, as to the evidence it admits of, to the invisible conception of a child in the womb. The resurrection and ascension, supposing them to have taken place, admitted of public and ocular demonstration, like that of the ascension of a balloon, or the sun at noon day, to all Jerusalem at least. A thing which every body is required to believe, requires that the proof and evidence of it should be equal to all, and universal; and as the public visibility of this last related act was the only evidence that could give sanction to the former part, the whole of it falls to the ground, because that evidence never was given. Instead of this, a small number of persons, not more than eight or nine, are introduced as proxies for the whole world, to say they *saw it*, and all the rest of the world are called upon to believe it. But it appears that Thomas did not believe the resurrection; and, as they say, would not believe without having ocular and manual demonstration himself. *So neither will I*; and the reason is equally as good for me, and for every other person, as for Thomas.

It is in vain to attempt to palliate or disguise this matter. The story, so far as relates to the supernatural part, has every mark of fraud and imposition stamped upon the face of it. Who were the authors of it is as impossible for us now to know, as it is for us to be assured that the books in which the account is related were written by the persons whose names they bear. The best surviving evidence we now have respecting this affair is the Jews. They are regularly descended from the people who lived in the time this resurrection and ascension is said to have happened, and they say *it is not true*. It has long appeared to me a strange inconsistency to cite the Jews as a proof of the truth of the story. It is just the same as if a man were to say, I will prove the truth of what I have told you, by producing the people who say it is false.

That such a person as Jesus Christ existed, and that he was crucified, which was the mode of execution at that day, are historical relations strictly within the limits of probability. He preached most excellent morality, and the equality of man; but he preached also against the corruptions and avarice of the Jewish priests; and this brought upon him the hatred and vengeance of the whole order of priesthood. The accusation which those priests brought against him was that of sedition and conspiracy against the Roman government, to which the Jews were then subject and tributary; and it is not improbable that the Roman government might have some secret apprehension of the effects of his doctrine as well as the Jewish priests; neither is it improbable that Jesus Christ had in contemplation the delivery of the Jewish nation from the bondage of the Romans. Between the two, however, this virtuous reformer and revolutionist lost his life.

It is upon this plain narrative of facts, together with another case I am going to mention, that the Christian Mythologists, calling themselves the Christian Church, have erected their fable, which for absurdity and extravagance is not exceeded by any thing that is to be found in the mythology of the ancients.

The ancient Mythologists tell us that the race of Giants made war against Jupiter, and that one of them threw a hundred rocks against him at one throw; that Jupiter defeated him with thunder, and confined him afterwards under Mount Etna; and that every time the Giant turns himself, Mount Etna belches fire. It is here easy to see that the circumstance of the mountain, that of its being a volcano, suggested the idea of the fable; and that the fable is made to fit and wind itself up with that circumstance.

The Christian Mythologists tell that their Satan made war against the Almighty, who defeated him, and confined him afterwards, not under a mountain, but in a pit. It is here easy to see that the first fable suggested the idea of the second; for the fable of Jupiter and the Giants was told many hundred years before that of Satan. . . .

The Christian Mythologists, after having confined Satan in a pit, were obliged to let him out again to bring on the sequel of the fable. He is then introduced into the garden of Eden in the shape of a snake, or a serpent, and in that shape he enters into familiar conversation with Eve, who is no ways surprised to hear a snake talk; and the issue of this tête-à-tête is, that he persuades her to eat an apple, and the eating of that apple damns all mankind.

After giving Satan this triumph over the whole creation, one would have supposed that the Church Mythologists would have been kind enough to send him back again to the pit; or, if they had not done this, that they would have put a mountain upon him, (for

they say that their faith can remove a mountain) or
have put him *under* a mountain, as the former Mythologists had done, to prevent his getting again among
the women, and doing more mischief. But instead of
this, they leave him at large, without even obliging
him to give his parole. The secret of which is, that
they could not do without him; and after being at the
trouble of making him, they bribed him to stay. They
promised him ALL the Jews, ALL the Turks by antici-
pation, nine-tenths of the world beside, and Mahomet
into the bargain. After this, who can doubt the bounti-
fulness of the Christian Mythology?

Having thus made an insurrection and a battle in
heaven, in which none of the combatants could be
either killed or wounded—put Satan into the pit—let
him out again—given him a triumph over the whole
creation—damned all mankind by the eating of an
apple, these Christian Mythologists bring the two ends
of their fable together. They represent this virtuous
and amiable man, Jesus Christ, to be at once both
God and man, and also the Son of God, celestially
begotten on purpose to be sacrificed, because, they
say, that Eve in her longing had eaten an apple.

Putting aside every thing that might excite laughter
by its absurdity, or detestation by its prophaneness,
and confining ourselves merely to an examination of
the parts, it is impossible to conceive a story more
derogatory to the Almighty, more inconsistent with
his wisdom, more contradictory to his power, than this
story is.

In order to make for it a foundation to rise upon,
the inventors were under the necessity of giving to the
being, whom they call Satan, a power equally as great,
if not greater, than they attribute to the Almighty.
They have not only given him the power of liberating
himself from the pit, after what they call his fall, but
they have made that power increase afterwards to in-
finity. Before this fall, they represent him only as an

angel of limited existence, as they represent the rest. After his fall, he becomes, by their account, omnipresent. He exists every where, and at the same time. He occupies the whole immensity of space.

Not content with this deification of Satan, they represent him as defeating by stratagem, in the shape of an animal of the creation, all the power and wisdom of the Almighty. They represent him as having compelled the Almighty to the *direct necessity* either of surrendering the whole of the creation to the government and sovereignty of this Satan, or of capitulating for its redemption by coming down upon earth, and exhibiting himself upon a cross in the shape of a man.

Had the inventors of this story told it the contrary way, that is, had they represented the Almighty as compelling Satan to exhibit *himself* on a cross in the shape of a snake, as a punishment for his new transgression, the story would have been less absurd, less contradictory. But instead of this, they make the transgressor triumph, and the Almighty fall.

That many good men have believed this strange fable, and lived very good lives under that belief (for credulity is not a crime) is what I have no doubt of. In the first place, they were educated to believe it, and they would have believed any thing else in the same manner. There are also many who have been so enthusiastically enraptured by what they conceived to be the infinite love of God to man, in making a sacrifice of himself, that the vehemence of the idea has forbidden and deterred them from examining into the absurdity and prophaneness of the story. The more unnatural any thing is, the more is it capable of becoming the object of dismal admiration.

But if objects for gratitude and admiration are our desire, do they not present themselves every hour to our eyes? Do we not see a fair creation prepared to receive us the instant we are born—a world furnished to our hands that cost us nothing? Is it we that light up the sun; that pour down the rain; and fill the earth with abundance? Whether we sleep or wake, the vast machinery of the universe still goes on. Are these things, and the blessings they indicate in future, nothing to us? Can our gross feelings be excited by no other subjects than tragedy and suicide? Or is the gloomy pride of man become so intolerable, that nothing can flatter it but a sacrifice of the Creator?

I know that this bold investigation will alarm many, but it would be paying too great a compliment to their credulity to forbear it on that account. The times and the subject demand it to be done. The suspicion that the theory of what is called the Christian church is fabulous, is becoming very extensive in all countries; and it will be a consolation to men staggering under that suspicion, and doubting what to believe and what to disbelieve, to see the subject freely investigated. I therefore pass on to an examination of the books called the Old and the New Testament.

These books, beginning with Genesis and ending with Revelations, (which by the bye is a book of riddles that requires a revelation to explain it) are, we are told, the word of God. It is, therefore, proper for us to know who told us so, that we may know what credit to give to the report. The answer to this question is, that nobody can tell, except that we tell one another so. The case, however, historically appears to be as follows:

When the Church Mythologists established their system, they collected all the writings they could find, and managed them as they pleased. It is a matter altogether of uncertainty to us whether such of the writings as now appear under the name of the Old and the New Testament, are in the same state in which those collectors say they found them; or whether they added, altered, abridged, or dressed them up.

Be this as it may, they decided by *vote* which of the books out of the collection they had made, should be the WORD OF GOD, and which should not. They rejected several; they voted others to be doubtful, such as the books called the Apocrypha; and those books which had a majority of votes, were voted to be the word of God. Had they voted otherwise, all the people since calling themselves Christians had believed otherwise; for the belief of the one comes from the vote of the other. Who the people were that did all this, we know nothing of; they call themselves by the general name of the church; and this is all we know of the matter. . . .

But some perhaps will say, Are we to have no word of God—No revelation? I answer yes. There is a Word of God; there is a revelation.

THE WORD OF GOD IS THE CREATION WE BEHOLD: And it is in *this word*, which no human invention can counterfeit or alter, that God speaketh universally to man.

Human language is local and changeable, and is therefore incapable of being used as the means of unchangeable and universal information. The idea that God sent Jesus Christ to publish, as they say, the glad tidings to all nations, from one end of the earth unto the other, is consistent only with the ignorance of those who know nothing of the extent of the world, and who believed, as those world-saviours believed, and continued to believe for several centuries, (and that in contradiction to the discoveries of philosophers and the experience of navigators,) that the earth was flat like a trencher; and that a man might walk to the end of it.

But how was Jesus Christ to make anything known to all nations? He could speak but one language, which was Hebrew; and there are in the world several hundred languages. Scarcely any two nations speak the same language, or understand each other; and as to translations, every man who knows any thing of languages, knows that it is impossible to translate from one language into another, not only without losing a great part of the original, but frequently of mistaking the sense; and besides all this, the art of printing was wholly unknown at the time Christ lived.

It is always necessary that the means that are to accomplish any end be equal to the accomplishment of that end, or the end cannot be accomplished. It is in this, that the difference between finite and infinite power and wisdom discovers itself. Man frequently fails in accomplishing his end, from a natural inability of the power to the purpose; and frequently from the want of wisdom to apply power properly. But it is impossible for infinite power and wisdom to fail as man faileth. The means it useth are always equal to the end: but human language, more especially as there is not an universal language, is incapable of being used as an universal means of unchangeable and uniform information; and therefore it is not the means that God useth in manifesting himself universally to man.

It is only in the CREATION that all our ideas and conceptions of a *word of God* can unite. The Creation speaketh an universal language, independently of human speech or human language, multiplied and various as they be. It is an ever existing original, which every man can read. It cannot be forged; it cannot be counterfeited; it cannot be lost; it cannot be altered; it cannot be suppressed. It does not depend upon the will of man whether it shall be published or not; it publishes itself from one end of the earth to the other. It preaches to all nations and to all worlds; and this *word of God* reveals to man all that is necessary for man to know of God.

Do we want to contemplate his power? We see it in the immensity of the creation. Do we want to contemplate his wisdom? We see it in the unchangeable order by which the incomprehensible Whole is governed. Do we want to contemplate his munificence?

We see it in the abundance with which he fills the earth. Do we want to contemplate his mercy? We see it in his not withholding that abundance even from the unthankful. In fine, do we want to know what God is? Search not the book called the scripture, which any human hand might make, but the scripture called the Creation.

The only idea man can affix to the name of God, is that of a *first cause*, the cause of all things. And, incomprehensibly difficult as it is for a man to conceive what a first cause is, he arrives at the belief of it, from the tenfold greater difficulty of disbelieving it. It is difficult beyond description to conceive that space can have no end; but it is more difficult to conceive an end. It is difficult beyond the power of man to conceive an eternal duration of what we call time; but it is more impossible to conceive a time when there shall be no time. In like manner of reasoning, every thing we behold carries in itself the internal evidence that it did not make itself. Every man is an evidence to himself, that he did not make himself; neither could his father make himself, nor his grandfather, nor any of his race; neither could any tree, plant, or animal make itself; and it is the conviction arising from this evidence, that carries us on, as it were, by necessity, to the belief of a first cause eternally existing, of a nature totally different to any material existence we know of, and by the power of which all things exist; and this first cause, man calls God. . . .

. . . I proceed to speak of the three principal means that have been employed in all ages, and perhaps in all countries, to impose upon mankind.

Those three means are Mystery, Miracle, and Prophecy. The first two are incompatible with true religion, and the third ought always to be suspected.

With respect to Mystery, everything we behold is, in one sense, a mystery to us. . . .

In the same sense that every thing may be said to be a mystery, so also may it be said that every thing is a miracle, and that no one thing is a greater miracle than another. The elephant, though larger, is not a greater miracle than a mite: nor a mountain a greater miracle than an atom. To an Almighty power, it is no more difficult to make the one than the other, and no more difficult to make a million of worlds than to make one. Every thing, therefore, is a miracle, in one sense; whilst, in the other sense, there is no such thing as a miracle. It is a miracle when compared to our power, and to our comprehension. It is not a miracle compared to the power that performs it. But as nothing in this description conveys the idea that is affixed to the word miracle, it is necessary to carry the inquiry further.

Mankind have conceived to themselves certain laws, by which what they call nature is supposed to act; and that a miracle is something contrary to the operation and effect of those laws. But unless we know the whole extent of those laws, and of what are commonly called, the powers of nature, we are not able to judge whether any thing that may appear to us wonderful or miraculous, be within, or be beyond, or be contrary to, her natural power of acting. . . .

If we are to suppose a miracle to be something so entirely out of the course of what is called nature, that she must go out of that course to accomplish it; and we see an account given of such a miracle by the person who said he saw it, it raises a question in the mind very easily decided, which is, Is it more probable that nature should go out of her course, or that a man should tell a lie? We have never seen, in our time, nature go out of her course; but we have good reason to believe that millions of lies have been told in the same time; it is, therefore, at least millions to one, that the reporter of a miracle tells a lie.

The story of the whale swallowing Jonah, though a whale is large enough to do it, borders greatly on the marvellous; but it would have approached nearer to the idea of a miracle, if Jonah had swallowed the whale. In this, which may serve for all cases of miracles, the matter would decide itself as before stated, namely, Is it more probable that a man should have swallowed a whale, or told a lie?

But suppose that Jonah had really swallowed the whale, and gone with it in his belly to Nineveh, and to convince the people that it was true have cast it up in their sight, of the full length and size of a whale, would they not have believed him to have been the devil instead of a prophet? or, if the whale had carried Jonah to Nineveh, and cast him up in the same public manner, would they not have believed the whale to have been the devil, and Jonah one of his imps?

The most extraordinary of all the things called miracles, related in the New Testament, is that of the devil flying away with Jesus Christ, and carrying him to the top of a high mountain; and to the top of the highest pinnacle of the temple, and showing him and promising to him all *the kingdoms of the world*. How happened it that he did not discover America? or is it only with *kingdoms* that his sooty highness has any interest?

I have too much respect for the moral character of Christ to believe that he told this whale of a miracle himself: neither is it easy to account for what purpose it could have been fabricated, unless it were to impose upon the connoisseurs of miracles, as is sometimes practised upon the connoisseurs of Queen Anne's farthings, and collectors of relics and antiquities; or to render the belief of miracles ridiculous, by outdoing miracle, as Don Quixote outdid chivalry; or to embarrass the belief of miracles, by making it doubtful by what power, whether of God or of the devil, any thing called a miracle was performed. It requires, however, a great deal of faith in the devil to believe this miracle.

In every point of view in which those things called miracles can be placed and considered, the reality of them is improbable, and their existence unnecessary. . . .

As mystery and miracle took charge of the past and the present, prophecy took charge of the future, and rounded the tenses of faith. It was not sufficient to know what had been done, but what would be done. The supposed prophet was the supposed historian of times to come; and if he happened, in shooting with a long bow of a thousand years, to strike within a thousand miles of a mark, the ingenuity of posterity could make it point-blank; and if he happened to be directly wrong, it was only to suppose, as in the case of Jonah and Nineveh, that God had repented himself, and changed his mind. What a fool do fabulous systems make of man!

It has been shewn, in a former part of this work, that the original meaning of the words *prophet* and *prophesying* has been changed, and that a prophet, in the sense of the word as now used, is a creature of modern invention; and it is owing to this change in the meaning of the words, that the flights and metaphors of the Jewish poets, and phrases and expressions now rendered obscure by our not being acquainted with the local circumstances to which they applied at the time they were used, have been erected into prophecies, and made to bend to explanations at the will and whimsical conceits of sectaries, expounders, and commentators. Every thing unintelligible was prophetical, and every thing insignificant was typical. A blunder would have served for a prophecy; and a dish-clout for a type. . . .

But it is with prophecy as it is with miracle. It could not answer the purpose even if it were real. Those to whom a prophecy should be told could not tell whether the man prophesied or lied, or whether it had been revealed to him or whether he conceited it; and if the thing that he prophesied, or pretended to prophesy, should happen, or some thing like it, among the multitude of things that are daily happening, nobody could again know whether he foreknew it, or guessed at it, or whether it was accidental. A prophet, therefore, is a character useless and unnecessary; and the safe side of the case is to guard against being imposed upon, by not giving credit to such relations.

Upon the whole, mystery, miracle, and prophecy, are appendages that belong to fabulous and not to true religion. They are the means by which so many *Lo heres!* and *Lo theres!* have been spread about the world, and religion been made into a trade. The success of one impostor gave encouragement to another, and the quieting salvo of doing *some good* by keeping up a *pious fraud* protected them from remorse.

Having now extended the subject to a greater length than I first intended, I shall bring it to a close by abstracting a summary from the whole.

First, That the idea or belief of a word of God existing in print, or in writing, or in speech, is inconsistent in itself for the reasons already assigned. These reasons, among many others, are the want of an universal language; the mutability of language; the errors to which translations are subject; the possibility of totally suppressing such a word; the probability of altering it, or of fabricating the whole, and imposing it upon the world.

Secondly, That the Creation we behold is the real and ever existing word of God, in which we cannot be deceived. It proclaimeth his power, it demonstrates his wisdom, it manifests his goodness and beneficence.

Thirdly, That the moral duty of man consists in imitating the moral goodness and beneficence of God manifested in the creation towards all his creatures. That seeing, as we daily do, the goodness of God to all men, it is an example calling upon all men to practise the same towards each other; and consequently that every thing of persecution and revenge between man and man, and every thing of cruelty to animals, is a violation of moral duty.

I trouble not myself about the manner of future existence. I content myself with believing, even to positive conviction, that the power that gave me existence is able to continue it, in any form and manner he pleases, either with or without this body; and it appears more probable to me that I shall continue to exist hereafter than that I should have had existence, as I now have, before that existence began.

It is certain that, in one point, all nations of the earth and all religions agree. All believe in a God, the things in which they disagree are the redundancies annexed to that belief; and therefore, if ever an universal religion should prevail, it will not be believing any thing new, but in getting rid of redundancies, and believing as man believed at first. Adam, if ever there was such a man, was created a Deist; but in the mean time, let every man follow, as he has a right to do, the religion and worship he prefers.

—A CITIZEN OF THE UNITED STATES OF AMERICA

AGRARIAN JUSTICE

OPPOSED TO AGRARIAN LAW,
AND TO AGRARIAN MONOPOLY,
BEING A PLAN FOR MELIORATING
THE CONDITION OF MAN, &C.
(SELECTIONS)

1797

Preface

The following little Piece was written in the winter of 1795 and 96; and, as I had not determined whether to publish it during the present war, or to wait till the commencement of a peace, it has lain by me, without alteration or addition, from the time it was written.

What has determined me to publish it now is a Sermon, preached by WATSON, *Bishop of Llandaff*. . . .

At the end of the Bishop's book is a List of Works he has written among which is the Sermon alluded to; it is entitled,

"THE WISDOM AND GOODNESS OF GOD, IN HAVING MADE BOTH RICH AND POOR; with an Appendix, containing REFLECTIONS ON THE PRESENT STATE OF ENGLAND AND FRANCE."

The error contained in the title of this Sermon determined me to publish my AGRARIAN JUSTICE. It is wrong to say that God made *Rich* and *Poor*; he made only *Male* and *Female*; and he gave them the earth for their inheritance.

Instead of preaching to encourage one part of mankind in insolence it would be better that Priests employed their time to render the general condition of man less miserable than it is. Practical religion consists in doing good; and the only way of serving God is, that of endeavouring to make his creation happy. All preaching that has not this for its object is nonsense and hypocrisy.

Thomas Paine

To preserve the benefits of what is called civilized life, and to remedy at the same time the evils it has produced, ought to be considered as one of the first objects of reformed legislation.

Whether that state that is proudly, perhaps erroneously, called civilization, has most promoted or most injured the general happiness of man is a question that may be strongly contested. —On one side, the spectator is dazzled by splendid appearances; on the other, he is shocked by extremes of wretchedness; both of which it has erected. The most affluent and the most miserable of the human race are to be found in the countries that are called civilized.

To understand what the state of society ought to be, it is necessary to have some idea of the natural and primitive state of man; such as it is at this day among the Indians of North America. There is not, in that state, any of those spectacles of human misery which poverty and want present to our eyes in all the towns and streets in Europe. Poverty, therefore, is a thing created by that which is called civilized life. It exists not in the natural state. On the other hand, the natural state is without those advantages which flow from Agriculture, Arts, Science and Manufactures.

The life of an Indian is a continual holiday, compared with the poor of Europe; and, on the other hand, it appears to be abject when compared to the rich. Civilization, therefore, or that which is so called, has operated two ways: to make one part of society more affluent, and the other more wretched, than would have been the lot of either in a natural state.

It is always possible to go from the natural to the civilized state, but it is never possible to go from the civilized to the natural state. The reason is that man in a natural state, subsisting by hunting, requires ten times the quantity of land to range over to procure himself sustenance, than would support him in a civilized state, where the earth is cultivated.

When therefore a country becomes populous by the additional aids of cultivation, arts, and science, there is a necessity of preserving things in that state; because without it there cannot be sustenance for more, perhaps, than a tenth part of its inhabitants. The thing therefore now to be done is to remedy the evils and preserve the benefits that have arisen to society, by passing from the natural to that which is called the civilized state.

Taking then the matter up on this ground, the first principle of civilization ought to have been, and ought still to be, that the condition of every person born into the world, after a state of civilization commences, ought not to be worse than if he had been born before that period.

But the fact is that the condition of millions, in every country in Europe, is far worse than if they had been born before civilization began, had been born among the Indians of North America of the present day. I will shew how this fact has happened.

It is a position not to be controverted, that the earth, in its natural, cultivated state, was, and ever would have continued to be, THE COMMON PROPERTY OF THE HUMAN RACE. In that state every man would have been born to property. He would have been a joint life-proprietor with the rest in the property of the soil, and in all its natural productions, vegetable and animal.

But the earth in its natural state, as before said, is

capable of supporting but a small number of inhabitants compared with what it is capable of doing in a cultivated state. And as it is impossible to separate the improvement made by cultivation, from the earth itself, upon which that improvement is made, the idea of landed property arose from that inseparable connection; but it is nevertheless true, that it is the value of the improvement, only, and not the earth itself, that is individual property. Every proprietor therefore of cultivated land owes to the community a *ground-rent* (for I know of no better term to express the idea) for the land which he holds; and it is from this ground-rent that the fund proposed in this plan is to issue.

It is deducible, as well from the nature of the thing as from all the stories transmitted to us, that the idea of landed property commenced with cultivation, and that there was no such thing, as landed property before that time. It could not exist in the first state of man, that of hunters. It did not exist in the second state, that of shepherds. Neither Abraham, Isaac, Jacob, nor Job, so far as the history of the Bible may be credited in probable things, were owners of land. Their property consisted, as is always enumerated in flocks and herds, they travelled with them from place to place. The frequent contentions at that time about the use of a well in the dry country of Arabia, where those people lived, also shew that there was no landed property. It was not admitted that land could be claimed as property.

There could be no such thing as landed property originally. Man did not make the earth, and, though he had a natural right to *occupy* it, he had no right to *locate* as *his property* in perpetuity any part of it: neither did the Creator of the earth open a land-office, from whence the first title-deeds should issue. Whence then, arose the idea of landed property? I answer as before, that when cultivation began, the idea of landed property began with it, from the impossibility of separating the improvement made by cultivation from the earth itself upon which that improvement was made. The value of the improvement so far exceeded the value of the natural earth, at that time, as to absorb it; till, in the end, the common right of all became confounded into the cultivated right of the individual. But there are nevertheless distinct species of rights, and will continue to be so long as the earth endures.

It is only by tracing things to their origin, that we can gain rightful ideas of them, and it is by gaining such ideas that we discover the boundary that divides right from wrong, and teaches every man to know his own. I have entitled this tract *Agrarian Justice* to distinguish it from *Agrarian Law*. Nothing could be more unjust than Agrarian Law in a country improved by cultivation; for though every man, as an inhabitant of the earth, is a joint proprietor of it in its natural state, it does not follow that he is a joint proprietor of cultivated earth. The additional value made by cultivation, after the system was admitted, became the property of those who did it, or who inherited it from them, or who purchased it. It had originally no owner. Whilst, therefore, I advocate the right, and interest myself in the hard case of all those who have been thrown out of their natural inheritance by the introduction of the system of landed property, I equally defend the right of the possessor to the part which is his.

Cultivation is at least one of the greatest natural improvements ever made by human invention. It has given to created earth a ten-fold value. But the landed monopoly, that began with it, has produced the greatest evil. It has dispossessed more than half the inhabitants of every nation of their natural inheritance, without providing for them, as ought to have been done, an indemnification for that loss, and has thereby created a species of poverty and wretchedness that did not exist before.

In advocating the case of the persons thus dispossessed, it is a right, and not a charity, that I am pleading for. But it is that kind of right which, being neglected at first, could not be brought forward afterwards till heaven had opened the way by a revolution in the system of government. Let us then do honour to revolutions by justice, and give currency to their principles by blessings.

Having thus in a few words, opened the merits of the case, I shall now proceed to the plan I have to propose, which is,

To create a National Fund, out of which there shall be paid to every person, when arrived at the age of twenty-one years, the sum of Fifteen Pounds *sterling, as a compensation in part, for the loss of his or her natural inheritance, by the introduction of the system of landed property.*

AND ALSO,

The sum of Ten Pounds *per annum, during life, to every person now living, of the age of fifty years, and to all others as they shall arrive at that age.*

Means By Which the Fund Is to Be Created

I have already established the principle, namely, that the earth, in its natural uncultivated state, was, and ever would have continued to be, the COMMON PROPERTY OF THE HUMAN RACE—that in that state, every person would have been born to property—and that the system of landed property, by its inseparable connection with cultivation, and with what is called civilized life, has absorbed the property of all those whom it dispossessed, without providing, as ought to have been done, an indemnification for that loss.

The fault, however, is not in the present possessors. No complaint is intended, or ought to be alleged against them, unless they adopt the crime by opposing justice. The fault is in the system, and it has stolen perceptibly upon the world, aided afterwards by the agrarian law of the sword. But the fault can be made to reform itself by successive generations, without diminishing or deranging the property of any of present possessors, and yet the operation of the fund can yet commence, and be in full activity the first year of its establishment, or soon after, as I shall shew.

It is proposed that the payments, as already stated, be made to every person, rich or poor. It is best to make it so, to prevent invidious distinctions. It is also right it should be so, because it is in lieu of the natural inheritance, which, as a right, belongs to every man, over and above property he may have created, or inherited from those who did. Such persons as do not chuse to receive it can throw it into the common fund.

Taking it then for granted, that no person ought to be in a worse condition when born under what is called a state of civilization, than he would have been, had he been born in a state of nature, and that civilization ought to have made, and ought still to make, provision for that purpose, it can only be done by subtracting from property a portion equal in value to the natural inheritance it has absorbed.

Various methods may be proposed for this purpose, but that which appears to be the best . . . is at the moment that property is passing by the death of one person to the possession of another. In this case, the bequeather gives nothing: the receiver pays nothing. The only matter to him is that the monopoly of natural inheritance, to which there never was a right, begins to cease in his person. A generous man would not wish it to continue, and a just man will rejoice to see it abolished. . . .

Though in a plan, in which justice and humanity are the foundation principles, interest ought not to be admitted into the calculation, yet it is always of advantage to the establishment of any plan to shew that it is beneficial as a matter of interest. The success of any proposed plan, submitted to public consideration, must finally depend on the numbers interested in supporting it, united with the justice of its principles.

The plan here proposed will benefit all, without injuring any. It will consolidate the interest of the republic with that of the individual. To the numerous class dispossessed of their natural inheritance by the system of landed property, it will be an act of national justice. To persons dying possessed of moderate fortunes, it will operate as a tontine to their children, more beneficial than the sum of money paid into the fund: and it will give to the accumulation of riches a degree of security that none of the old governments of Europe, now tottering on their foundations, can give. . . .

An army of principles will penetrate where an army of soldiers cannot—It will succeed where diplomatic management would fail—It is neither the Rhine, the Channel, nor the Ocean, that can arrest progress—It will march on the horizon of the world, and it will conquer.

SUGGESTED READINGS

Scholarship on Thomas Paine's life and work has blossomed so much in recent years that several new works have appeared. Readers will find some of the titles listed below to be useful in exploring more about this exciting writer and activist.

Aldridge, A. Owen. *Man of Reason: The Life of Thomas Paine*. Philadelphia: J. B. Lippincott, 1959.

——. *Thomas Paine's American Ideology*. Newark: University of Delaware Press, 1984.

Ayer, A. J. *Thomas Paine*. London: Secker and Warburg, 1988.

Blakemore, Steven. *Crisis in Representation: Thomas Paine, Mary Wollstonecraft, Helen Maria Williams, and the Rewriting of the French Revolution*. Madison, NJ: Fairleigh Dickinson University Press, 1997.

Claeys, Gregory. *Thomas Paine: Social and Political Thought*. Boston: Unwin, Hyman, 1989.

Davidson, Edward H., and William J. Scheick. *Paine, Scripture, and Authority: "The Age of Reason" as Religious and Political Idea*. Bethlehem, PA: Lehigh University Press, 1994.

DeLony, Eric. "Tom Paine's Bridge: The Man Who Wrote *Common Sense* Was Just As Much of a Revolutionary in the Field of Engineering." *American Heri-*

tage of Invention and Technology 15 (Spring 2000): 38–45.

Dyck, Ian, ed. *Citizen of the World: Essay on Thomas Paine*. London: Christopher Helm, 1987.

Foner, Eric. *Tom Paine and Revolutionary America*. Oxford: Oxford University Press, 1976.

Fruchtman, Jack, Jr. *Thomas Paine and the Religion of Nature*. Baltimore: Johns Hopkins University Press, 1993.

———. *Thomas Paine: Apostle of Freedom*. New York: Four Walls Eight Windows, 1994; rept., 1996.

Hawke, David Freeman. *Paine*. New York: Harper and Row, 1974; rept., Norton, 1992.

Keane, John. *Tom Paine: A Political Life*. Boston: Little, Brown, 1995.

O'Brien, P. *Debate Aborted, 1789–91: Priestley, Paine, Burke and the Revolution in France*. Edinburgh: Pentland Press, 1996.

Philp, Mark. *Paine*. Past Masters Series. Oxford: Oxford University Press, 1989.

Scheuermann, Mona. *In Praise of Poverty: Hannah More Counters Thomas Paine and the Radical Threat*. Lexington: University Press of Kentucky, 2002.

Williamson, Audrey. *Thomas Paine: His Life, Work and Times*. London: George Allen and Unwin, 1973.

Wilson, David A. *Paine and Cobbett: The Transatlantic Connection*. Kingston and Montreal: McGill-Queen's University Press, 1988.

Wilson, Jerome D., and William F. Ricketson. *Thomas Paine*. Boston: Twayne Publishers, 1989.

For Younger Readers

Fish, Becky Durost, and Bruce Fish. *Tom Paine: Political Writer*. Broomall, PA: Chelsea Press, 1999.

Kaye, Harvey J. *Thomas Paine: Firebrand of the Revolution*. New York: Oxford University Press, 2000.

McCarthy, Pat. *Tom Paine: Revolutionary Patriot and Writer*. Berkeley Heights, NJ: Enslow, 2001.

McCartin, Brian. *Thomas Paine:* Common Sense *and Revolutionary Pamphleteer*. New York: PowerKids Press, 2002.

Meltzer, Milton. *Tom Paine: Voice of Revolution*. New York: Franklin Watts, 1996.

READ THE TOP 20
SIGNET CLASSICS

1984 BY GEORGE ORWELL

ANIMAL FARM BY GEORGE ORWELL

FRANKENSTEIN BY MARY SHELLEY

THE INFERNO BY DANTE

BEOWULF (BURTON RAFFEL, TRANSLATOR)

HAMLET BY WILLIAM SHAKESPEARE

HEART OF DARKNESS & THE SECRET SHARER
    BY JOSEPH CONRAD

NARRATIVE OF THE LIFE OF FREDERICK DOUGLASS
    BY FREDERICK DOUGLASS

THE SCARLET LETTER BY NATHANIEL HAWTHORNE

NECTAR IN A SIEVE BY KAMALA MARKANDAYA

A TALE OF TWO CITIES BY CHARLES DICKENS

ALICE'S ADVENTURES IN WONDERLAND &
        THROUGH THE LOOKING GLASS BY LEWIS CARROLL

ROMEO AND JULIET BY WILLIAM SHAKESPEARE

ETHAN FROME BY EDITH WHARTON

A MIDSUMMER NIGHT'S DREAM BY WILLIAM SHAKESPEARE

MACBETH BY WILLIAM SHAKESPEARE

OTHELLO BY WILLIAM SHAKESPEARE

THE ADVENTURES OF HUCKLEBERRY FINN BY MARK TWAIN

ONE DAY IN THE LIFE OF IVAN DENISOVICH
    BY ALEXANDER SOLZHENITSYN

JANE EYRE BY CHARLOTTE BRONTË